MASTERING

OMNIS ®

3

STEVEN MALLER

TAB TAB BOOKS Inc.
Blue Ridge Summit, PA 17214

FIRST EDITION
SECOND PRINTING

Copyright © 1986 by Steven Maller
Printed in the United States of America

Library of Congress Cataloging in Publication Data

Maller, Steven.
Mastering Omnis 3.

Includes index.
1. Omnis 3 (Computer program) 2. Data base manage-
ment. 3. Business—Data processing. I. Title.
II. Title: Mastering Omnis three.
HF5548.4.055M35 1986   658'.05574   86-5758
ISBN 0-8306-0374-3
ISBN 0-8306-0474-X (pbk.)

Front cover: courtesy of Blyth Software

For Annie, Obbie, Lottie and Lou.
You all believed in me, and I hope I've made you proud.

Contents

Acknowledgment

A sincere thanks to the people who helped make this book possible:
  Stephen Heffernan and Bill Schjelderup and Steve Kronin at Blyth Software, for their tireless support.
  Jacquie Hale at The Training Company, for showing me the fine points of this craft.
  Living Videotext, publishers of ThinkTank, the weapon for the terminally disorganized.
  Harold, Judith, Dan, Cindy, and Lar, my all-weather cheering section.
  . . . and Andrea, the inspiration for everything I do.

If my theory of relativity is proven successful, Germany will claim me as a German and France shall declare that I am a citizen of the world. Should my theory prove untrue, France will say that I am a German and Germany will say that I am a Jew.
—Albert Einstein

```
┌─────────────────────────┐
│ Omnis 3                 │
├─────────────────────────┤
│     The DataBasics      │
│     Useful Reports      │
│     Search Formats      │
│     Custom Menus        │
│     Sequences           │
│     More Sequences      │
│     Expansion           │
│     Connections         │
│     The Array           │
├─────────────────────────┤
│ Introduction            │
└─────────────────────────┘
```

On January 24, 1984, Apple Computer made outrageous claims about the future of computing and introduced their little computer called Macintosh. At 128K, that box was no heavyweight. Although the early software efforts were admirable, it wasn't until almost a year later and the introduction of the 512K machine that the Mac came into its own. Multiplan gave way to Jazz and Excel, MacPaint began to look simple next to MacDraw and PageMaker, and Habadex was outclassed by Omnis 3. The traditional measure of the machismo of a computer is database management software, and now the Macintosh had Omnis 3.

Welcome to *Mastering Omnis 3!*

This book is a working tour through the immense functionality and utility of the database manager Omnis 3. As the book progresses, we will be adding components on to a growing system of small business applications. Even though the book is generously illustrated, this is meant to be a hands-on experience. In order to derive full benefit from this book, you should be prepared to spend some time building these modules along with the book. The pace is certainly flexible, and the course of the exericises in the book can take you anywhere from a few days to a few months, depending mostly on your level of committment.

The book is meant to cater to the database novice and the casual user, not the experienced developer. We travel from the very genesis of the database all the way up to very sophisticated file-management techniques. The journey is not a rocky one, but it's not automatic, either. Many potholes are uncovered along the way, some not until they're fallen into. Even experienced users of database software are encouraged to come along for the ride from the very beginnings, as the review and the introduction to the language of Omnis 3 will be an asset as you build your expertise.

Each of the chapters of the book is divided into three sections. The beginning of each chapter poses a *Problem*. Each chapter's problem is based on an imaginary computer store. Included in the book are data management situations common to all businesses: inventory, personnel, invoicing, customer accounting, etc.. The second section is the *Plan*. This section outlines a plan of attack chosen to take on that chapter's problem. This section introduces the terminology and concepts necessary to achieve the desired solution. The third section of each chapter is the *Steps*. This section dictates the actual process involved in building the solution from the Plan section. Included in this section are pictures of what your screen should look like during the Steps, as well as pertinent data such as customer or part lists. In the Steps section, the actual steps are set off by a mark (□) and are *italicized* for emphasis. The rest of the text in those sections is just necessary commentary.

The structure of the book is meant to serve two purposes: first you will work through successive chapters dealing with significant features of the software; and second, if you follow the steps in each chapter, you will have built a small system of useful small business applications by the end of this book. This system is not meant to be commercial-quality, and those readers who have experience with systems of this nature will no doubt have stylistic differences with one or another of the approaches. However, the goal is to familiarize you with the capabilities of Omnis 3, and subsequently enable you to have the freedom to use the software in its most flexible and effective way.

Let's meet your imaginary client now, The Work Station. This family-owned retail computer store was opened in September of 1984 in San Francisco. Hard work and perseverance have paid off well for the Kleins; they have seen their business grow to be quite successful. Recently, however, they realized that expansion would be quite impossible without more effective controls and management. Their manual paperwork system was beginning to show its limitations, so they decided to design a new system.

The scenario for the course of the book is this: The Work Station has hired an outside consultant (you) to do the work, and they have wisely chosen Omnis 3 to help them.

Most of their design goals are direct replacements for existing manual systems such as invoicing, inventory control, costing, and salesperson support. However, many more things are possible in a computer-based business system. Among other things, complex reports detailing and comparing the profitablilty of invoices used to be too time-consuming. You and Omnis 3 will make many new things possible.

I realize that you probably don't own a computer store! As a matter of fact, very few of you will ever have the occasion to build a system of this magnitude. However, this construction experience will surely help you to understand how Omnis 3 works.

The way this book is written, it is possible for you to skip around among the chapters with little regard for their actual order in the book. However, if you intend to actually follow the steps and build the system, I strongly recommend that you follow the order of the chapters. Quite a few features introduced into our application in the later chapters will not work 'as advertised' without support from earlier features.

Now let's get started!

Starting the
Customer Database

The Problem: In the computer business, things change very quickly. Our computer store, The Work Station, has a growing list of customers and is in need of a system to track these customers. Often a customer finds that a recently purchased piece of hardware or software has been updated or replaced with a new and improved version. The salesperson needs to make the customer aware of this change.

The desired solution is for the store to print a standard postcard along with mailing labels for all of their customers (Fig. 1-1). It is also useful to have customers ''on file,'' so when a person calls on the telephone, their information can be instantly accessed. If a salesperson knows that the customer on the phone owns two Macintoshes, or that he recently purchased an AppleTalk network, that salesperson will be better equipped to service the customer's needs. This database also could be used to keep track of prospects.

Let's design a system to answer this need.

THE PLAN

The first move to make in the designing of a database is to map out the structure of the data. The Work Station's request is fairly basic. In order to output mailing labels, we must first create a file for their customer list. The data we will track is listed below:

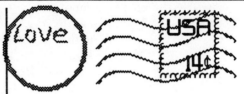

The Work Station proudly announces the arrival of Version 14.78 of Apple Computer's Switcher™!

Registered users are encouraged to drop by our store and pick up their FREE upgrade package. (just remember to bring along your original disk...)

If you are not a registered owner, we have the new version of Switcher™ ON SALE for

$17.96

250 Main St. • San Francisco
(415) 921-3333

Roger Woo, DDS.
4330 Arguello St.
Suite 4
Oakland, CA 94335

Fig. 1-1. The Work Station's desired standard mailing postcard.

Customer Name
Contact person   (In a business, the person to whom you speak)
Customer ID #   (A new wrinkle: let's assign ID numbers to each customer.)

Address
City
State
Zip
Phone number
Phone extension
System owned   (Notes—i.e., own equipment now, or are they a prospect?)

There are more fields that you could add, no doubt, but a useful feature of Omnis 3 is its ability to add to a database, even after it has been in use for a while.

DataBasics

The pieces of information outlined above combine to form a *Record*. The record is the structural unit of the database. Each record in a *File* contains the same identical record structure. Consider a paper filing system for a moment. Can you imagine the confusion in a personnel database if each employee filled out a slightly different form? The information would certainly all be there, but retrieving it would take an inordinate amount of time. This is the reason that record structure must be consistent. Omnis 3 expects all records in a file to share the same structure.

The individual components of a record are called *Fields*. Fields are what hold the actual data for a file, and they're made up of two parts: the *Field name* and the *Data* itself. The field name is what Omnis 3 uses to refer to that field, and therefore each field name must be unique. (Would you give two of your children the same name?) The data is the information you enter at the keyboard, and it must be stored in a specific format depending on what type of data it is (numeric, character, date, etc.). Incorporating the ideas covered above, we can ascertain that the big picture looks something like Fig. 1-2.

Now that we have the big picture straight, let's talk about Omnis 3. There is one preliminary step to creating a database: creating a *Library*. Omnis 3 keeps all of the descriptive information about a database in a large file called a library. This file can actually contain information on many related databases, but more on that later in the book.

File Formats

The first step towards creating a database with Omnis 3 is creating a *File format*. The descriptions of each field are saved in a File format. From that point on, the File format serves as the foundation for the database; any major changes to the structure must be done there.

Each field must be given a *name*, a *type*, a *length* (or number of *decimals*), and be marked as to whether it is indexed. Let's talk about each of these.

In addition to what has already been discussed above, *Field names* must be seven letters or less, with no punctuation or symbols. This is somewhat limiting, but you'll be amazed at how creative you'll get with seven letters!

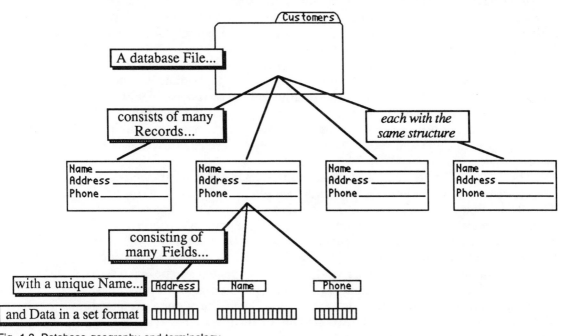

Fig. 1-2. Database geography and terminology.

The *Field type* is a multiple-choice question. There are a number of set types, and you must choose among them. The choices are:

Character	Normal text fields with ASCII sort order.
National	Similar to character, but sort order is alphabetic (and international).
Number	Numeric, with adjustable amount of decimal precision.
Boolean	A logical (True/False or Yes/No) field.
Date	Stores calendar dates.
Sequence	The record number of that record; not an editable field.

The *field length* setting is for *Character* and *National fields* only. Omnis 3 needs to know how much room to reserve in the file for the entries in these fields. If the length were constant at 60 characters (Omnis 3's maximum), you would fill up your disks very quickly, and most of the space would be wasted. Don't be too prudent, however, because this is also the maximum length a text string is allowed to be for that field. It never fails that you will reserve 35 spaces for a name, and the next day a customer with a 36-character name will walk in your door!

Numeric fields, on the other hand, are always set at nine characters because computers store numbers in a more compact way than text. However, you must specify the number of *decimals* for a Numeric field (up to the maximum of 6). This also determines the *precision* with which Omnis 3 will perform calculations.

As far as the other field types go, they are fairly simple. The format for *Date* fields are based on your Macintosh's "International" configuration, and normally won't be altered. *Boolean* fields are logical (true/false or yes/no) fields, and will only accept input consistent with this scheme.

The *Sequence* field is a place holder that contains the *record number* of that record, and is labeled "for internal use only" by Omnis 3. If you have entered 35 records into a file, then the next record input will be record number 36. Sequence fields may be viewed, printed, and used in calculations, but they can't be edited or deleted. Also, sequence numbers are never reassigned (i.e., if there are 35 records in a file and record 22 is deleted, the next record will still be record 36).

The last—and most complicated—attributes for a field are the *indexing* characteristics. With no indexing, records in a file are referred to in order of their record numbers. This is sometimes all right, but often the needs of a user are more complex. You might usually prefer to look at your salespeople listing ordered by gross sales, but you may later want to see the list ordered by gross profit, or margin percentage. It would be time-consuming for Omnis 3 to search and sort through all your records each time you wanted to look at these printouts. But if those fields are indexed, Omnis 3 will already know the order! When you add records to an Omnis 3 file, the program stays one step ahead of you and will maintain up to 12 different indexes. Indexing also speeds up searches for information, such as the price for a part in your inventory.

Indexes can be kept for the full length of any field (up to 60 characters) but, just like with field lengths, that takes up room in the file. Typically you might limit your indexes in a complex database to the first handful of characters to save space, but that can be judgement call. Limiting the number will simply lower the precision for the index. If you have a 3-character index length on a Customer name field, there is no guarantee that *Johns* won't be listed before *Johannsen*. Depending on the application, that might or might not be acceptable. It surely won't hurt to opt for the full number for that field, but you can save space by being frugal.

A note about file formats: A thoughtful feature of Omnis 3 is its ability to let you make changes to a File format at any time, even after you have entered data into the file. This is fairly complex for a program to do, much like making an adjustment to the foundation of a house. It's not too much trouble to do before the concrete has set, but imagine the difficulty involved if you waited until after the house was finished! Remember, the File format is the foundation of a database. But there is a way (covered in a later chapter) to reorganize all the data and indexes if you need to make a change to the file after data has been entered.

Once the File format is complete and safely tucked away inside the Library, you can start work on the next step of database construction: an Entry layout.

Entry Layouts

File formats need to have a "front end," or a layout displayed on the screen, to guide the user through entry of data. This front end is called an *Entry layout*.

At its most basic, an Entry layout is a list of each of the fields and a space for data, with the Field names listed nearby so you can see where to enter the data. Also shown on the screen with an Entry layout is a series of buttons to facilitate basic operations like inserting, deleting, and editing records, finding a record, printing, and searching for records. These on-screen buttons are accompanied by a menu duplicating their functions, and ⌘-key equivalents are added for some of the button commands. Later in the book you will discover more fascinating details about Entry layouts:

1) They actually consist of 12 individual screens each, allowing great versatility in screen design.
2) Screen buttons can be customized.
3) There can be a custom Macintosh pulldown menu associated with an Entry layout.
4) You can use Omnis 3's programming language to build programs, or command sequences for your database.
5) You can control access to any Entry layout through the use of passwords.

As you work your way through Omnis 3, you will spend time with each of the tremendous variety of tools available.

Once this first basic Entry layout is completed, you can enter the first group of The Work Station's customers.

Data Entry

When you enter data, you are actually carrying on a conversation with an Entry layout. There is no trick to entering data; it is the most time-consuming and critical part of the construction of a database. I wish I could tell you that there is a better way, but until computers can read our minds or understand spoken words, we are stuck with our keyboards and disk drives.

Omnis 3 has a number of tools to assist you along the way. First, you have the option of aborting input at any time by clicking an onscreen button marked Cancel. Second, you can always go back and edit or delete a record if an input mistake was made. Omnis 3 also fully supports the Clipboard, so a particularly lengthy field that must be repeated across a number of records can be copied to the Clipboard, then "pasted" into each of the other records. Finally, there is no need to save your file periodically. As with most database programs, Omnis 3 saves each record to the disk as you complete its entry.

Omnis 3 uses a term that may be unfamiliar to those of you who have worked with other database software. The Insert command appends (adds records) to a file. Needless to say, you will use this command quite often!

In order to enter data, you must first create a *Data file*. Along with the Library file, these two files are all that you'll see on your diskette when using a database; the formatting, layouts, and related characteristics of the database are in a Library file, while the raw data is kept in the Data file.

Once the data is input, you can get some useful reports from the database. To produce reports, you must first define a *Report format*.

Report Formats

Last but not least, one of Omnis 3's most flexible areas is the Report formats. In order to output information from a database, you have to do what is essentially the reverse of an Entry layout. Instead of deciding how the information is to be input, you use a similar screen editor to define how the information is to be put out. However, Report formats offer even more flexibility.

You decide which fields to output, where to put them, whether or not to keep running totals, perform calculations "on the fly," print page headers, print mailing labels, and much more. You can output to a disk file, the screen, ImageWriter, LaserWriter, or any printer you can connect to a Macintosh.

For this application, we were asked to have the system output mailing labels for the post card announcements. To do this you must create a Report format.

The first part of a report is generally the *Heading* section, which would print at the top of each page. However, this particular Report format does not need to have headers and footers, as it will be printing directly to continuous mailing labels. The only section we need to create is the *Detail* section. The fields in this section are printed once for every record in the report—just like an Entry layout, which is only created once. We also don't need every field to be printed, since mailing labels are quite simple.

Just like the Entry layout, text can be typed directly on to the Report format if there is to be descriptive information, such as a Heading which might say "The Work Station Customers." Again, the labels don't need anything like this, so we can skip this for now. All we need to do is line up the fields correctly and leave enough space for the label.

Now let's get to it!

THE STEPS

The first step in using Omnis 3 is starting the program. In order to run it, you'll need a Macintosh with at least 512K of memory and a hard disk or at least 800K of disk storage (two single-sided drives or one double-sided drive). The possible configurations are detailed in your Omnis 3 user's guide. The only recommendation I can make in addition to those in the manual is that you seriously consider the purchase of a hard disk system for your Macintosh. The performance advantages far outweigh the obvious difference in price.

In order to start Omnis 3, you will need to see the Omnis 3 *Program* icon shown in Fig. 1-3. You may also see some *Library* or *Data* icons, but you needn't bother with those now.

☐ *Double click the Omnis 3 **Program** icon to start the program.*

Once the program has started, the first window that you will see will be the one shown in Fig. 1-4.

Remember, the first step towards creating a database is creating a *Library* file. (If you had double-clicked an icon other than the program, then that Library would have been opened automatically.) This is the file that will hold all the descriptive information about this new database. We'll name it "WorkStation."

☐ *Click the **New Library** button, as shown in Fig. 1-4.*
☐ *Type **WorkStation** in the dialog box which appears. (Fig. 1-5.)*
☐ *Click **OK**.*

After a few seconds, the disk stops spinning and you have a blank desktop from which to start. Notice there are three menus in addition to the ever-present ⌘ menu: the *File, Edit,* and *Options* menus. The Edit menu is standard Macintosh fare. The File menu controls changing to a different Library file, and other Omnis 3 internal settings. The Options menu enables work with File formats, Entry layouts, Report formats, Search formats, and Menus. We can use this menu to create the first part of a database, the File format.

File Formats

Choose File formats from the Options menu and you are soon greeted with Omnis 3's standard "pick one from this list" dialog box. Obviously there aren't

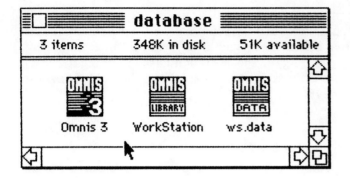

Fig. 1-3. Omnis 3's three different icons.

any File formats to choose from yet, so you must create one from scratch:

- ☐ Click **New.**
- ☐ Type **CUSTS.**
- ☐ Press **Return.**

Omnis 3 is now presenting you with the File format window (Fig. 1-6). It is here that you will make all modifications to File formats. Notice there are two main areas: the field listings with numbers from 1-120 (only 1-20 are shown, but you have a scroll bar) and the field attribute setting controls along the right side of the screen.

Remember the listing of fields from the ''Plan?'' Here they are again:

Customer Name
Contact person   (In a business, the person to whom you speak)
Customer ID #   (A new wrinkle: let's assign ID numbers to each cus-
                      tomer.)
Address
City
State
Zip

Fig. 1-4. Requesting a New Library.

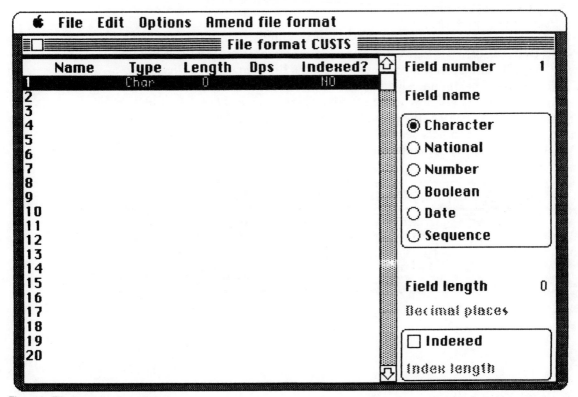

Fig. 1-5. Entering the Library name.

Phone number
Phone extension
System owned   (Notes - i.e., own equipment now, or are they a
                     prospect?)

Let's go through and set up the CUSTS File format for these fields. The first

Fig. 1-6. File format entry window.

field is the Customer's name. Remember, we are limited to seven characters for Field names, so we'll have to abbreviate.

☐ Press **Tab** to move the selection area to the **Field name** setting.
☐ Type **CSTNAME** for the first Field name.
☐ Click **National** to set this as an international text field.
☐ Press **Tab** to move the selection area to the **Field length** setting.
☐ Type **30** for the first field's length.
☐ Click **Indexed** to tell Omnis 3 to keep an index on this field. (We'll leave the index length set at 30.)

Now that the attributes have been set for field 1, we can move through the rest of the fields.

☐ Click the mouse on line 2 to start work on that field (Fig. 1-7).
☐ Press **Tab** to move to **Field name.**
☐ Type **CONTACT** for the second Field name.
☐ Click **National.**
☐ Press **Tab** to move to **Field length.**
☐ Type **20** for the field's length.
☐ CONTACT doesn't need to be indexed, so that's all for this field.
☐ Click the mouse on line 3.

Now I'll leave it up to you to set the rest of the fields. Don't fret, this isn't a test. As a matter of fact, I'll give you all the answers right now. Figure 1-8 shows what this File format should look like when it's finished. Each of the indexes can be left at its maximum value for this exercise. Notice that there are two address fields. This is to allow input of suite, floor, apartment, or box numbers in the second field. Also, the CUSTID field is set as a *sequence*, so it doesn't have a length or decimals setting.

Any mistakes can be corrected by clicking on that line, then making the

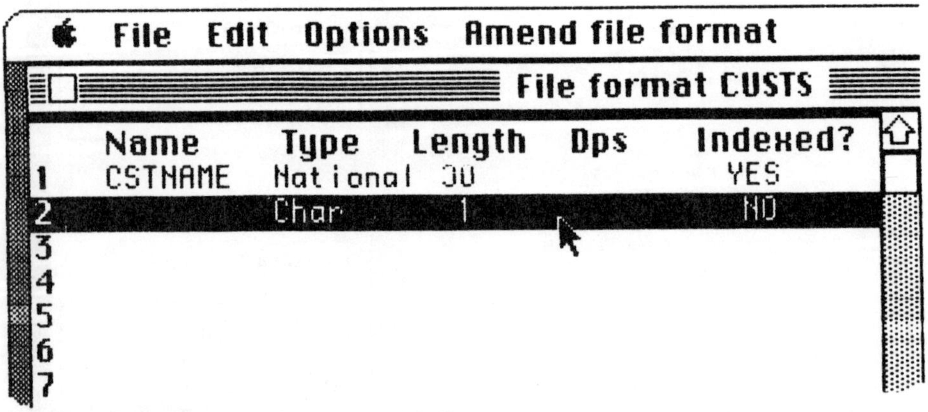

Fig. 1-7. Adding the second field.

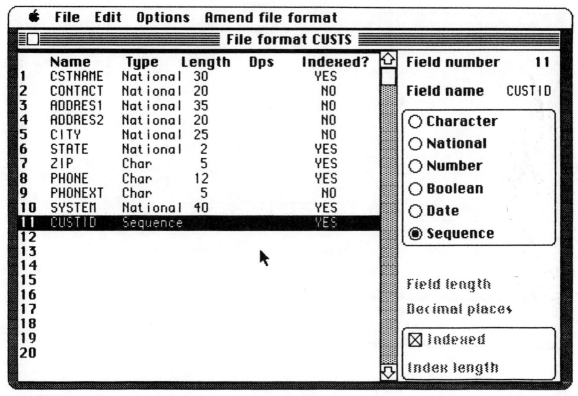

Fig. 1-8. The complete CUSTS File format.

necessary changes on the right side of the window. Once the File format has
been set properly, you can save it.

☐ *Click the window's **Close** box to save this File format in the Library file.*

Entry Layouts

Now that the file has been properly configured, so we can prepare the Entry layout, which is supposed to resemble the Customer card pictured in Fig.
1-9; we'll be able come fairly close.

☐ *Choose **Entry layouts** from the Options menu.*
☐ *Click the **New** button.*
☐ *Type **CSTENTR***
☐ *Press **Return.***

You are now presented with the *Entry layouts* window, where you can design
your input screens. You can think of it as a blank canvas, similar to MacPaint's
screen. Here you can place fields, helpful text, and even some graphic information. Notice at the bottom right corner is a position box displaying a column
and row number. This tells you the cursor's exact coordinates, which is helpful

```
┌─────────────────────────────────────────────────────────────────────┐
│                                                                       │
│  The Work Station                    Customer ID #  17                │
│  Customer record card                                   _____      │
│                                                                       │
│ ─────────────────────────────────────────────────────────────────── │
│  Customer Name:          Roger Woo, DDS.                              │
│  Contact person's name:  Sally                                        │
│  Address:                4330 Arguello St.                            │
│                          Suite 4                                      │
│  City:                   Oakland                                      │
│  State:                  CA                                           │
│  Zip:                    94335                                        │
│  Phone number:  415-338-0900      Extension:                         │
│                                                                       │
│  System owned: Macintosh (2), Omnis 3, LaserWriter                   │
│                                                                       │
│                                                                       │
│                                                                       │
│                                                                       │
│                                                                       │
└─────────────────────────────────────────────────────────────────────┘
```

Fig. 1-9. The Work Station's existing notecards.

when aligning fields or text. Right now it's in the upper left corner, or (Col 1/Row 1).

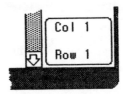

The fields will be placed similarly to the way they are found on the card in Fig. 1-8.

☐ *Move the cursor to* **(Col 6/Row 3)** *by clicking the mouse until the position box looks like this:*

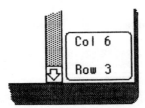

(If you accidentally double-click the mouse, you may open the field windows. Don't worry, just click *Cancel* to close them).

Before we go on, make sure that the *Automatic names window* option is

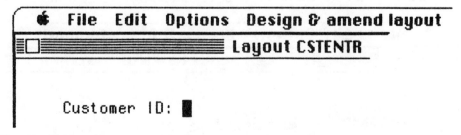

Fig. 1-10. This is how the "Automatic names window" item should be set.

Design & amend layout

Undo all changes

Field   ⌘F
Rectangle   ⌘R
Reorder   ⌘0
Remove button margin
Print layout details

Bold text
Normal text

✓Automatic names window
Display numbers

turned on. If it is on, it will have a ✓ next to it, as in Fig. 1-10.

☐ Open the **Design & amend layout** menu and look. If there is a ✓ mark, just close the menu; if there isn't a ✓ mark, choose **Automatic names window** from the menu.
☐ Type **Customer ID:**
☐ Press the space bar once.

Your screen should now look like Fig. 1-11.

☐ Click the **Field** button at the right of the screen.

Your screen now has the windows shown in Fig. 1-12. The front window is simply a list of the Field names for the File format in use, CUSTS. The window underneath is the Field description window. Let's get rid of the Field names first.

🍎 File   Edit   Options   Design & amend layout

Layout CSTENTR

Customer ID: █

Fig. 1-11. The screen as it should appear after the name is typed onto the layout.

13

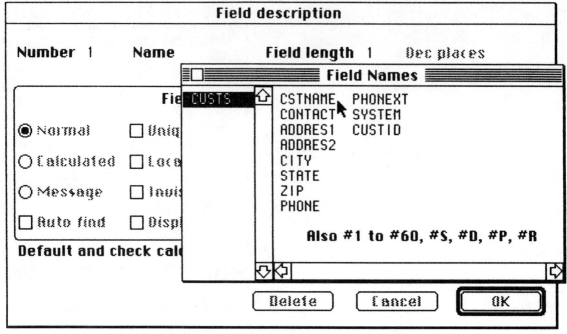

Fig. 1-12 The Omnis 3 Names window.

☐ *Click the mouse on **CUSTID** Field name.*

Notice that Omnis 3 centers the Fieldname for you.

The Field description window, which is now fully visible, allows you to enter all of the pertinent information about the selected field in your Entry layout. You can set the display length (the data length is set in the File format), justification, and defaults, and check your calculations here. There is so much information in this one window, it will take a number of chapters before you have discovered all the details.

We'll use the default Field length, so that's all for this field.

☐ *Press **Tab** twice.*

☐ *Click **OK** to set this field.*

The field is shown as in Fig. 1-13. The funny block over the "C" is just the cursor superimposed over the field. The box surrounding the field name shows

Fig. 1-13. After the CUSTID field is set.

14

the area that will be available for data input when this Entry layout is actually used.

We'll skip one line here, and put the Customer name field underneath.

☐ *Move the cursor to (Col 6/Row 5).*
☐ *Type Customer Name:*
☐ *Press the space bar once.*

Uh-oh. The two names won't end up aligned properly. However, there are editing keys which work on the Format screens: *Tab* and *Backspace* insert or delete spaces to the right or left of the cursor. (The space bar does not insert spaces.) Let's see how they work and continue constructing the Entry layout.

☐ *Place the cursor on the "C" of Customer Name:*
☐ *Press Backspace twice to delete the extra spaces. (Go ahead and experiment with Tab and Backspace, but just be sure to get the labels aligned when you're done.)*
☐ *Move the cursor to (Col 19/Row 5).*
☐ *Click the Field button.*
☐ *Click the CSTNAME Field name.*
☐ *Press Tab.*
☐ *Note the default field length is 30, the same as in the File format. We'll leave it set.*
☐ *Press Return.*
☐ *Enter the rest of the fields as shown in Fig. 1-14.*

Once all the fields have been set, let's make a couple of refinements. First of

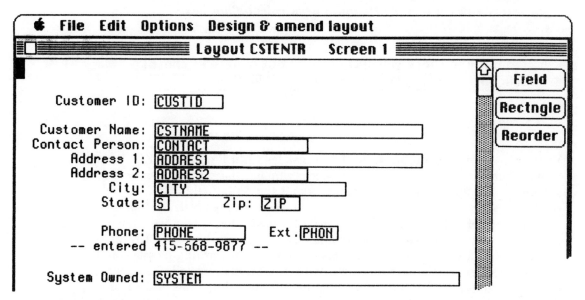

Fig. 1-14. Complete CSTENTR layout.

all, most of The Work Station's customers are from California, so it doesn't make sense to force the users of the system type "CA" every time they pass this field. We can supply a *Default* value for a field in the Field description box. You *can* edit a field's information, so let's call up the STATE field and add a default:

☐ *Double-click on the field box for **STATE** (all you can see is the "S" right now). The Field description box appears.*
☐ *Press **Tab** twice to the **Default:Check calculations** box.*
☐ *Type **'CA'** (Make sure to include the quotes as shown below, or else Omnis 3 will look for a Field called CA. The single quotes denote a string.)*

Default and check calculations (format is default:check)

```
'CA'
```

☐ *Click **OK.***

We need to check the operator's input to verify that they entered a phone number for the customer, and that it is a valid number. That is the other half of the *Default:Check calculations* option, checking data. This can get quite complex, but we'll use a simple example here. By the way, since both the Default and the Check calculation are entered into the same box they must be separated by a colon (:). Even if there is only a Check calculation, it must be started with a colon, as in the next example:

☐ *Double-click on the field box for **PHONE.***
☐ *Press **Tab** twice to the **Default:Check calculations** box.*
☐ *Type **:CHK(PHONE, '000-000-0000', '999-999-9999')**, thus:*

Default and check calculations (format is default:check)

```
:CHK(PHONE,'000-000-0000','999-999-9999')
```

☐ *Click **OK.***

You are probably wondering what this translates to in English. CHK( ) is an Omnis 3 *function* which compares the three *arguments* (parts of the expression), and makes sure the first falls between the second and third. In this case, it makes sure that users don't enter a phone number without an area code, or that they don't fudge and enter a letter "O" instead of a zero. That is why we have the note on the entry layout about the format for the phone number. The CHK function is useful in validating input because it will post a warning message and prevent the user from continuing until the situation is corrected. As we progress through the book, you'll see many more built-in functions and become familiar with their use.

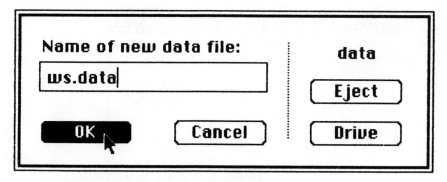

Fig. 1-15. Data file name entry.

There is one small item to attend to before you race off and enter data using this new Entry layout: create a *Data file* so that Omnis 3 will have somewhere to store the data that is input using the newly created Entry layout.

☐ Choose **Change data files** from the Options menu.
☐ Click **New data file.**
☐ Type **ws.data** (see Fig. 1-15).
☐ Click **OK.**

Now you're ready to input some customers!

Data Entry

The most time-intensive part of database management is obviously the entry of data. The best-designed File formats are for naught if the data can't be input easily and efficiently. Omnis 3 makes data entry rather straightforward, and offers a few tools to make it easier. First, these are some keys that move you around on the data entry screen:

Tab	Moves forward to the next field.
Shift-Tab	Moves backward to the previous field.
Backspace	Corrects typing errors within fields.
Return	Completes the current record and saves it to disk.

Of course, the mouse can move you quickly from one field to another, and the *Edit* menu commands (Cut, Paste, etc.) are fully functional during input.
Without further noise, let's enter 11 customers.

☐ Click **Enter data** as in Fig. 1-16.

The data entry screen appears. Recognize it? It's the Entry layout you just finished with. Let's have a quick tour before you start. There are a number of buttons up the right side of the window. Of these, *Next* and *Insert* will be the ones you use here. There is also a new menu, the *Enter data* menu. In order to input

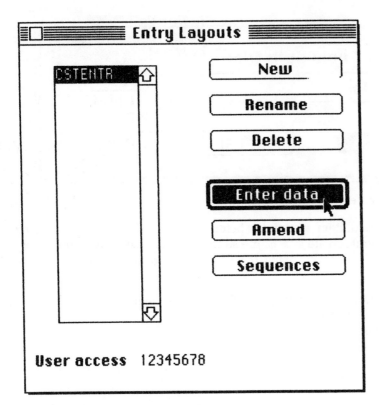

Fig. 1-16. Entry layout choosing window.

data, you use the Insert command. Needless to say, this is the most-used command in Omnis 3, so it is accessible a number of different ways: click the onscreen button, choose Insert from the *Enter data* menu, or press ⌘ (Fig. 1-17).

To complete a record, you can either press *Return* or click the *OK* button at the lower right corner of the window (Fig. 1-18). The *Cancel* button aborts entry of the current record and clears the fields. The scroll bar at the right of the window would be active if your Entry layout had utilized any more of its 12 available screens.

The data which you will enter is listed in Fig. 1-19. Take your time with each record, and be deliberate. If you make a mistake, you can use the *Cancel*, *Edit*, or *Delete* commands to correct it. Try to input the records in the order presented so our Customer ID numbers will be the same. However, if you have to delete a record, they will be off a bit. Don't worry about that; it's definitely not crucial. Take note that the CUSTID field will always show a zero when you are entering data. Sequence fields are set only when the record is saved to disk. Go to it, and I'll see you when you're done.

☐ *Enter the data from Fig. 1-19.*

There, wasn't that fun?

You can use the *Next* and *Previous* buttons to step a record a time through your database and review the records. If you entered an invalid phone number

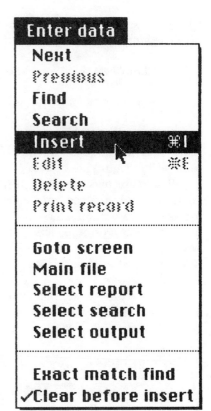

Fig. 1-17. The Options menu.

(did you?) you got an alert like the one in Fig. 1-20. This is the result of the CHK() function which you put in the PHONE field. Rather annoying, but it can save you a lot of rekeying of data.

Speaking of rekeying data, let me encourage you to make a *backup copy* of your work files right now. Even the best-designed software or the top brand of disk sometimes fails. Quit Omnis 3 now and use the Finder to drag the *WorkStation* (Library) and *ws.data* (Data) icons to a spare floppy disk. It's a good habit to get into, and someday it will save you a lot of grief.

Report Formats

Now that there has been a herculean effort and all that data has been entered, we have to remember The Work Station's request: mailing labels. In order to output any type of report with Omnis 3, you have to define a *Report format*. A report format is similar to an Entry layout in that you "paint" a screen to show what you want to output, and where it is to go.

For this report, we need to output a mailing label with the NAME, ADDRES1, ADDRES2, CITY, STATE, and ZIP fields.

In this section, you'll be introduced to *temporary fields*, Omnis 3's memory "variables." These are available for times when, for example, you want to combine two fields for a printout, but still keep them stored separately in the file. You can use a function to combine them in a *Calculated temporary field*. The simplest way to describe how all this works is to go ahead and do it.

- ☐ Choose **Reports** *from the Options menu.*
- ☐ Click **New.**
- ☐ Enter **LABELS** *as the name of this Report (Fig. 1-21).*

You are now looking at the Layout for report LABELS. This screen is similar to the Entry layout design window. You have an *Amend report* menu, and buttons on the right side.

Report formats are divided into *sections*. The most common ones are the *Heading* and *Detail* sections. As a matter of fact, there would be no report without the Detail section, since this is the part of the report which is repeated once for every record printed. This particular report has no use for headings (because we're just printing on adhesive labels), but page headings can give a polished look to almost any report. We'll work with all of the advanced report features in later chapters.

First we have to set the proper section on the screen. Notice that you have a similar cursor as when you were in the Entry layouts, and it is moved in the same manner. You also have the same *Editing* keys (Tab and Backspace). As

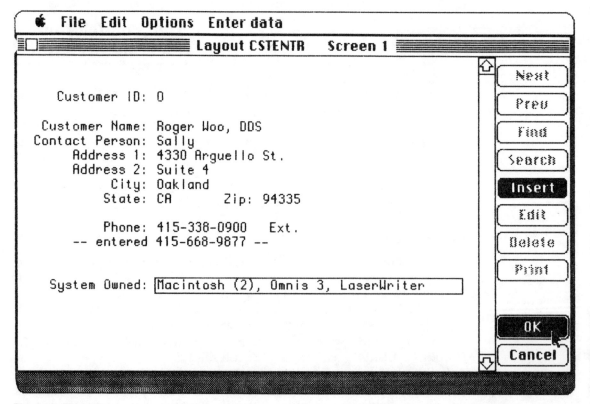

Fig. 1-18. Data entry.

```
The Work Station's Customer list                    Name:      Mary Sommers
- - - - - - - - - -                                 Contact:
                                                    Address:   678 Castro St.
Name:      Roger Woo, DDS                                      Apt. 4B
Contact:   Sally                                    City,ST,Zip: San Francisco, CA  94119
Address:   4330 Arguello St.                        Phone:     415-922-1614 ext.
           Suite 4                                  System:    Mac Plus,Word,IW2
City,ST,Zip: Oakland, CA  94335                     - - - - - - - - - -
Phone:     415-338-0900 ext.
System:    Macintosh (2), Omnis 3, LaserWriter      Name:      Ron McMannis
- - - - - - - - - -                                 Contact:
                                                    Address:   18C Jersey Street
Name:      David's Sound Service
Contact:   David                                    City,ST,Zip: San Francisco, CA  94113
Address:   270 First St.                            Phone:     415-567-1790 ext.
                                                    System:    DG One,Mac,Word,IW2,SmartModem
City,ST,Zip: San Francisco, CA  94120               - - - - - - - - - -
Phone:     415-228-5591 ext.
System:    Macintosh,IW2,Excel,Omnis3               Name:      Radical Departures Clothing
- - - - - - - - - -                                 Contact:   Cynthia
                                                    Address:   747 Hart St.
Name:      Steve's Carpets                                     Unit #3
Contact:   Steve                                    City,ST,Zip: Los Angeles, CA  90044
Address:   25550 Mission St                         Phone:     213-622-8844 ext.
           2nd floor                                System:    Mac,Omnis3,LaserWriter,MacDraw
City,ST,Zip: San Mateo, CA  94220                   - - - - - - - - - -
Phone:     415-336-8750 ext.
System:    Mac,IW2,HD20,Excel,Word                  Name:      Sandra Jacoby Associates
- - - - - - - - - -                                 Contact:   Sandy
                                                    Address:   450 Montgomery St.
Name:      Guitar WorkShop                                     Suite 2105
Contact:   Jim Brown                                City,ST,Zip: San Francisco, CA  94102
Address:   76 Elizabeth St.                         Phone:     415-543-9000 ext.239
                                                    System:    Mac(7),LaserWriter,HD20(2),Omnis3
City,ST,Zip: San Francisco, CA  94105               - - - - - - - - - -
Phone:     415-621-3900 ext.
System:    IBM XT,Epson,dBASE,WordStar              Name:      Pacific Utilities
- - - - - - - - - -                                 Contact:   Jeff Smith
                                                    Address:   100 Market St.
Name:      Axiom Design                                        11th floor
Contact:   Andrea                                   City,ST,Zip: San Francisco, CA  94120
Address:   494 27th Street                          Phone:     415-361-2222 ext.2153
           Suite 330                                System:    Mac(9),LaserWriter,Omnis3,HD20(8)
City,ST,Zip: San Francisco, CA  94121
Phone:     415-229-8540 ext.                        - - - - - - - - - -
System:    Interested in graphics...
- - - - - - - - - -

Name:      Dr. Harold Martin
Contact:   Jerri
Address:   155 Cedar
           Suite 210
City,ST,Zip: Mill Valley, CA  94880
Phone:     415-782-7600 ext.
System:    Mac,LaserWriter,Omnis3,HD20
```

Fig. 1-19. Customer list.

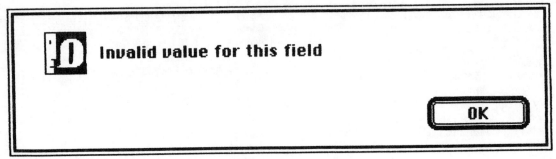

Fig. 1-20. The warning when the data doesn't match the :Check calculation.

with the Entry layouts, make sure the *Automatic names window* option in the
Amend report menu is marked with a ✓ mark.

☐ Place the cursor at the upper left corner *(Col 1/Row 1)*.
☐ Click the **Section** button.
☐ Click the **Detail section** button in the Section description window (Fig.
   1-22).
☐ Click **OK**.

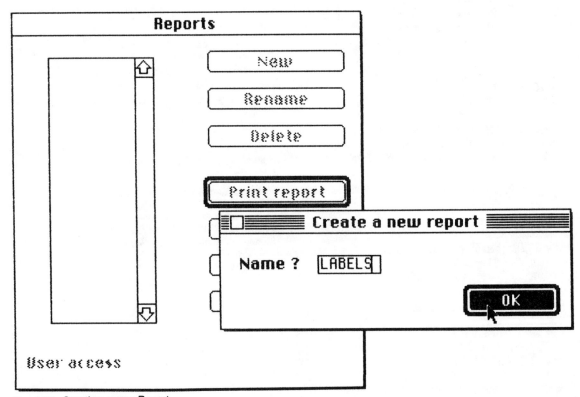

Fig. 1-21. Creating a new Report.

Fig. 1-22. Report section being set.

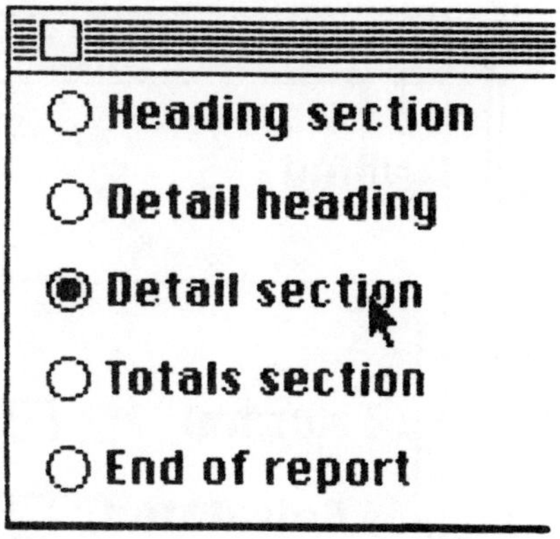

- [ ] Move the cursor down one row to *(Col 1/Row 2)*.
- [ ] Click the **Field** button.
- [ ] Click **CSTNAME** as the name for this first field.
- [ ] Press **Return** to accept all the defaults.
- [ ] Move the cursor down one row to *(Col 1/Row 3)*.
- [ ] Click the **Field** button.
- [ ] Click **ADDRES1** as the name for this field.
- [ ] Press **Return** to accept all the defaults.
- [ ] Move the cursor down one row.
- [ ] Click the **Field** button.
- [ ] Click **ADDRES2** as the name for this field.
- [ ] Press **Return** to accept all the defaults.

Now all that's left to set is the CITY, STATE, and ZIP fields. However, there are a lot of combined spaces in all of those fields, and there are no doubt a few blank spaces at the end of the CITY field in each of the records. Therefore, we can make use of a *Calculated temporary field* here. We can use the CON( ) function to *concatenate* (stick together) the three fields, along with a few blank spaces in between, into one long String. We have to use a *temporary string field* (#S), because there are 60 temporary fields for numeric values (1 through 60), but they do not work with Character or National fields very well.

- [ ] Move the cursor down one row.
- [ ] Click the **Field** button.
- [ ] Type **#S** as the name for this field. (Don't worry about the **Automatic names** window: it goes away if you press a key.)
- [ ] Press **Tab** to the Field length.
- [ ] Type **45** for the length.
- [ ] Click the **Calculated** button, as shown in Fig. 1-23.

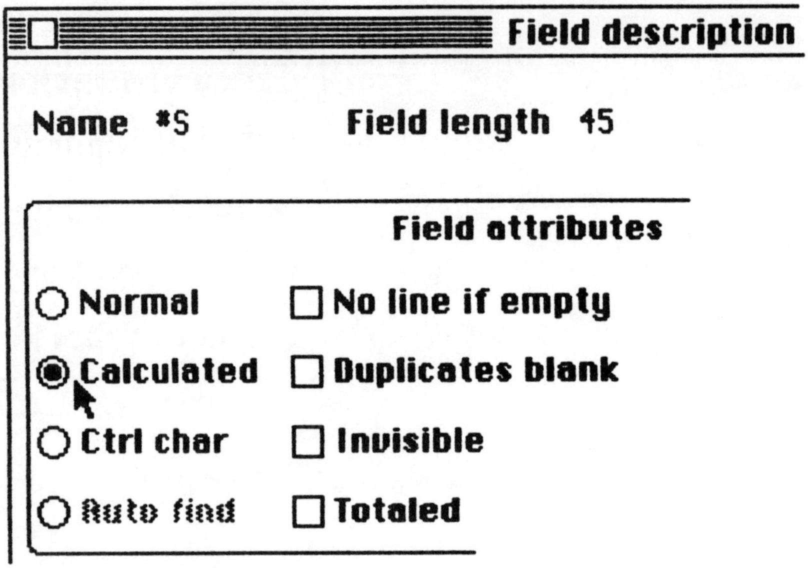

Field description

Name *S   Field length 45

Field attributes

○ Normal   ☐ No line if empty

⦿ Calculated   ☐ Duplicates blank

○ Ctrl char   ☐ Invisible

○ Auto find   ☐ Totaled

Fig. 1-23. Setting the field attributes.

☐ Press **Tab** to the **Calculation** box.
☐ Type CON(CITY,', ',STATE,' ',ZIP), like this:

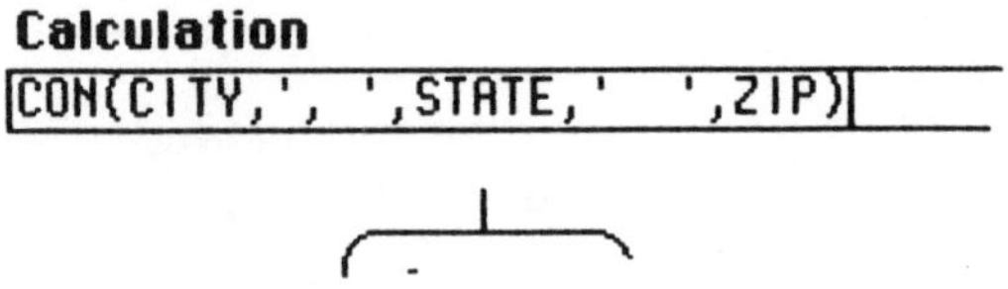

Calculation

CON(CITY,', ',STATE,'   ',ZIP)

☐ Press **Return** to save this field.

There is no doubt an explanation in order about the CON( ) function as it was used here. It can stick together any number of character strings into one long one. In this case it is used to glue the following: the CITY field, a comma and a space, the STATE field, a few spaces, and the ZIP field. Remember, anything placed between single quotes is treated by Omnis 3 as a character string.

Now let's finish up this report. We need to leave two blank lines at the end, because a standard mailing label has space for six lines, and we've only used four. The final Section of a report is called *End of report*. Let's finish now.

☐ Move the cursor down three rows to *(Col 1/Row 8)*.
☐ Click the **Section** button.
☐ Click the **End of report** button.
☐ Click **OK.**

Your screen should now look like Fig. 1-24. If not, you can edit it using a vari-

24

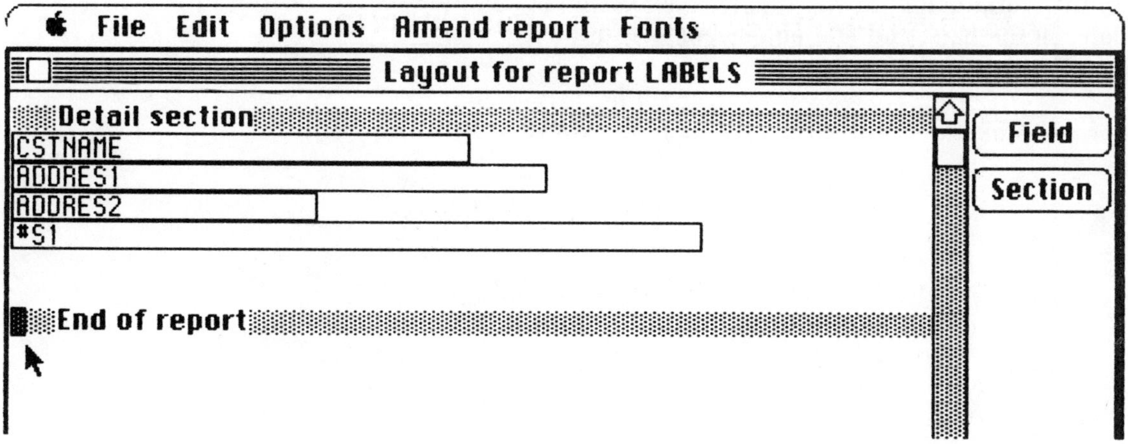
File Edit Options Amend report Fonts
Layout for report LABELS
Detail section
CSTNAME
ADDRES1
ADDRES2
#S1
End of report
Field
Section

Fig. 1-24. The finished LABELS report.

ety of tools. In the menu are the *Delete line* and *Insert line* commands. *Insert line* will add those extra blank lines if you forgot them, and *Delete line* will trim things up if you overshot. Remember, the Tab and Backspace keys work here, too, if your fields are out of alignment.

Now let's print this layout, and see what it looks like.

☐ *Choose* ***Print 'LABELS'*** from the Options menu.
☐ *When you're prompted for output (Fig. 1-25) click* ***Screen.***

You should then get a printout on your screen. You can click the *Next page* or *Prev page* buttons to look through the report, and click *Finish* to end the report.

You can now feed those pesky labels into your ImageWriter and choose *Print 'LABELS'* from the *Options* menu again, except choose *Printer* instead of *Screen*, and the labels should be output correctly. It may take a few tries to get the printout aligned with the labels, but it will work eventually.

By the way, be careful if you are using the peel-off labels with tractor feed holes; they will peel off inside your printer if you roll them backwards out of the printer. Take it from one who knows: it is not easy to clean out your printer.

In case it isn't clearly obvious, the LABELS report is now a permanent part

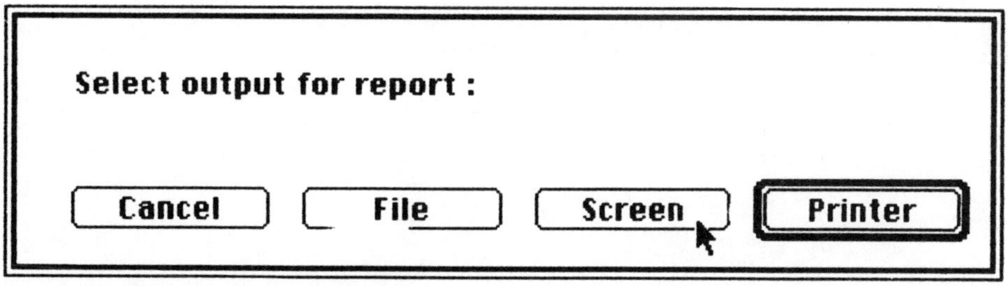
Select output for report :
Cancel
File
Screen
Printer

Fig. 1-25. Selecting the desired output.

of the WorkStation Library file, and can be run at any time. We will call it up later in the book and add enhancements to it.

The last step is . . .

☐ *Make a backup copy of your files. NOW!*

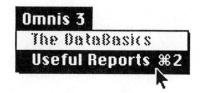
Expanding
the Customer File

The Problem: Now that the management at The Work Station has seen how easy it is to develop an Omnis 3 database, they want to expand the file we built in Chapter 1. They would like to account for the individual salespeople in each customer's record, and to add a "notes" field for miscellaneous data on a customer, such as the last phone contact or spouse's name. Once this data is added to the existing customer records, they want to give the salespeople a print-out of all their customers, along with a list of those customers' telephone numbers.

THE PLAN

The first order of business is to adjust the CUSTS File format. We need to add two fields, one for a salesperson's name and another for notes. These will be text fields, so the National field type should be appropriate. The length of the salesperson field should be sufficient for an average surname, so we'll set that at 15 characters. The length for the notes field ideally would be expandable, but in the interest of simplicity we'll set it at 60 characters (Omnis 3's single-field maximum). The salesperson's name should be indexed, because we will quickly reorder the database by that field when we do the requested report. This is not all that needs to be done, however.

The File Format

As you remember from the first chapter, the File format is the "foundation" of a database. Therefore we have a bit of work to do in order to rebuild our original file. Luckily, Omnis 3 has a built-in facility to handle such things: the *Reorganize data* command. This command rebuilds the file format, then copies each record in the Data file one field at a time back into this new file format. This ensures that each customer's record is given two new blank fields, instead of any other, less attractive result. (If you didn't activate this command, the results would be unpredictable at best, and the file would be left in a disorganized state.) Omnis 3 will also reindex the database. Because new fields have been created and the individual positions of the records in the file have changed, the indexes must be rebuilt or they will no longer be valid.

While all this sounds very complicated, it is remarkably fast. Even with a large database, you will rarely see this command take more than a short while to run. Your database here should take only a few seconds. If you had to do this by hand, as with many other less powerful programs, it might take you days!

The Entry Layout

Once the File format is amended, we can go to work on the Entry layout. If you remember from the last chapter, we built the CSTENTR Entry layout to handle data entry for each individual customer. There are two ways of approaching the problem here. The first is to design a new Entry layout that has only the Customer's name, the Salesperson's name, and the Notes field. This would certainly be appropriate for updating the existing customer records, and it would be simple to design because as it only has three fields. But what about new customers when they are entered into the database? Obviously we would make an extra step for users, because they would have to use two different Entry layouts in order to add each new customer. The other approach is to simply modify the CSTENTR layout and add the two new fields to it instead.

Now that the layout has become more complex, we should "pretty up" the screen a little bit. Omnis 3 can draw rectangles and lines in a number of different patterns on your Entry layouts. We can use some rectangles on the screen to break it up into sections, making it easier on the user's eyes. Amending an Entry layout is not nearly as complicated as amending a File format, since the former is not directly connected to the data structure of your files. We simply make our changes, then close the window, saving them in the Library. The next time we choose to "Enter data using CSTENTR," Omnis 3 will use this new version.

Data Entry

The next order of business is inputting salespeople. (The notes field will be used in the next chapter.) Rather than cycling through each customer's record using the Next button, we can use the *Find* command to get at the records in the order they appear on the list. Omnis 3 can do an "exact match find" or (more commonly) a match on however many characters you entered for the Find; if no match is found, you are shown an alert box explaining this. Then Omnis 3 advances to the record with the closest index value past the one requested.

This feature only works with indexed fields, so now you see one reason for using indexes.

Using the Find command, for instance, we can enter "Dr." into the NAME field, and Omnis 3 will find Dr. Harold Martin's record. Or we could enter "415-228-5591" into the PHONE field to find David's Sound Service. Remember, any indexed field can be used in a Find operation.

Once the correct record is found, the *Edit* command is used to add the salesperson's name to the record. After the record is edited, the OK button is clicked and Omnis 3 updates the file.

The Report Format

The Work Station requested listings of their customers by salesperson. We should design a new Report format for this. It would be counterproductive to modify the LABELS format, since we will be able to make use of it for more mailings in the future. Omnis 3 has a limit of 240 total Entry layouts and Report formats that can be contained in a Library, so we will make the system as flexible as possible by building individual reports for each different purpose.

This report will use some features of reports which you haven't yet seen. One is the capability of specifying a *Sort field* or fields. When a report is printed with no specific sorting instructions, the records are output in the order of the first indexed field in the file format (in this case, the alphabetical order of the Customer names). In order to obtain a meaningful report, we need to have Omnis 3 sort the output records by Salesperson name. This way, the customers for each salesperson will be listed in succession, one salesperson at a time.

We will also work more with the characteristics settings within the field description box. One of these is *Duplicates blank*, which tells Omnis 3 to evaluate each field in the Detail section; if the data for that field in the previous record was the same as the current record, it leaves the field blank. This will be clearer when you see the example.

To recap, we will amend the CUSTS File format, reorganize the Data file, amend the CSTENTR Entry layout, enter the salespeople's names in the appropriate customers' records, and finally design a new Report format to output the records in the desired fashion.

THE STEPS

The process of expanding our customer file breaks down into a number of distinct steps. We must make adjustments in the CUSTS format, then readjust the Entry layout to suit, and then add salespersons' names to the records. Last, we must accommodate the added information in our reporting procedures.

The File Format

The first step here is to open the old file format and make the necessary adjustments. The format's name is CUSTS.

☐ Choose **File formats** from the Options menu.

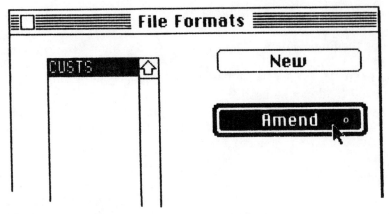

Fig. 2-1. Recalling a File format for modification.

☐ *Make sure that **CUSTS** is selected (highlighted).*
☐ *Click **Amend** as shown in Fig. 2-1.*

The *Amend file format* menu is now visible, along with the window that is titled
"File format CUSTS." This is the File format which you created in Chapter 1.
Right now the #1 field, CSTNAME, is highlighted, and its characteristics are
displayed on the right side of the window: National, 30 characters, and indexed.

What we want to do with this screen is add two new fields to the list. To
do this, we have to start with a blank field slot.

☐ *Click on the #12 slot, as shown in Fig. 2-2.*

	Name	Type	Length	Dps	Indexed?
1	CSTNAME	National	30		YES
2	CONTACT	National	20		NO
3	ADDRES1	National	35		NO
4	ADDRES2	National	20		NO
5	CITY	National	25		NO
6	STATE	National	2		YES
7	ZIP	Char	5		YES
8	PHONE	Char	12		YES
9	PHONEXT	Char	5		NO
10	SYSTEM	National	40		YES
11	CUSTID	Sequence			YES
12		Char	1		NO
13					
14					

Title above table: **File format CUSTS**

Fig. 2-2. Adding to the format.

- ☐ Press **Tab** to the **Field name** box.
- ☐ Type **SLSPRSN**
- ☐ Press **Tab.**
- ☐ Press the space bar once to change the field type to **National.**
- ☐ Press **Tab** to the **Field length** box.
- ☐ Type **15**
- ☐ Click **Indexed.**
- ☐ Click on the #13 slot to complete field #12.

Notice the shortcut introduced here? If you are highlighting a box with a column of Macintosh "radio buttons," you can step through them by pressing the spacebar. In this case, we wanted the second button, so we pressed the spacebar once.

We also have to add the notes field. You can follow the steps above and fill in the information for this field (Fig. 2-3). Remember, this will be *field #13*. If you were to enter the following information for #12, you would replace the SLSPRSN field which you just entered. Go ahead, here's the information for #13:

Field name	**NOTES**
Field type	**National**
Field length	**60**
Indexed?	**No**

Before this File format is closed, we need to perform the critical step: reorganizing the Data file.

- ☐ Choose **Reorganize data** from the **Amend file format** menu, as in Fig. 2-4.

	Name	Type	Length	Ops	Indexed?
1	CSTNAME	National	30		YES
2	CONTACT	National	20		NO
3	ADDRES1	National	35		NO
4	ADDRES2	National	20		NO
5	CITY	National	25		NO
6	STATE	National	2		YES
7	ZIP	Char	5		YES
8	PHONE	Char	12		YES
9	PHONEXT	Char	5		NO
10	SYSTEM	National	40		YES
11	CUSTID	Sequence			YES
12	SLSPRSN	National	15		YES
13	NOTES	National	60		NO

Fig. 2-3. The updated CUSTS file.

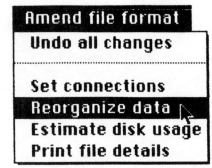

Amend file format

Undo all changes

Set connections

Reorganize data

Estimate disk usage

Print file details

Fig. 2-4. The Reorganize data command being selected.

Notice that the window disappears and it is replaced by the dialog box in Fig. 2-5. Acknowledge the warning! In this case, we are working with a very small Data file, so there is little danger of corrupting our data. If we were working on a large file, however, it is *likely* (due to the extremely sensitive nature of this operation) that our data would be damaged if there were a problem such as a disk error or a power loss.

☐ Click **Full reorganization.**

You will notice some messages flashing by as Omnis 3 rebuilds the File format and the Data file. As you watch this happen, try to appreciate the relative ease with which you can develop database given this capability.

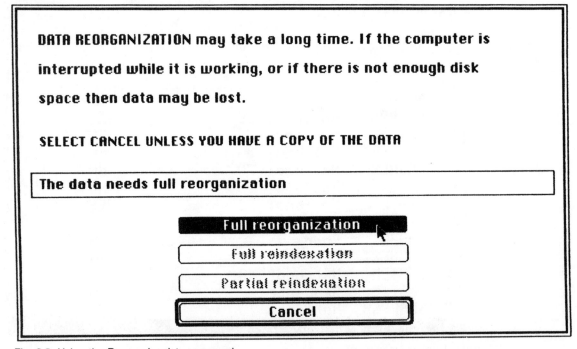

Fig. 2-5. Using the Reorganize data command.

The Entry Layout

Now that the File format has been changed, you can make the necessary adjustments to the Entry layout. These changes are rather basic: add the two new fields to the entry screen we've been working with. We have been using CSTENTR, and there is no reason to abandon the work that has been put into that layout. We can open it up again and amend it quite easily.

☐ *Choose **Entry layouts** from the Options menu.*
☐ *Highlight the **CSTENTR** layout by clicking on it.*
☐ *Click **Amend.***

This screen should be familiar by now. It is the *Amend layout* window and menu. The project this time is the addition of two fields. There is nothing fancy about them, so I'll just list their individual characteristics, and let you go through their placement. See Fig. 2-6 for the final screen.

Field name	***SLSPRSN***
Position (col,row)	***19,16***
Display length	***15***
Characteristics?	*(none)*
Justification	***Left***
Default:Check?	*(none)*

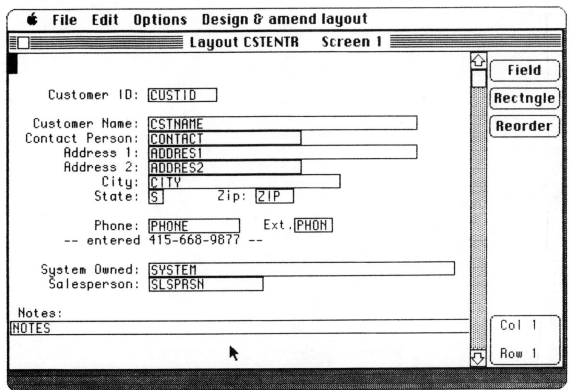

Fig. 2-6. The updated CSTENTR Entry layout.

```
Customer ID: CUSTID

    Customer Name: CSTNAME
    Contact Person: CONTACT
       Address 1: ADDRES1
       Address 2: ADDRES2
            City: CITY
           State: S          Zip: ZIP

        Phone: PHONE          Ext. PHON

    System Owned: SYSTEM
    Salesperson: SLSPRSN
```

Fig. 2-7. Setting up the Rectangle button by selecting the area for the rectangle.

Field name	**NOTES**
Position (col,row)	**1,19**
Display length	**60**
Characteristics?	(none)
Justification	**Left**
Default:Check?	**'Place notes about the customer here . . .'**

Remember, if there is a any horizontal discrepancy between your screen and mine, you can use the Tab and Backspace keys to insert and delete spaces. If there is a field on the wrong line, you can insert or delete a line using the menu.

Looking at this screen, we can surmise that it is getting a little busy. Luckily, you have access to limited drawing capability with Omnis 3 (well, this *is* the Macintosh!). Follow along with these steps. Incidentally, just as you might think, if you click and drag the mouse on the layout screen you can select large areas at once. This comes in handy for many operations, including cutting and pasting, changing fonts, and drawing graphics.

☐ **Click and drag** the mouse to highlight the area shown in Fig. 2-7.
☐ Click the **Rectngle** button once:
☐ Click the mouse on the layout to cancel the selection.

You now have the desired rectangle as a part of your Entry layout.

The last order of business is to adjust one more of the fields due to a user request. The majority of The Work Station's customers are from the 415 area code, so the input people want to have the first part of the phone number default to that number. That is no problem, but remember we already have a CHK() function in that field. We have to be certain that the total *Default:Check* expression fits in the box allotted to it; if it fails to fit, Omnis 3 will discard it. Don't worry, we'll be OK for the time being.

□ *Double-click on the **PHONE** field box.*
□ *Click the mouse in front of the existing :**Check** expression.*
□ *Add this **Default** to the existing expression:*

Default and check calculations (format is default:check)
```
'415-000-0000':CHK(PHONE,'000-000-0000','999-999-9999')
```

□ *Click **OK** to save the changes.*

The Entry layout is finally complete. Do you see how complex one of these can become in a short time? However, the many tools Omnis 3 gives you make this task very easy. In later chapters you will see even more of these tools.

Data Entry

Now that the Entry layout has been changed, we can go to work updating the existing customers. At this time, we won't be using the NOTES field, but we will be adding Salespersons' names to each of our existing 11 customers. (If you have used another list, or have added more of your own, you can improvise a bit here)

The most obvious way to do this would be to use the Next button to cycle through each of the customers, look up the appropriate record on the list, then Edit the record. However, let's use another feature of Omnis 3, the Find command. As I covered in the Plan section, the Find command can work on any Indexed field, and is quite flexible about input. What we will do here is tell Omnis 3 you want to Enter data using the Entry layout, then proceed to Find each customer, editing their Salesperson field.

□ *Choose **Entry layouts** from the **Options** menu.*
□ *Highlight the **CSTENTR** layout.*
□ *Double-click that name.*

Note the shortcut: whenever a button in one of Omnis 3's "picking" boxes is highlighted, its command will be the action that takes place if you double-click a name within that box. Here, the *Enter data* button is highlighted.

Now let's look at the list of salespeople in Fig. 2-8. We'll work from this picture. (This listing is similar to the reports that we will be generating at the

```
┌─────────────────────────────────────────┐
│                                           │
│   Shelley ............ Sandra Jacoby Associates│
│                   Radical Departures Clothing│
│                   David's Sound Service   │
│                   Ron McMannis            │
│                                           │
│                                           │
│   Mack ............... Guitar WorkShop    │
│                   Axiom Design            │
│                   Steve's Carpets         │
│                   Mary Sommers            │
│                                           │
│                                           │
│   Otto ............... Roger Woo, DDS     │
│                   Dr. Harold Martin       │
│                   Pacific Utilities       │
│                                           │
└─────────────────────────────────────────┘
```

Fig. 2-8. The salespeople and their customers.

end of this chapter.)

- ☐ First, make sure that the **Exact match find** setting is not checked in the **Enter data** menu. If it is checked, simply choose that item again to uncheck it.
- ☐ Tab to box.
- ☐ Click the **Find** button.
- ☐ Type **Sandra** as in Fig. 2-9.
- ☐ Click **OK.**

Notice that we didn't have to type the entire name of the customer. Just the first few characters of their name was enough for Omnis 3 to find the record for Sandra Jacoby Associates. Now let's enter *Shelley* as their salesperson.

- ☐ Click the **Edit** button.
- ☐ Click the mouse on the **Salesperson** field as shown in Fig. 2-10.
- ☐ Type **Shelley.**
- ☐ Press **Return.**

Whenever you see an highlighted button (i.e., the OK button in Fig. 2-10) on the screen, pressing the Return key will perform the same function as clicking the mouse on that button would do. The rest of the names need to be entered now. Use Fig. 2-8 as a guide in entering the names. When you have finished entering the salespeople, you should cycle through the records manually using the *Next* and *Prev* buttons to check your work.

Next we will create a report to list these additions to the file.

Report Format

The Work Station's request was for us to develop a report that listed all the Customers by Salesperson. Because this report is sufficiently different from the previous format we created (LABELS), we will create a new format.

☐ Choose **Reports** from the **Options** menu.
☐ Click **New**.
☐ Type **PRS** as the name for the report.
☐ Press **Return**.

As before, you are presented with a blank report format screen.

Now we'll add a practical, cosmetic touch to this report: a page header. This part of the report will print at the top of each page of this report, regardless of how long it is. This is quite convenient, since it would be impossible to do that manually. We'll keep this one simple, but you'll see that this is by no means the limit to what you can do with headers. We will do more extensive work with them in later chapters. If you remember from the previous chapter, reports are divided into *Sections*. The last report only had two: *Detail* and the *End of report*. This section will use a third kind: the *Heading* section.

☐ Make sure the cursor is at **Col 1/Row 1.**
☐ Click the **Section** button.
☐ Click the **Heading** button as in Fig. 2-11.

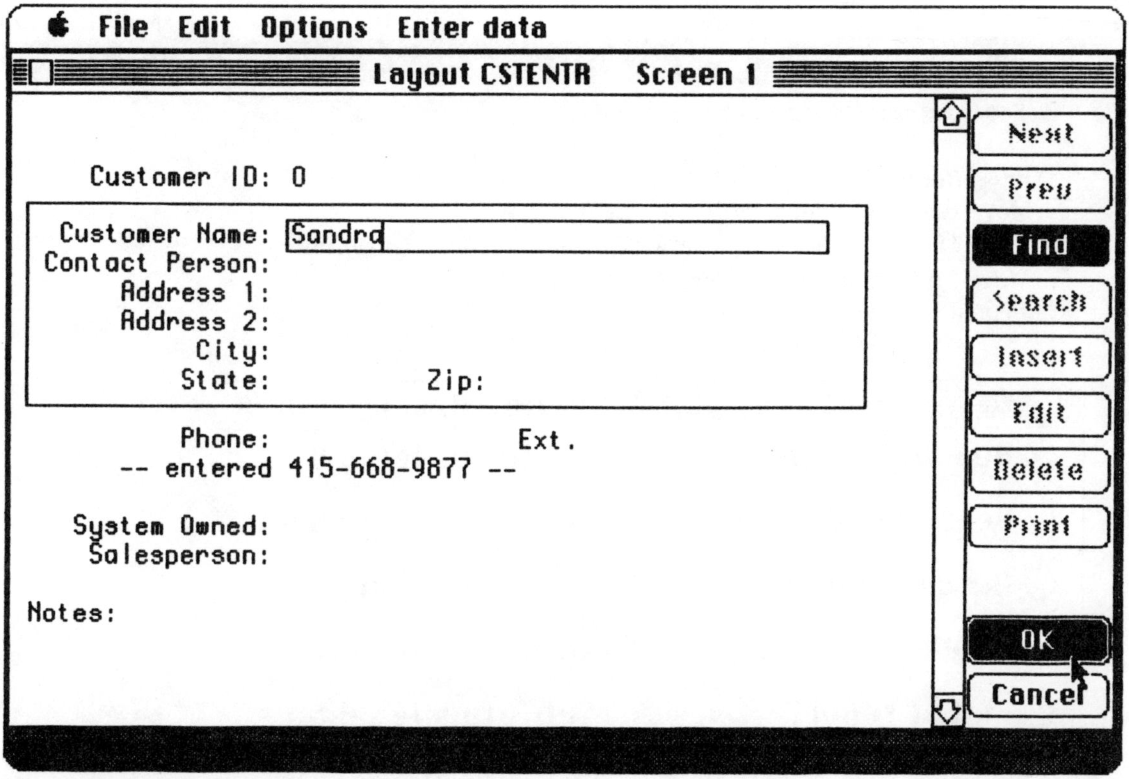

Fig. 2-9. Using the Find command.

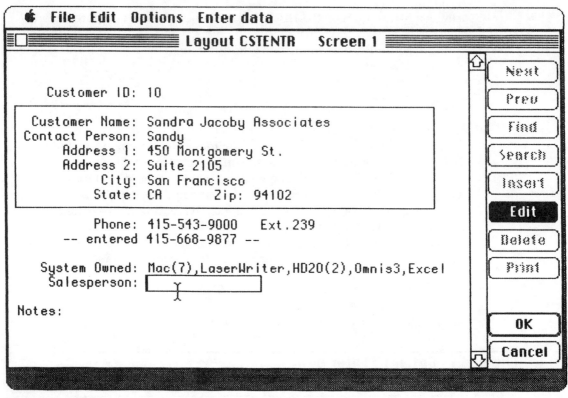

Fig. 2-10. Editing the record after it is found.

☐ Press **Return.**
☐ Move the cursor down one row to *Col 1/Row 2.*
☐ Type **The Work Stations's Salespeople and Their Customers**
☐ Move the cursor down one row to *Col 1/Row 3.*
☐ Type a dashed line across the page.

Fig. 2-11. The sections window.

Sort fields for report PRS

	Field Name	Descending	Upper case	Subtotals
1	SLSPRSN	☐	☐	☐
2		☐	☐	☐
3		☐	☐	☐
4		☐	☐	☐

Fig. 2-12. Print the report!

☐ Move the cursor down one row to *Col 1/Row 4.*
☐ Click the *Section* button.
☐ Click the *Detail* button.
☐ Press *Return.*

The next few steps are similar to the last report: we decide what fields to use, and where to put them. We will try it once in a relatively raw format, and then embellish it and incorporate more features. We can use the two most obvious fields first, Salesperson and Customer name, and we'll leave the display lengths set at the default File format lengths (15 and 30, respectively).

☐ Move the cursor down one row to *Col 1/Row 5.*
☐ Click the *Field* button.
☐ Type *SLSPRSN*
☐ (If the Automatic names window is showing, you can click on that name.)
☐ Press *Return* to accept all the defaults.
☐ Move the cursor to the space shown in Fig. 2-12.
☐ Click the *Field* button.
☐ Type *CSTNAME.*
☐ (If the Automatic names window is showing, just click on that name.)
☐ Press *Return* to accept the defaults.
☐ Move the cursor down one row to *Col 1/Row 6.*
☐ Click the *Section* button.
☐ Click the *End of report* button.
☐ Press *Return.*

The simple part of the layout is complete now. Notice that there is no blank line before the end-of-report marker. This will cause the records to be printed right below one another. If you wanted to skip a line between records, you could simply leave one blank line before the End of report section. Remember, the entire Detail section, *including blank lines,* is printed once for each record in the report. Let's print it and see how it works so far.

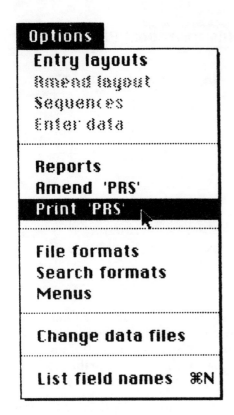

Options

Entry layouts
Amend layout
Sequences
Enter data

Reports
Amend 'PRS'
Print 'PRS'

File formats
Search formats
Menus

Change data files

List field names   ⌘N

Fig. 2-13. Accessing the Sort fields window.

☐ *As in Fig. 2-13, choose* **Print 'PRS'.**

There! Each customer is listed along with their Salesperson. Needless to say, this report is not too terribly useful as it stands. The Salespeople and Customers are not listed in any particular order, so we have some more work to do. Let's set up the report to be sorted by Salesperson's name.

☐ *As in Fig. 2-14, click* **Sort fields.**
☐ *Click the mouse next to the number 1.*
☐ *Type* **SLSPRSN.**
☐ *Press* **Return.**
☐ *As in Fig. 2-13, choose* **Print 'PRS'.**

The report is sorted as we wanted. The next revision to this report is probably apparent in this last printout. There is no reason to repeat each of the salespeople's names for each customer, and it would make the report easier to read if we eliminated this duplication. Let's see what we can do about this.

When Omnis 3 prints a report, it scans through the field description box of each field before it is printed for any special instructions pertaining to the report. For instance, you can specify a field to be right-justified, or to be left blank if the field is zero. Normally Omnis 3 will print a zero in that field if it

40

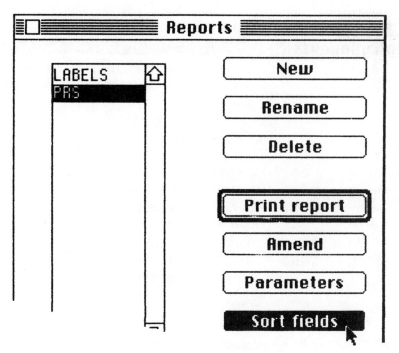

Fig. 2-14. The Sort fields.

is empty, but sometimes that is not desired. Here we'll use another of these settings.

- ☐ Choose *Amend 'PRS'*.
- ☐ Double-click on the field box for *SLSPRSN*.
- ☐ Check the *Duplicates blank* option as in Fig. 2-15.
- ☐ Choose *Print 'PRS'*.

The report should be printed as in Fig. 2-16. Notice that this is very close to the way we wanted the report. There is only one piece missing, the phone

---

Field attributes

◉ Normal   ☐ No line if empty   ☐ Zero shown empty

◯ Calculated   ☒ Duplicates blank   ☐ Shown like (1.23.4)

◯ Ctrl char   ☐ Invisible   ☐ Shown like 1.23-4.5

◯ Auto find   ☐ Totaled

Fig. 2-15. The attributes.

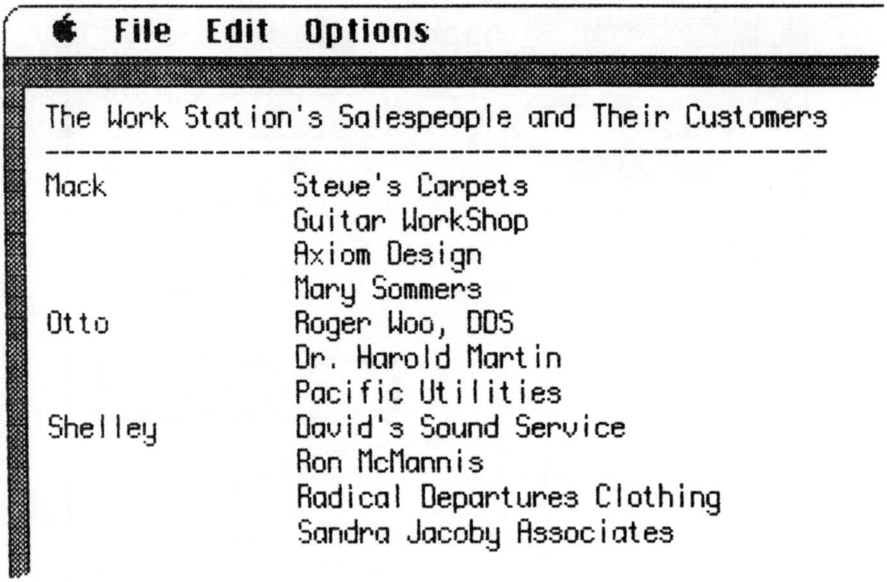

```
 🍎  File  Edit  Options

The Work Station's Salespeople and Their Customers
--------------------------------------------------
Mack            Steve's Carpets
                Guitar WorkShop
                Axiom Design
                Mary Sommers
Otto            Roger Woo, DDS
                Dr. Harold Martin
                Pacific Utilities
Shelley         David's Sound Service
                Ron McMannis
                Radical Departures Clothing
                Sandra Jacoby Associates
```

Fig. 2-16. The first printing.

numbers. These can be added as the other fields were, but let's go for a more cosmetic look than we have now.

If the salespeople are going to use the database to look up customers' names, we should add the CONTACT field to this report. After all, they will need to know whom to talk to if they call the customer. However, we don't really need to add another complete field to this report. The way we can work around this is to use the CON() function to surround the Contact person's name with parentheses and glue it onto the end of the customer's name. We can also use that function to glue the word "ext." together with the extension. Let's see how it all works.

☐ Choose **Amend 'PRS'**.
☐ Double-click on the **CSTNAME** field box.
☐ Change the field name to **#S**.
☐ Change the field length to **40**.
☐ Set it as **Calculated**.
☐ Set the **Calculation** so:

Calculation
```
CON(CSTNAME,' (',CONTACT,')')
```

☐ Click **OK**.
☐ Scroll the window right with the horizontal scroll bar.
☐ Put the **PHONE** field at **col #58**. (You know how by now.)
☐ Make sure the name is **PHONE**.

☐ *Leave the field length as-is at 12.*
☐ *Place the next field at **col #71** (Fig. 2-17).*

☐ *Set the field name as **#S** (another copy of the temporary string field).*
☐ *Set the length as **10.***
☐ *Set it as **Calculated.***
☐ *Set the **Calculation** as shown below:*

Calculation

    CON('ext.',PHONEXT)

That should do it for this field, and this report. Go ahead and print it. Your report should look like the one in Fig. 2-18. This is a useful report for all parties concerned. The salespeople get a listing of their customers, along with their phone numbers, and The Work Station's management gets an idea of their people's performance.

The next chapter will continue to build on the utility of the examples in this chapter. If you are so inclined, make a backup copy of the Library and Data files now, and experiment a bit with them. If you use the *Duplicate* command

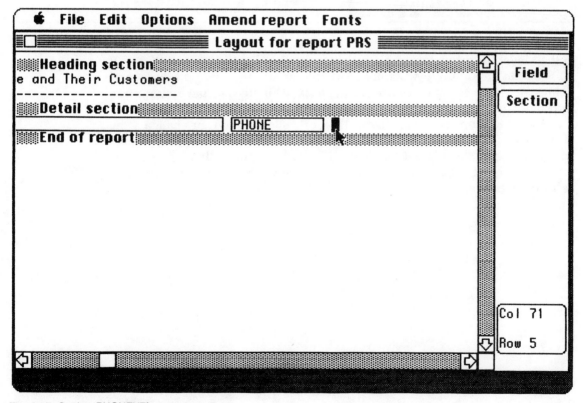

Fig. 2-17. Setting PHONEXT's temporary field.

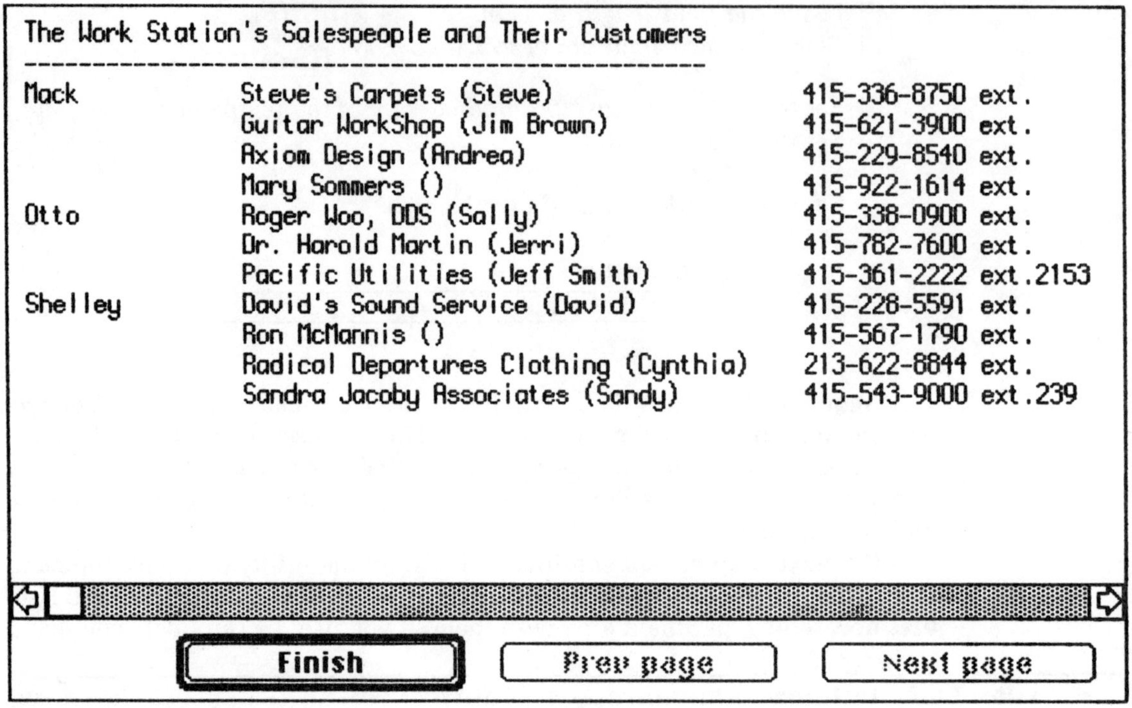

```
The Work Station's Salespeople and Their Customers
---------------------------------------------------
Mack          Steve's Carpets (Steve)            415-336-8750 ext.
              Guitar WorkShop (Jim Brown)        415-621-3900 ext.
              Axiom Design (Andrea)              415-229-8540 ext.
              Mary Sommers ()                    415-922-1614 ext.
Otto          Roger Woo, DDS (Sally)             415-338-0900 ext.
              Dr. Harold Martin (Jerri)          415-782-7600 ext.
              Pacific Utilities (Jeff Smith)     415-361-2222 ext.2153
Shelley       David's Sound Service (David)      415-228-5591 ext.
              Ron McMannis ()                    415-567-1790 ext.
              Radical Departures Clothing (Cynthia)  213-622-8844 ext.
              Sandra Jacoby Associates (Sandy)   415-543-9000 ext.239
```

◁ ▯ ▷

[**Finish**]   [Prev page]   [Next page]

Fig. 2-18. The final report.

in the Finder, be aware that you can then work with the files named *"Copy of Workstation"* and *"Copy of ws.data."* If you do, use the *Change Library* and *Change data files* commands once you are back in Omnis 3 to make sure you're working with the correct files!

See what happens if you change the Sort fields around, or change some of the settings in the Field characteristics boxes. But remember, *always* play with a *backup* of the original file. It is very easy to accidentally modify or corrupt a File format or your Data file. If you don't have a recent backup, you may be in for a good deal of work.

Searching and Sorting the Database

The Problem. The problem for this chapter involves the NOTES field that you added in the last chapter. The sales personnel at The Work Station have a request: they would like to be able to print a listing of their customers based on a particular word or phrase that had been entered previously in the notes field.

Here is a scenario: The Work Station receives a new version of a page layout program for the Macintosh that is optimized for the LaserWriter. The salespeople want to be able to contact all their customers who have a LaserWriter or are interested in one. This dictates that they should be able to search for every customer that has the word "Laser" in the NOTES or SYSTEM field.

THE PLAN

This latest assignment will expand upon what we have worked with in the previous chapters. We will continue with the same File format, CUSTS. The purpose in this chapter is to make use of the second field added in the last chapter, the NOTES field. The request was to have one line's worth of free-form space available in addition to the SYSTEM field. This field can be used for whatever the salesperson thinks is appropriate: customer's budget, family information, their prospective purchases, etc.

The first task is to enter some Notes on the 11 customers entered so far. As in previous chapters, if you have been adventurous and expanded upon your customer base, you'll have to improvise a little bit here. However, this chapter's example does not depend on having the data entered in the exact manner as the book.

In order to enter the Notes for the customers, we'll have to Enter data using the CSTENTR Entry layout again. As before, we can use the Find command to ease the process of locating each customer's record. Once located, the record can be edited, the Notes field filled in, and then saved. We can also Edit any of the other fields in that record, with the exception of the CUSTID field, which is a Sequence field. Remember from Chapter 1 that Sequence fields can be used like any other field, with the exception of entering and editing data. They can be used in reports, for Finds, or for Sort fields.

Report Format

Reports are the heart of a good database system, because they are the means of communication with the outside world. They are the "hard copy" that managers and analysts rely on for their decision-making process.

Once the file has been updated with the new information, you can move on and work on the new report. Although this one is similar to the previous chapter's report, we'll do a new one in the interest of getting more practice with report formats.

This report will use a couple of new tricks, as well as some familiar methods from the previous chapters. From this point on in the book, we will be presenting various hints and tips in context with the examples. These shortcuts are aimed at the more experienced users, but the novices among you who are working along here should also take note of them.

There is a need for more detail in this report, and we'll see how we can make a report more "intelligent" using more of the characteristics from the field box on the layout. This report will have to be a little smarter than the previous one in order to filter out unwanted records and fields when it is printed.

Search Formats

An important part of The Work Station's request was the ability to perform a search of the database for a particular group of records when the report is printed. Search formats are a fascinating and very powerful area of Omnis 3. With a properly configured format, you can have Omnis 3 evaluate a tremendous number of conditions, filter out unwanted data, and concentrate on just the records that match preselected criteria.

Criterion is an old logic term which literally means a *test* or *condition*. The mathematical laws of logic are based on a simple system first described by George Boole. There are only two possible answers to every conceivable problem, true or false. However, the power of the system comes in the science of combining these true/false questions (or criteria) into a logical expression. This may sound awfully mathematical, but it really isn't. Consider this example problem:

> We need a printout of customers who live in California or Nevada, and have Omnis 3. They also must be a customer of Otto's, because he is the person entering this Search format.

This translates into this logical expression:

```
STATE = 'CA'  OR  STATE = 'NV'
              AND
   SYSTEM CONTAINS 'Omnis'
              AND
      SLSPRSN = 'Otto'
```

Omnis 3 will then go on to evaluate every record in the database against these criteria, each record returning a True or a False depending on whether or not it passed this test.

Now notice the terminology, or *operators* in the expression. There is an OR in there, along with a couple AND tests. The rule here is that an AND connecting two logical statements means that both must be true for that part of the expression to be true. Conversely (a good logical word!), an OR test means that any of the OR-connected statements can be true to make that part true. So this means that even if a record isn't from California, it could pass if it were from Nevada, as long as they owned Omnis 3 and were a customer of Otto's. Incidentally, if more than one part of an OR-connected expression is true, that has no extra significance to the rest of the expression. Remember, an expression can only be true or false, therefore it cannot be ''more true'' than another true statement.

Knowing what we do about the database, we know that the SYSTEM field is a ''free-form'' field, so the data can be anywhere within it. What this means is that we can't say ''is equal to,'' as we can in the other parts of this expression. Therefore we can say that the field *contains* the substring ''Omnis'' somewhere within. We can be more specific if need be, and ask that the field *begin with* the text. There are also a number of operators for doing numeric comparisons, such as *greater than* (>), *less than* (<), and so on.

Using all these powerful statement parts, you can build very complex and useful logical expressions for your searches. Omnis 3 allows up to 50 lines of logical statements to make up one Search format. That is more that this small database would ever need, but you would be surprised how quickly you can get very particular about your searches with freedom like this!

Using Search and Report Together

Using a Search format with a report is very simple. A window you have not seen yet is the *Parameters* window. With this screen you can set many of the default actions Omnis 3 is to take when your report is printed. A couple of these options relate to Search formats.

First, you can decide if you want to have a Search format in use and, if so, which one. (Search formats are named just like Report formats and Entry layouts.) This insures that a commonly used report will be almost totally automatic, saving you the trouble of defining and assigning the Search each time you make a change to the Report.

Second, you can tell Omnis 3 to display the selected Search format each time you print a report. This is useful with a ''generic'' report, where you might often use slightly different Search criteria. It is also insurance, showing you what Search you have selected before you print the report. This feature could end up saving you from disaster! Imagine if you assumed the Search format is set for one setting, but it was actually set for something very different. It would be terribly embarrasing if your manager asked you for a list of names only for those customers with outstanding balances of greater than $2000, and you accidentally left the Search format set for a calculation of BALANCE < = 2000 (less than or equal to $2000). It would not be obvious by the printout if the actual balances didn't appear on the report. You would have quite a bit of explaining to do to a lot of angry customers!

Aside from a Search format, we also need to design another Report format. This one will be somewhat similar to the format from Chapter 2, but there are enough subtle differences to warrant another go at it. As with any endeavor, practice with Omnis 3 makes perfect! We'll work with some more of the settings in the Field characteristics boxes, and talk about hints and tricks for more visually effective reports. We'll also talk about the various output options available with a report, and give examples of how each could be used.

THE STEPS

To refamiliarize yourself with this database, open up the CSTENTR Entry layout and review it. Also, be sure that you're using the correct Library file (*Work-Station*) and Data file (*ws.data*).

☐ Choose **Entry layouts** from the Options menu.
☐ Double-click the **CSTENTR** layout name (Fig. 3-1).

Take a second to reacquaint yourself with the individual fields and the field description boxes before we go on.

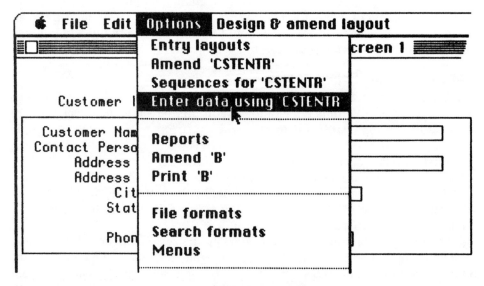

Fig. 3-1. Choosing to enter data with the CSTENTR Entry layout.

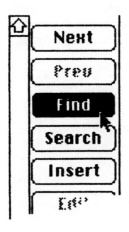
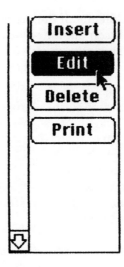

Fig. 3-2. The Edit and Find buttons on the Entry layout.

New data must be entered before we can go farther in this chapter. What we need to do is fill in the Notes field on those Customers that have some information that needs to be saved in their files. Before you race off and do it, remember to use the Find and Edit commands as we did in Chapter 2 (Fig. 3-2). Below you will find the Customers for whom we have entries to make in the NOTES field. Notice not all of them are listed.

☐ Using the **Find** and **Edit** commands, enter the notes shown in Fig. 3-3 for the listed Customers.

Steve's Carpets Wants the 1 meg upgrade for his Mac	Axiom Design Needs MacWrite upgrade
Mary Sommers Getting married 4 April	Roger Woo, DDS Wants to buy another Mac
Dr. Harold Martin Wants to buy a Mac Plus	Pacific Utilities Wants Laser upgrade
David's Sound Service Ask about a trade for a Stereo for the store	Ron McMannis Wants a service contract; IW repaired 14 March
Radical Departures Clothing Owner's name is Andrea Lynn.	Sandra Jacoby Associates Accountants; interested in financial packages

Fig. 3-3. The Customers and their NOTES fields.

Remember, you could also Edit any of the other fields in these records if need be. The Edit command works on an entire Record, not just a selected Field.

The hard part is over! Now we can move on to more interesting matters.

Search Format

As we said before, the Search formats are essentially a open-ended affair. They can (and will) get very complex, so we are going to work with a fairly straightforward example in this report. The salespeople at The Work Station want to be able to search through the NOTES and SYSTEM fields for a match on "Laser." Let's see how to do that.

First we must create a new Search format. Search formats are handled much like File formats, Entry layouts, and Report formats: they are named and then saved in the Library file for future use.

☐ Choose **Search formats** from the **Options** menu (Fig. 3-4).
☐ Click **New**.
☐ Type **SYSNOTE**
☐ Press **Return**.

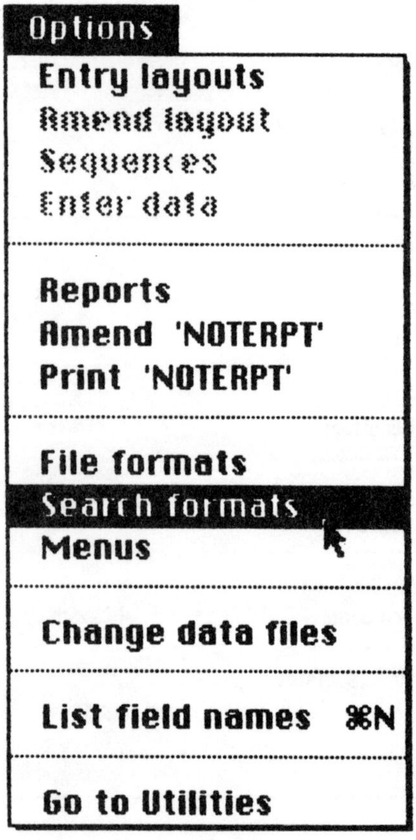

Options

Entry layouts
Amend layout
Sequences
Enter data

Reports
Amend 'NOTERPT'
Print 'NOTERPT'

File formats
Search formats
Menus

Change data files

List field names ⌘N

Go to Utilities

Fig. 3-4. Choosing the Search formats command from the Options menu.

You are now looking at the Search format window. It is comprised of four major areas. The topmost section is the scrolling list of statements. They are not actually typed, but are entered by clicking the mouse on choices of operators, field names, and criteria.

The other three sections on the screen are reserved for the "verb," the "adjective," and the "subject" and "object" of the expression. If your memory is a bit dim, here's a quick refresher in functional grammar. In a sentence such as "John is older than Robert," there are four parts. *John* is the subject, *is* is the verb, *older* is a predicate adjective describing the subject, and *Robert* is the object of the expression (strictly speaking, of the preposition *than*). Why is this important? In a logical expression, there must be at least one of each of these components. Here are the components as they relate to logical comparisons in Omnis 3:

Subject	**Comparison field.**
Verb	**Comparison/Calculation/AND/OR box.**
Adjective	**Comparison type box.**
Object	**Comparison value.**

Following this logic, a simple request like "All customers whose balance is less

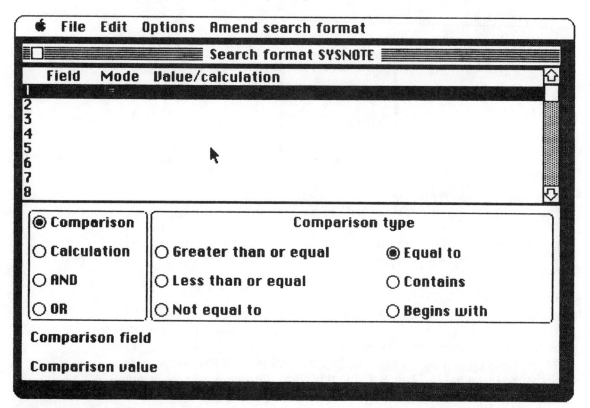

Fig. 3-5. The Search format window.

than 2000" breaks out like this:

Subject	**Balance.**
Verb	**Is** (implied).
Adjective	**less than** (<).
Object	**2000.**

Following this thought, this is almost the exact pieces of data that would be entered into this Omnis 3 window to set up a search like the one described (Fig. 3-5).

We need to start somewhere on this. Our request was for a search across both the NOTES field and SYSTEM field for the key word "Laser." Let's start with one of these fields.

☐ Press **Tab** three times to put the cursor in the **Comparison field** box.
☐ Type **NOTES**
☐ Click **Comparison** in the box above.
☐ Click **Contains** in the box to the right (as in Fig. 3-6).
☐ Press **Tab** twice to the **Comparison value** box.
☐ Type **Laser** as in Fig. 3-7.
☐ Click the mouse on line #2.
☐ Click **OR:**

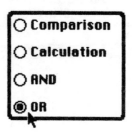

☐ Click the mouse on line #3.
☐ Following the above steps, set the next criterion as in Fig. 3-8.

Now the Search should be set up as shown in Fig. 3-8. Click the close box of this window and store it safely away.

Report Format

This report will be somewhat more complex than the previous ones. Using some Omnis 3 tricks, we can make this report "smart" about its output. The goal here is to produce a report that lists Salesperson's customers if they have some reference to the word "Laser" in their NOTES or SYSTEM fields. Following what was covered in Chapter 2, the report can also be sorted by Salesperson's name so their customer's records will be grouped by Salesperson.

The first step is obviously to create a new Report format.

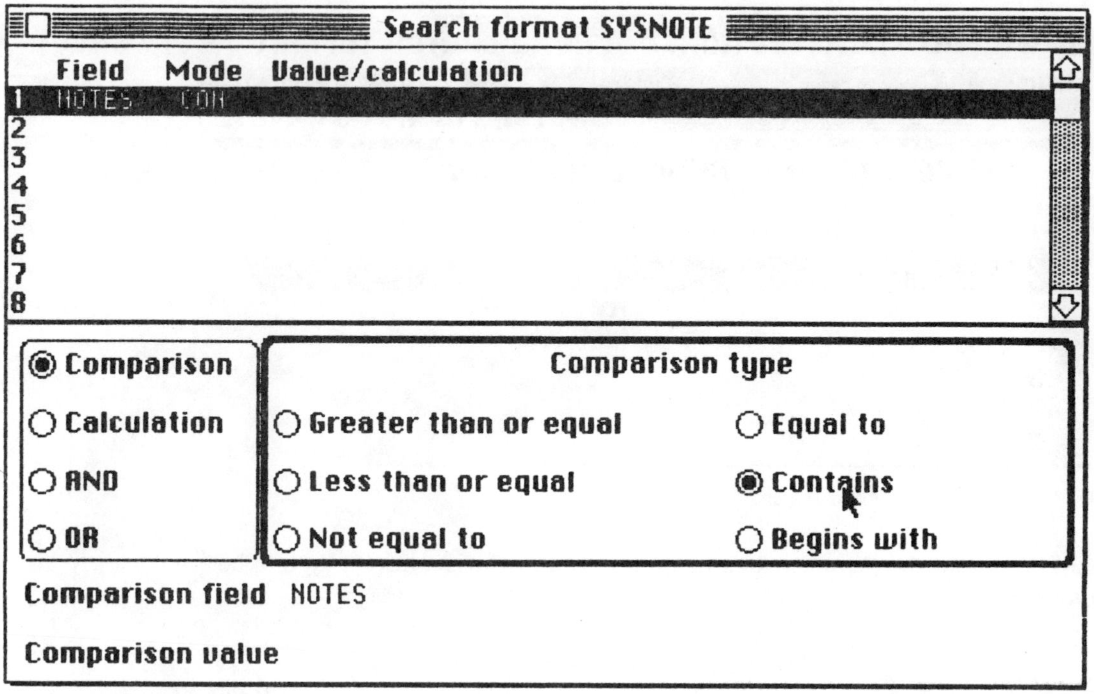

Fig. 3-6. Building the search.

□ Create a New report format named **NOTERPT** (Fig. 3-9).

We'll use a page heading for this report, for a more asthetic appearance. To do so, you must create a heading section (Fig. 3-10).

□ Click the **Section** button.
□ Click **Heading section**.
□ Press **Return**.

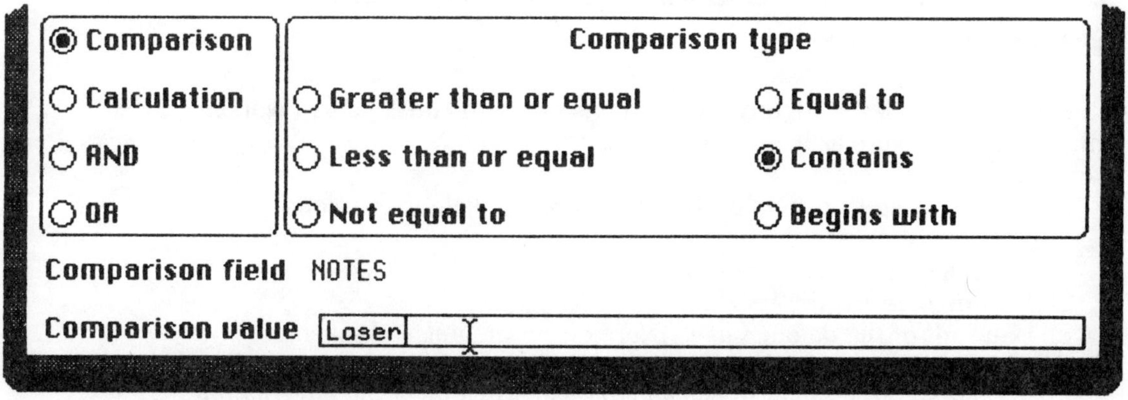

Fig. 3-7. Adding the field comparison value.

Search format SYSNOTE

	Field	Mode	Value/calculation
1	NOTES	CON	Laser
2		OR	
3	SYSTEM	CON	Laser
4			
5			
6			
7			
8			

Fig. 3-8. The final look of the search.

Now, we can put in the page heading—nothing too fancy, but enough to be explanatory.

☐ *Type the heading as shown in Fig. 3-10.*
☐ *You may have to scroll the window to the right with the scroll bar to complete the entire heading.*

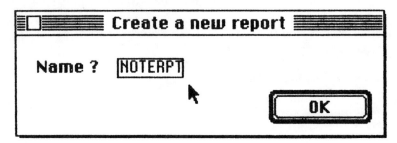

Create a new report

Name ? NOTERPT

OK

Fig. 3-9. The new report's name.

The Detail section is slightly more complex than the ones you've worked with before. Stay close as we build this together.

☐ *Set the Detail section at the row directly below the equal signs (= = = = = = =).*
☐ *Click the mouse as shown in Fig. 3-11.*
☐ *Set this field as **CSTNAME***
☐ *Leave all of the defaults as-is (Normal, nothing else checked).*
☐ *Set the other two fields as shown in Fig. 3-12.*
☐ *Set the SLSPRSN field to be centered when displayed by clicking the **Center** button:*

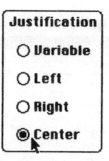

The next field is a bit tricky. We want to line up the PHONEXT field beneath the PHONE field for clarity in our report. Also, we should use the CON() function to glue together "ext." to the actual extension. However, not all of the customers in the database have a telephone extension. Ideally, that line would only be inserted only if there were something in the PHONEXT field in that rec-

░Heading section░░░
Notes On The Work Station's Customers   Salesperson
=====================================   ================

Fig. 3-10. The Heading section for NOTERPT.

ord. The way to do that is to use an *invisible field*. This is a field that is just as active as any other field in an Omnis 3 report; it can be used in calculations, for formatting, etc. However, it is not printed with the report. We'll set the next field (PHONEXT) as *invisible*, and *No line if empty*. You'll also see that you can use more than one copy of a field in a report.

☐ *Double click as shown in Fig. 3-13.*
☐ *Set this field as shown in Fig. 3-14. (Be sure to set the Field length as 1 (one), as it will be invisible, and we don't want its box to take up undue room in the layout window.)*

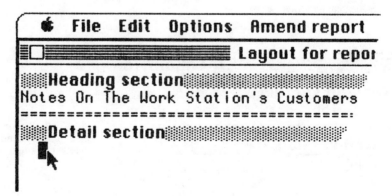

Fig. 3-11. Placement for the first field of the Detail section.

☐ *Once you have the field set correctly, it should look like this:*

Detail section
CSTNAME

☐ *Set the next field directly under the beginning of the PHONE field.*
☐ *Set its characteristics as shown in Fig. 3-15.*
☐ *Set the next two fields as shown in Fig. 3-16. Leave the default settings as is for both (Normal, nothing else checked).*
☐ *Type a line of underscores across the window to the point shown in Fig. 3-17.*
☐ *Set the **End of report** section on the line directly below the underscores.*

Now the report should be set up as shown in Fig. 3-18. There are two steps left here: set the *Sort fields* and adjust the *Parameters* for the report.

Sort Fields and Parameters

This report is probably destined for each of the individual salespeople, so we will want to separate their customers as much as possible. Obviously, sorting by salesperson will divide the customers up. The ideal way to go, how-

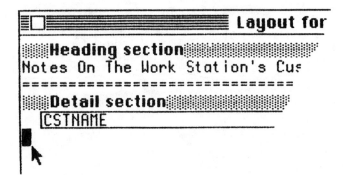

Fig. 3-12. Horizontal placement of the fields .

Fig. 3-13. Placement of the field to take advantage of the "No line if empty" feature.

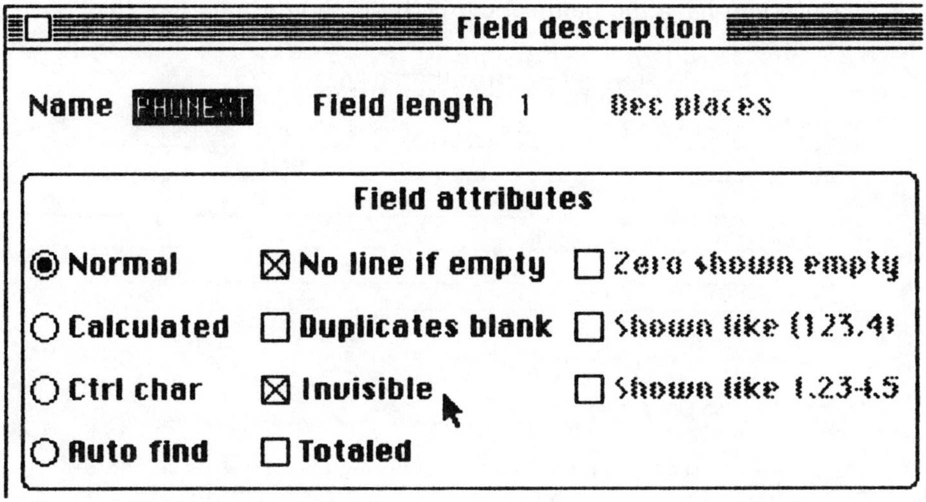

Field description

Name PHONEXT Field length 1 Dec places

Field attributes

- ● **Normal**   ☒ **No line if empty**   ☐ Zero shown empty
- ○ **Calculated** ☐ **Duplicates blank**   ☐ Shown like (123.4)
- ○ **Ctrl char**   ☒ **Invisible**   ☐ Shown like 1.23-4.5
- ○ **Auto find**   ☐ **Totaled**

Fig. 3-14. Attributes for PHONEXT.

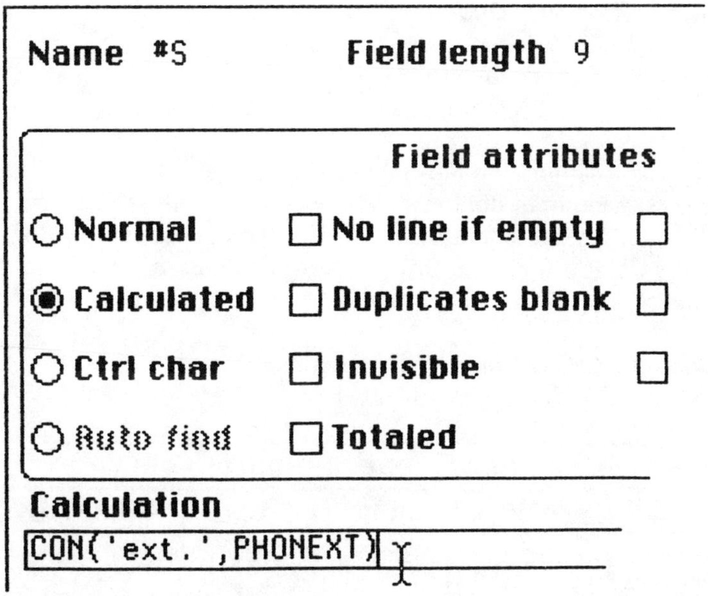

Name **#**S   Field length 9

Field attributes

- ○ **Normal**   ☐ **No line if empty**   ☐
- ● **Calculated** ☐ **Duplicates blank**   ☐
- ○ **Ctrl char**   ☐ **Invisible**   ☐
- ○ **Auto find**   ☐ **Totaled**

Calculation

```
CON('ext.',PHONEXT)
```

Fig. 3-15. The string calculation for the #S field.

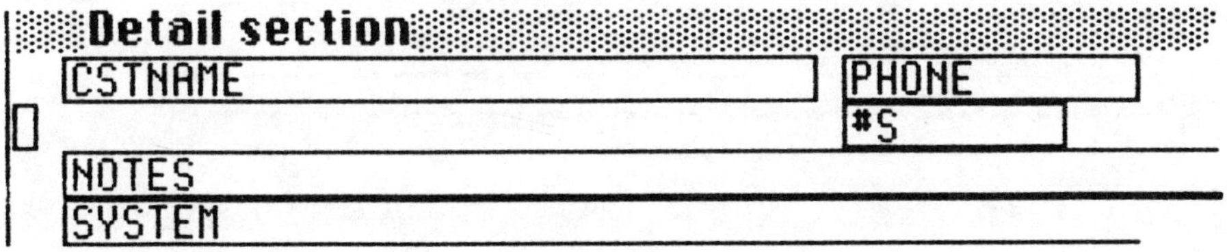

Detail section

```
CSTNAME                          PHONE
                                 #S
NOTES
SYSTEM
```

Fig. 3-16. Latest look of the report.

```
::::Heading section::::::::::::::::::::::::::::::::::::::::::::::::::::::::::::::
Notes On The Work Station's Customers
===================================================
::::Detail section::::::::::::::::::::::::::::::::::::::::::::::::::::::::::::::
 ┌─────────────────────────────────────┐  ┌────────┐
 │CSTNAME                               │  │PHONE   │
□│                                      │  │#S      │
 └──────────────────────────────────────────────────┘
 ┌──────┐
 │NOTES │
 │SYSTEM│
 └─────────────────────────────────────────────────┘
 ─────────────────────────────────────────────────
```

Fig. 3-17. A dashed line typed across the layout.

ever, would be to break the page each time we reach a new salesperson in the list. These characteristics can be set in the *Sort fields* window.

☐ *To get to the Sort fields window, close the current window by choosing* **Reports** *from the* **Options** *menu.*
☐ *Select* **NOTERPT.**
☐ *Click the* **Sort fields** *button.*
☐ *Set the SLSPRSN field as shown in Fig. 3-19*

The last step is to adjust the *Parameters* for this report. Parameters determine such things as whether or not to use Macintosh fonts, the size of the report, output options, and printer defaults. We need to change the defaults for the Search. Note that the default for the Search format is 0. This means there's no search format currently in use.

☐ *Choose* **Reports** *from the* **Options** *menu.*
☐ *Select* **NOTERPT.**

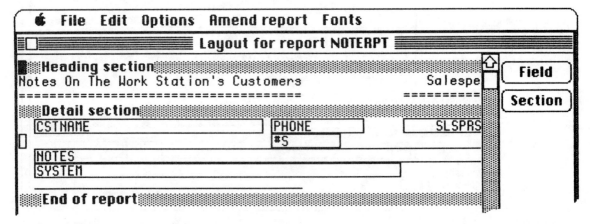

Fig. 3-18. The final look of the report.

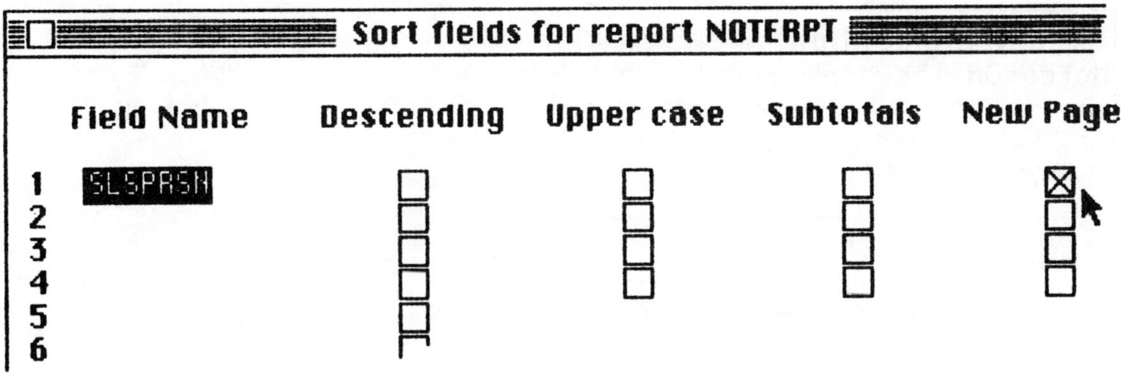

Fig. 3-19. Sort fields for NOTERPT.

☐ Click the **Parameters** button.
☐ Click the **Change search format?** check box.
☐ For the Search format, type **SYSNOTE** as in Fig. 3-20.
☐ Close the window to finish setting the Parameters.

All that's left to do now is print the report. Remember, we set the Parameters so that we would see the Search format before the report is printed. There's no reason to change it, but it is good practice to review it before you print the Report. As noted earlier in this chapter, failing to set a Search format properly before printing a report could result in disaster!

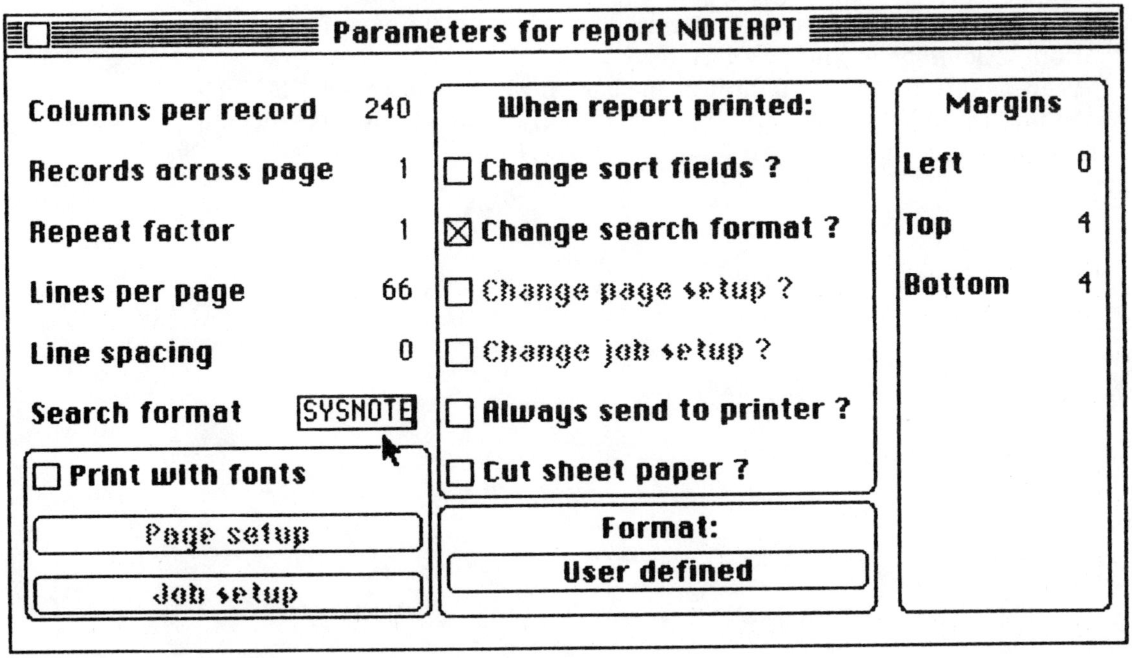

Fig. 3-20. Adding the Search as a parameter for the report.

```
┌──────────────────────────────────────────────────────────────────
│ Notes on The Work Station's Customers              Salesperson
│ =====================================              =================
│    Radical Departures Clothing      213-622-8844        Shelley
│    Owner's name is Andrea Lynn.
│    Mac,Omnis3,LaserWriter,MacDraw
│    ─────────────────────────────────────────
│    Sandra Jacoby Associates         415-543-9000        Shelley
│                                        ext.239
│    Accountants; interested in financial packages
│    Mac(7),LaserWriter,HD20(2),Omnis3,Excel
│    ─────────────────────────────────────────
│
```

Fig. 3-21. The report printed to the screen.

☐ Choose **Print 'NOTERPT'** from the **Options** menu.
☐ Review the **Search format 'SYSNOTE'** window.
☐ Click the close box if the window looks correct.
☐ Select the desired output option.

If all went as planned, each Salesperson's customers printed out a different page, and each customer printed had the word "Laser" appear somewhere in the NOTES or SYSTEM field. Figure 3-21 shows an example of the output. This report was output to the screen, but you should feel free to experiment with your output options if you haven't already.

Now that we have worked through the basics, we can work a bit with some of the fun features that set Omnis 3 apart from the competition, like custom menus and command sequences.

```
 Omnis 3
   The DataBasics
   Useful Reports
   Search Formats
  Custom Menus  ⌘4
```

Automating the System

The Problem. At The Work Station, the users of this growing system have noticed how issuing the correct Omnis 3 commands is getting more involved. For instance, entering new customers or printing a desired report is now a three-step process. The user needs to first choose Entry layouts or Reports from the Options menu. They then have to remember the Omnis 3 name we have given to that layout, such as CSTENTR or NOTERPT. Finally, they have to click the desired button, either Enter data or Print.

They have asked us to automate this system as much as possible.

THE PLAN

This chapter's request is a common one for consultants. The client wouldn't have called in a consultant if they could produce an acceptable system themselves.

People who design systems exclusively for their own use rarely go to the trouble to make these applications "pretty." With most popular database software, this task has always been an arduous one at best. These programs' cryptic, complex programming languages, combined with machines with no standard user interface, made "programming" other machines a task that only an expert would dare take on. The Macintosh and Omnis 3 have changed all that. This chapter will demonstrate just how simple it is to include a "standard" Macintosh feature in your database applications: the *pull-down menu*.

Omnis 3 Menus

The goal in this section is to produce a pull-down menu for use with this application. The four capabilities which we have built in to this application so far are:

1) Enter and/or Edit customer data.
2) Print mail labels.
3) Print a Salespersons' listing of customers.
4) Print a customer list matching a Search of SYSTEM and NOTES.

Omnis 3 has a straightforward mechanism for building menus. There are two types; both appear the same on the screen, but they are very different in how they are implemented. The first and easiest to implement is the standard-type menu, which is the type we'll use in this chapter. It involves virtually no programming and can be implemented in a matter of minutes once the basic ideas are demonstrated.

The second and more complex type of menu is built into Entry layouts. These menus are more complex in that they can contain and trigger *sequences*, or stored lists of Omnis 3 commands. These sequences can execute Omnis 3 commands and call other sequences. They can also perform calculations and make decisions based on their results. They are more powerful (and difficult to implement) than the standard menu described in this chapter. Sequences will be used in Chapter 5.

A standard menu is designed in a manner quite similar to that used to design Entry layouts and Report formats. As a matter of fact, the term that should have been used is "Menu format." However, they are simply called Menus. They are given a name of seven (or fewer) characters, and are saved in the Library file.

There is one "special" menu recognized by Omnis 3. If you create a menu named STARTUP, that menu will be installed in the Menu bar in place of the Options menu when that Library file is opened. The Options menu will still be available, but will be hidden from view until it is needed. There is an option in the File menu that has read *Hide Options menu* until now. When Omnis 3 actually hides the Options menu from view, that item in the File menu becomes *Show Options menu*. The Options menu can be accessed at any time using this command, so the user is not locked out of changing to any of the Library items (Entry layouts or Report formats). What this feature does is eliminate the confusion that the options menu might cause to an uninitiated user. You will see in this chapter that none of the commands in the Options menu are absolutely necessary for simply inputting data or producing reports.

Input and output options can be controlled using a custom Menu. Each item in the menu is associated with a short list of simple Omnis 3 commands. Just like the Macintosh itself, Omnis 3 determines for you which item the user chose from the list, and executes the commands associated with it.

The commands in the list are chosen from a group of five. The first four are commands available from the Options menu:

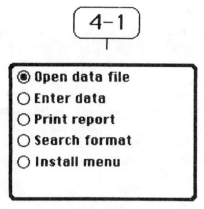

The last command choice listed below might be unfamiliar. Its function is to call other menus or sequences. The items perform the following functions:

Open data file   Sets the current data file. Useful when opening an existing Library file with which you wish to work.

Enter data   Opens an Entry layout for data entry. If there are any Sequences associated with that layout, they are initiated (more on sequences in Chapter 5).

Print report   Uses the named Report format to output a report. Follows the parameters settings you have set for that report.

Search format   Makes the named Search format the current one. All operations (Find, Next, Previous, etc.) will follow this search's rules until the Search is cleared, or another one is chosen.

Install menu   Retrieves the named Menu and installs it in the Menu bar.

Choosing from this list of commands, you can set up an application to have straightforward choices for the user. Good interface design can be the difference between a useful and useless system! If users cannot make intuitive choices while running a program, you are only making things harder by adding a level of complexity to an already confusing situation. Ideally, the user is given just a few simple choices. The menu which we will construct will look like this:

The Work Station
Enter customers

Print mail labels
Print Salesperson list
Search System & Notes

The Macintosh User Interface

Throughout the rest of this book, sound programming and software design principles will be introduced in hopes of helping you understand the interaction of software with a user. You are working with the most advanced personal computer in the industry. What makes it so advanced is not the hardware itself; the advantage that it has over most other personal computers is its software user interface, i.e., the manner in which the hardware interacts with the user. Omnis 3 makes it possible for you to construct, within certain limits, applications which can take advantage of the features of the Macintosh User Interface. We will work as much as possible with the Mac users in mind, since many of you will be building applications for other users.

THE STEPS

As with each of the previous chapters, you should confirm that you have the correct Library file and Data file open. You should keep a separate file for each of these chapters, so if something terrible happens, you can start over without having to return to Chapter 1! Use the Finder's *Duplicate* command to create files called *"Copy of WorkStation"* and *"Copy of ws.data"*. Then rename them to "end of chap 3" or whatever is appropriate for you.

The first step in constructing an Omnis 3 Menu is to create a new Menu in your Library:

☐ *Choose* **Menus** *from the* **Options** *menu.*
☐ *Click* **New.**
☐ *Enter the name as shown in Fig. 4-1.*

After a moment you are greeted with the *Menu format* window (Fig. 4-2). A quick tour is in order here. Starting from the upper left corner of the window, the word Title is highlighted. This is where the title of your menu will go. This is the word or words that is displayed on the menu bar when your Menu is *installed*, or active. Right now, the menu bar has five Menus installed: , File, Edit, Options, and Amend menu. Obviously, these are all built-in Omnis 3 menus, but your menu will appear up there as if it, too, were part of the Omnis 3 program.

Moving to the right, the Commands window is empty now, but that is where

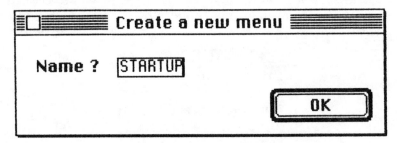

Fig. 4-1. The magic name for an Omnis 3 menu format.

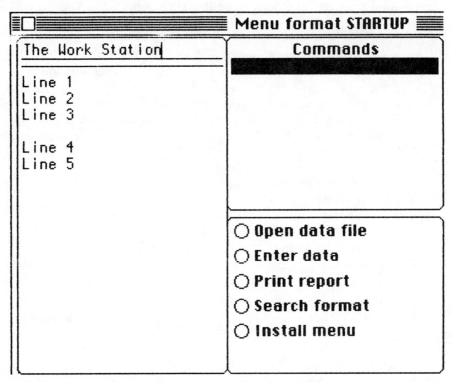

The Work Station|

| Line 1 |
| Line 2 |
| Line 3 |
| |
| Line 4 |
| Line 5 |

Menu format STARTUP

Commands

○ **Open data file**

○ **Enter data**

○ **Print report**

○ **Search format**

○ **Install menu**

Fig. 4-2. The Menu format screen with the name of our new menu entered.

you will eventually put your command list for each item in this menu. At the far right is a long window that is currently almost empty. This is the message area for the window.

At the middle of the command is the list of commands which were detailed earlier. Each of these commands needs additional information, such as a name of an Entry layout, of the name of a Data file. The message area is where this information will be entered.

At the bottom of the screen (not shown in Fig. 4-2) is an interesting area. It is here that you can control user access to each item in this menu. Users can be assigned passwords, and Omnis 3 will "check their IDs" before allowing access to this menu. We will work more with passwords in later chapters.

This menu will be appropriately titled "The Work Station." Enter the title now:

☐ *Double-click the mouse on the word **Title**.*
☐ *Type **The Work Station** (Fig. 4-2).*

Even the title of a menu can have commands associated with it. You might think, "How can the user choose the title of a menu?" You cannot, in fact, choose the title to issue that command. The commands associated with the title of a menu are executed whenever the Menu is installed. If you think back for a moment, that affords you a tremendous amount of control in Omnis 3 applications. Remember, if Omnis 3 finds a menu called STARTUP in a Library that is being opened, it installs it. Now we see that Omnis 3 will also execute whatever commands are associated with the title of a menu when it is installed. This means that the commands attached to the title of the STARTUP menu will always execute first thing when that Library is opened.

If we ponder this for a moment, at this point in the construction of this application, there is really only one requirement for this database to operate properly. That is the fact that the Data file ''ws.data'' should be opened when this database is opened. We can enter this command now.

☐ Click the **Open data file** button.
☐ Tab to the **Name** box.
☐ Type **ws.data**

Name

ws.data

That command is now saved as the default startup command.

The first menu item for the STARTUP menu shown in Fig. 4-3 is ''Enter customers'':

☐ Click Line 1.
☐ Type **Enter customers**
☐ Click the **Enter data** button.
☐ Tab to **Name.**
☐ Type **CSTENTR** (as in Fig. 4-3)

Notice that there is another box below the Name box. This value in this

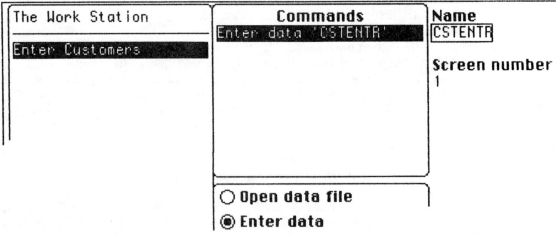

Fig. 4-3. The first menu command.

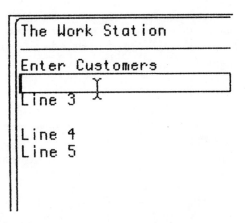

Fig. 4-4. Leaving the second menu line blank.

box determines which screen of your Entry layout the user will be using. The default is always Screen 1. Remember, you have access to up to 12 screens in an Entry layout.

In our proposed *The Work Station* menu early in the chapter, did you notice a dotted line across the slot where the next item would normally be found? This is standard Macintosh fare, since it could be confusing if menus were long continuous lists of commands. Most Mac menus have this dotted-line division between sections.

Using Omnis 3, you can easily divide your menus for clarity just like regular Macintosh menus. If you leave a line blank in a menu, it is replaced by one of those dotted lines. A dividing line is appropriate here, because input commands should be separated from the output commands. This is a stylistic matter, but you should stick to the Macintosh User Interface to maintain continuity in your programs. So let's leave this next line blank:

☐ *Click Line 2.*
☐ *Press **Backspace** as in Fig. 4-4.*

The next three items in the menu are for outputting the previously constructed Report formats. There are more options to set when setting up a Report in a menu. You have to attend to the Sort fields, the Search formats, and various output options. The next item is *"Print mail labels."*

☐ *Click Line 3.*
☐ *Type **Print mail labels***
☐ *Click **Print report.***
☐ *Tab to **Name.***
☐ *Type **LABELS***
☐ *Click **Clear search** and **Send to printer.***

Your window should now look like Fig. 4-5. Obviously, setting the *Clear search* option here defeats the capability of doing selective mailing labels, but this Menu can be easily amended later on and that option added.

Here are the settings for the last two menu items. Set them yourself.

	Item name	Action	Options
1)	*Print salesperson list*	Print report *'PRS'*	- *Change search* - *Clear search* - *Prompt for output*
2)	*Search System & Notes*	Print report *'NOTERPT'*	- *Use default search* - *Prompt for output*

The last order of business here is to eliminate "Line 5"; otherwise it will show up on the menu. To do this, click on that line and then either press Backspace or choose *Delete line* from the *Amend menu* menu (Fig. 4-6).

Now that the menu is complete, you can print its details. Whenever you are building an Omnis 3 format of any kind, there is always an item in the *Amend menu* entitled *Print . . . details*. With this command, you can get a complete list of every detail from that particular format.

☐ Choose **Print menu details** from the **Amend menu** menu.

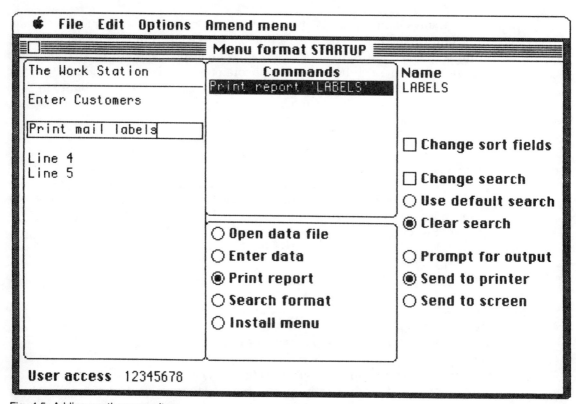

Fig. 4-5. Adding another menu item.

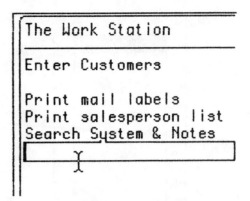

Fig. 4-6. Deleting the last line of the menu.

Now that you've printed the details of this format, compare them with Fig. 4-7.

If the Menu appears to be configured correctly, it can then be installed. If not, make the necessary changes before installing it. To install a menu is quite simple.

☐ *Click the window's close box to save the Menu.*
☐ *Click **Install** as in Fig. 4-8*

Notice that the menu is now installed! Go ahead and try it out. Notice that it automates the various reports dramatically.

To see how Omnis 3's automatic startup mechanism works, do this:

☐ *Choose **Select library**.*

```
----------------------------------------------------------------------------
MENU FORMAT STARTUP                                                   PAGE  1

TEXT                      COMMANDS                   OPTIONS
----------------------------------------------------------------------------
Menu title
----------
The Work Station          Open data file 'ws.data'

Menu lines
----------
Enter Customers           Enter data 'CSTENTR'       Screen number 1

. . . . . . . . . . . . . . . . . . . .

Print mail labels         Print report 'LABELS'      Clear search
                                                     Send to printer

Print Salesperson list    Print report 'PRS'         Clear search
                                                     Prompt for output

Search System & Notes     Print report 'NOTERPT'     Use default search
                                                     Prompt for output
```

Fig. 4-7. The details of the menu.

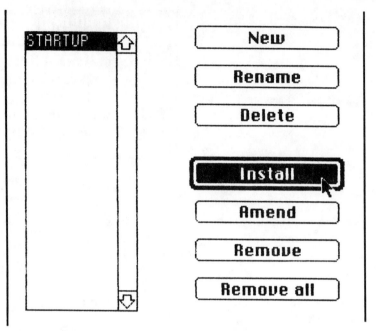

Fig. 4-8. Installing the menu on the menu bar.

    ☐ *Choose* **WorkStation** *and open it.*

This command closes all database files and clears Omnis 3's memory. Selecting a Library opens its files and initiates whatever startup features you may have built in. Look at the menu bar (see Fig. 4-9). Doesn't that look professional? All with very little time spent.

    If you ever need to make changes to a Menu, choose *Menus* from the Options menu, then click *Amend*. The modified menu will automatically be installed once you finish editing it. To make that Menu active, you have use the *Install* command. You can use more than one command for each menu item, up to eight per item. We only used one for each in the interest of simplicity. You will see in the next chapter that there are more choices and more items available for Sequences than for these standard-type menus.

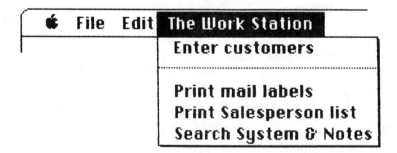

Fig. 4-9. Your new menu!

Omnis 3

The DataBasics

Useful Reports

Search Formats

Custom Menus

Sequences ⌘5

Improving the System

The Problem: Fascinated by the enhancements to the program that we made in the last chapter, the management of The Work Station has requested that we step up the pace in automating their system. They would like a more understandable data entry menu, better safeguards against accidental deletion of customer records, and the ability to turn on and off the Search format from within the CSTENTR Entry layout.

THE PLAN

The thrust of the work in this chapter, as well as the next, will be with the data entry portion of the program. Using Omnis 3's *sequences,* we will be optomizing the CSTENTR Entry layout that we built in Chapter 1, and we'll have a look at the more complex type of custom menu.

Until now we have been using Omnis 3's built-in *Enter data* menu and its corresponding onscreen buttons for entering data. The *Enter data* menu has a number of options that are not needed in this application, and are actually confusing to the users. One of The Work Station's requests was for a more user-friendly interface, so we can simplify things by eliminating unused commands.

They requested that users be able to turn on and off the Search from within the Entry layout. Remember, we defined the Search format SYSNOTE to look through the SYSTEM and NOTES fields for occurrences of the word "Laser." Even if you worked with the database a bit, you may not have noticed the one side effect of setting the Search format: once the Search was in force, *all* operations respected the rules of the Search. For instance, if you click Next or Previous, Omnis 3 takes you to the next record *that matches the Search*. It would be preferable to have access to a "switch" that allows us to turn off the Search from within the Entry layout. This is one limitation of Omnis 3: there is no simple way of telling the program to "zero out" the Search. However, we will discover a clever work-around to that limitation, and learn more about the logic behind the scenes.

The last area of work for this chapter is to build a safeguard against an accidental deletion of a Customer record. Using sequences, you can create your own Dialog and Alert boxes. These are standard Macintosh window types that generally appear over whatever is on the screen. They are used to request input, ask a question, or warn the user of a potentially dangerous situation. A key to successful programming is the anticipation of binds users may get themselves into, and being able to continually offer them an escape route in your program. We'll see how to use a sequence to "intercept" a user requests to delete a record, warn them of the action about to take place, then offer them the opportunity to change their mind.

What Are Sequences?

Sequences are stored lists of Omnis 3 actions. These lists can be as simple as one command, or as complex as a whole series of commands, calculations, and conditional branches. But before we talk about the sequences themselves, let's talk about what they are and how they are entered and stored.

The commands contained within sequences are virtually identical to those that you would initiate from the keyboard; almost every menu command can be found in the sequence "language." I put the word in quotes because Omnis 3's "language" is unlike any conventional programming language. In most languages, you have a text editor into which you must enter a series of lines containing keywords and logical grammar. For instance:

```
STORE (100/SomeNumber) TO Variable;
IF (Variable > 25)
     THEN DO one thing;
ELSE
     DO another thing;
```

The next step is usually to attempt to run the program. And the subsequent step is invariably watching your program stop because of a grammatical or spelling error. In conventional languages, the omission of just one semicolon, or one letter of a command (i.e., THN instead of THEN), will cause the host program to stop the execution of your creation. Or you may get a result that was not what you wanted because the program read your instructions literally, one of your mistakes actually changing the meaning of the expression.

The Omnis 3 way is remarkably different, while still being somewhat familiar. Its language uses much the same terminology as older programming languages, but its method of building programs is what sets it above the rest.

72

○ Find/next/etc	○ Redraw screen	○ Message
○ Edit/insert	○ Goto screen	○ Calculate
○ Delete	○ Set main file	○ Test
○ Print	○ Select	○ If/repeat/etc
○ Clear data	○ Set options	○ Call/quit

Fig. 5-1. The main list of sequences.

There is very little actual text entry needed to build a sequence. Instead of having to work with an awkward text editor and picky syntax checker, you can let Omnis 3 *write* the program for you. Commands and logical keywords are all represented as a series of onscreen buttons. You need only click on the appropriate commands in the order in which they should be executed, and Omnis 3 "writes" the sequence for you. If there is any typing to do, it is most likely just an occasional entry of a filename or a field name. And even field names can be chosen from the Names window, which is available from anywhere in Omnis 3.

Figure 5-1 shows the main list of commands available in sequences. Each one of these choices, however, has anywhere from two to over a dozen different variations. After clicking on this first choice, you are presented with a secondary screen to clarify your choice. For instance, if we clicked the *Find/next/etc.* button above, we would be presented with the secondary screen shown in Fig. 5-2. Once in this screen, we can decide exactly what command we want to have executed. (We'll discuss each of the sequence command options in detail in Chapter 6.)

Each sequence can be associated with a custom menu item. In the last chapter we discussed the two types of Omnis 3 menus: standard menus and those associated with sequences. Standard menu items are simpler than sequences because they only have a few possibilities, are incapable of performing

Find/next/etc		Another command
◉ Next	○ Find (prompted)	○ Search
○ Previous	○ Find	○ Find last
Index field		☐ Exact match
Calculation		

Fig. 5-2. The secondary screen for Find/next/etc.

calculations, and are unable to do logical testing and branching. Sequences, though, can do all of this.

Sequence Limitations

Sequence menus are limited to 19 lines. Each of these lines, or menu items, has a maximum of 60 commands associated with it. The total size of all the stored commands in the library file must be less than 30,000 bytes. That is a rather abstract limit, though, because Omnis 3 stores the sequences in a compact format. You will probably never approach this limit.

How Can I Use Sequences?

The actual answer to the above question is: for almost anything that Omnis 3 can do! It is best to describe the capabilities by example. In this chapter's problem, The Work Station's requests all have to do with further automation of their growing system. Let's look at how sequences can solve this problem.

The most basic request was to do away with Omnis 3's needlessly complex *Enter data* menu (see Fig. 5-3). The authors of Omnis 3 acknowledged this, and they built in a mechanism to take care of that complaint: a command to hide the Enter data menu when a particular Entry layout screen is displayed. Ob-

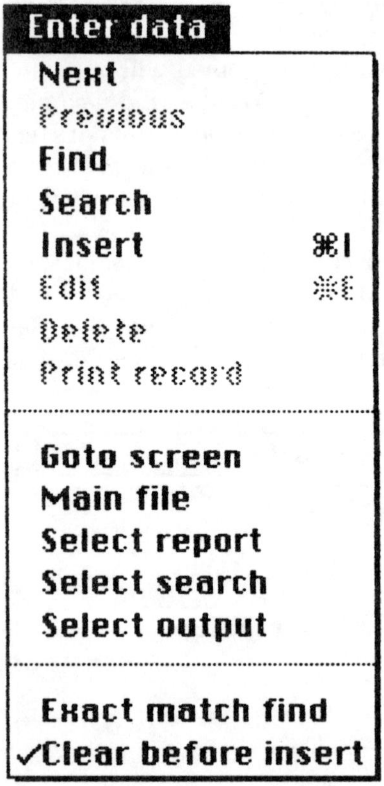

Enter data

Next
Previous
Find
Search
Insert   ⌘I
Edit   ⌘E
Delete
Print record

Fig. 5-3. Omnis 3's "standard" Enter data menu.

Goto screen
Main file
Select report
Select search
Select output

Exact match find
✓Clear before insert

viously, there has to be a substitute menu, because some commands are still needed. This is where you must define your own menu for that Entry layout. As you will soon learn, it is so easy to define your own Omnis 3 menus that you will probably never rely on the *Enter data* menu again.

Returning to the question, "How Can I Use Sequences?", here are the examples.

One of the requests was to be able to turn on and turn off the Search format SYSNOTE from within the Entry layout. You may have found that there is no direct command in Omnis 3 to "turn off", or deactivate a Search format once it is made current. If you were interested in looking at all the customers who have the word "Laser" in their records, you would activate the SYSNOTE Search that was built in Chapter 3. After that, all commands issued from within the Entry layout would "respect" the Search. If you click the *Next* button, Omnis 3 would display the next record that matches the Search. This is sometimes desired, but you might then need to return to the more global view, exclusive of any Search. Omnis 3 does not provide a "Clear Search" command in the Enter data menu. Using sequences, unfortunately, you have no explicit "Clear Search" command, either.

Here you can use a clever sequence to fake out Omnis 3! There is a command *Select a Search* available from the Sequences choices. What we will do is create a new Search format (we'll name it ZERO for clarity), and leave it blank. This effectively tells Omnis 3 "Give me all the records regardless of content." Therefore, the command to use in this sequence for our "Clear Search" command is:

Select the Search format named 'ZERO'

You could issue this same command by using the *Options* menu, but that would involve exiting the Entry layout, and is a much clumsier method. This new command can be accessible in our custom menu, and it will be very easy to issue.

How Do Sequences Work?

The internal technical details of sequences are very complex; they are not appropriate for discussion here. However, it is simple to discuss metaphorically what happens inside the Macintosh when a sequence is running.

When using the Macintosh, a user is never talking directly to the hardware. There is an intermediate level: *software*. Software is the arcane set of instructions that does everything from copying files to making your alarm clock accessory beep at a preset time. The software interprets the user's actions, such as which menu item has been selected. It then determines the appropriate actions to take, such as printing a document or drawing a circle on the screen, and it translates these instructions into a format recognizable to the machine. The built-in software of the Macintosh, the *operating system* contained in the read-only memory (ROM) chips, takes over and does the dirty work of actually

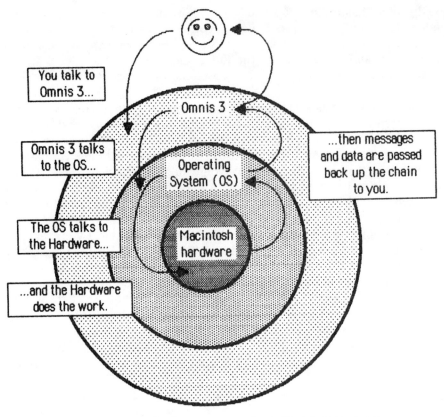

Fig. 5-4. The levels of communication between you and your Macintosh hardware.

moving the printer mechanism, or blackening the correct dots on your screen to make a circle. Noted computer expert and philosopher Stephen Heffernan once explained it to me with the very simple picture shown in Fig. 5-4.

When working with Omnis 3, a user is conversing with the software. Omnis 3 requests data, and the user enters it using the keyboard or the mouse. Building a Report format is a good example. The user clicks in a particular spot on the screen and tells Omnis 3 to put a field there. He then decides that he wants that particular field centered, and to be left blank if it is equal to zero. Omnis 3 all the while is "taking notes" on the user's actions. The characteristics are stored in a very efficient format, unreadable to you and me, taking up only a few bytes of storage in the Library file. When Omnis 3 prints that report, it looks up this information and acts accordingly. None of this would be possible without the hardware, but the user never speaks directly to the hardware: "Spin the disk now and put these bytes in this spot on my disk." Omnis 3 is handling all that interaction for you.

When you run a sequence, you are simply adding another layer to the picture. The sequence becomes your interface to the machine, running Omnis 3 for you. It is pressing the keys, clicking the mouse, and making the decisions for you. The system now looks like Fig. 5-5. Omnis 3 is still conversing with the operating system, which is still running the machine. However, there is a new insulating layer around Omnis 3, your sequence; as long as your sequence is running, you are having a relationship with that sequence, not Omnis 3.

In effect, building a sequence is just like writing your own program. Don't be intimidated, because Omnis 3 does most of the hard work for you. You will find that "programming" Omnis 3 is much easier than you ever imagined, and you might even think it's fun!

Now let's try it!

THE STEPS

If you have made any major changes to the database on your own, make sure you are now back to the version of the Work Station Library file from the end of the last chapter. Once you have done that, we need to open up the *Sequence* editing window.

☐ *Choose **Entry layouts** from the Options menu.*

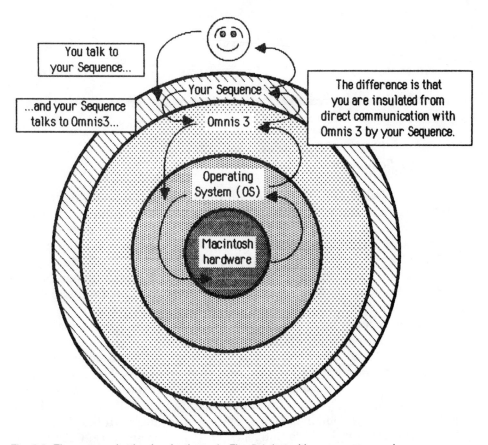

You talk to your Sequence...

...and your Sequence talks to Omnis3...

The difference is that you are insulated from direct communication with Omnis 3 by your Sequence.

Your Sequence

Omnis 3

Operating System (OS)

Macintosh hardware

Fig. 5-5. The communication levels shown in Fig. 5-4, but with a sequence running.

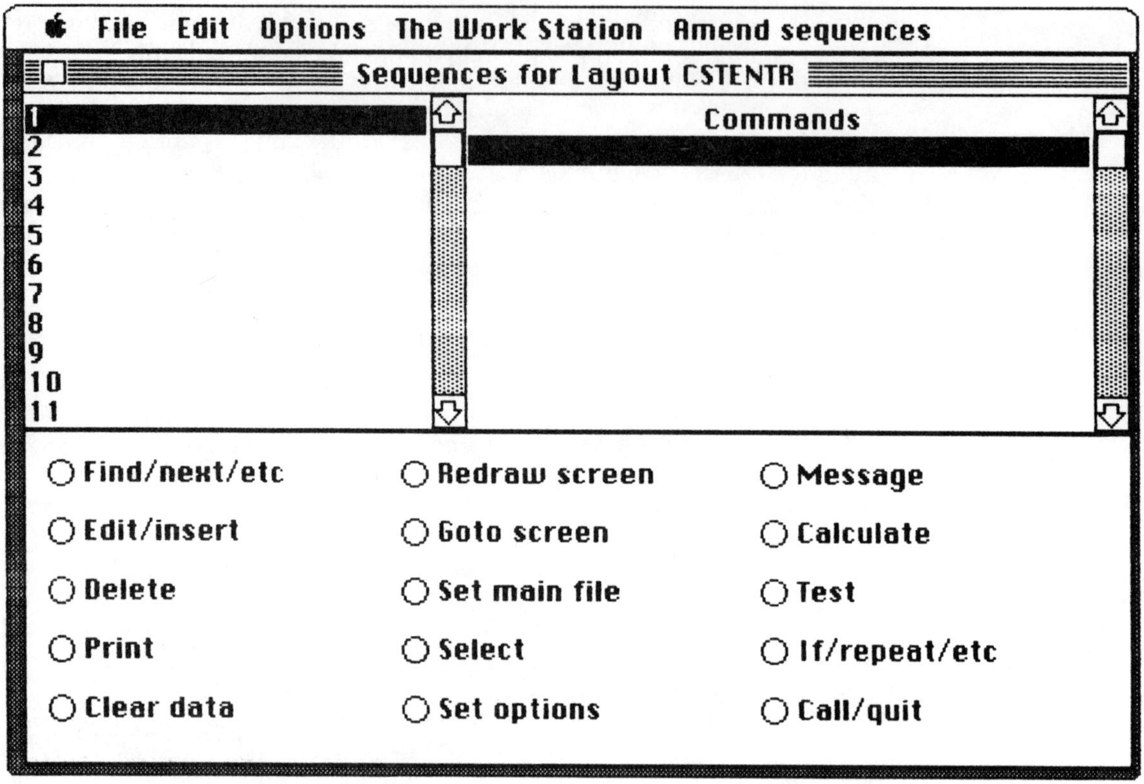
File Edit Options The Work Station Amend sequences
Sequences for Layout CSTENTR
1
2
3
4
5
6
7
8
9
10
11
Commands
Find/next/etc
Edit/insert
Delete
Print
Clear data
Redraw screen
Goto screen
Set main file
Select
Set options
Message
Calculate
Test
If/repeat/etc
Call/quit
Fig. 5-6. The Sequence editing window.

- ☐ *Select the **CSTENTR** layout.*
- ☐ *Click **Sequences.***

You are presented with the *Sequence* editing window (Fig. 5-6), with which you will create and edit all your sequences. There are three sections in this window (see Fig. 5-7).

Let's take a tour around this new window. We already talked about the bottom section, which contains all of the primary command choices, in the Plan above. Each of the choices shown in this section are *categories* (rather than actual commands), leading to a selection of related commands from which you make your ultimate choice.

The small window at the left is a scrolling list of the sequences for that Entry layout. As you put together the actions for a sequence, you must also give that sequence a name. Here, Omnis 3 breaks away from the regular limitation of seven characters imposed on most internal names (e.g., CSTENTR, NOTERPT). You can give more normal names to sequences, using the upper and lower cases, spaces, and limited punctuation (e.g., "Print a record," or "Print Joe's report"). Numbers 1-19 are reserved for use with the Custom Sequence Menu for each layout's Entry layout. If #1 has an entry, Omnis 3 expects the next 18 sequences to be menu choices or blank. It starts reading down, assigning each sequence name as a choice on the menu. It reads all the way through #19, but looks from the bottom up for the first name, and ends the menu there. This is so you won't have unsightly dashed lines at the end of your menu.

The last section (at the upper right) contains the list of commands for each sequence. Notice that it, too, has a scroll bar, enabling you to review more complex sequences. However, this small window does not have "word-wrap" (like word processors) and there is no horizontal scroll bar, so it will often be necessary for you to use a command in the *Amend Sequences* menu (*Print sequence details*) to see the sequences in their entirety.

Let's start with a simple version of a new *Enter data* menu. First, the regular Omnis 3 *Enter data* menu has to be disabled.

☐ Choose **Set menu options.**
☐ *Clear the two check boxes shown in Fig. 5-8.*
☐ *Close this window.*

The second option in the box determines whether or not your menu will have an item at the end entitled *Show* (or *Hide*) *Enter data* menu. This could be desirable for a database for your own use, but remember that this is for a client;

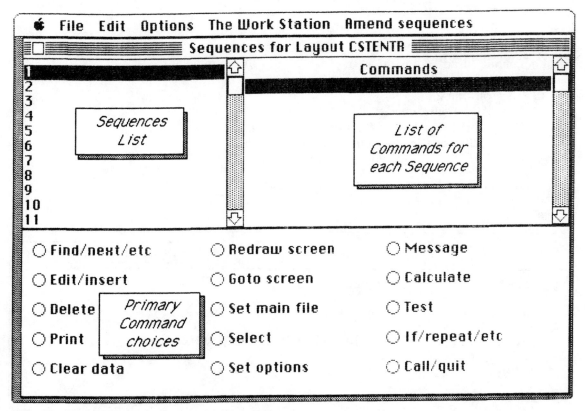

Fig. 5-7. The geography of the Sequence editing window.

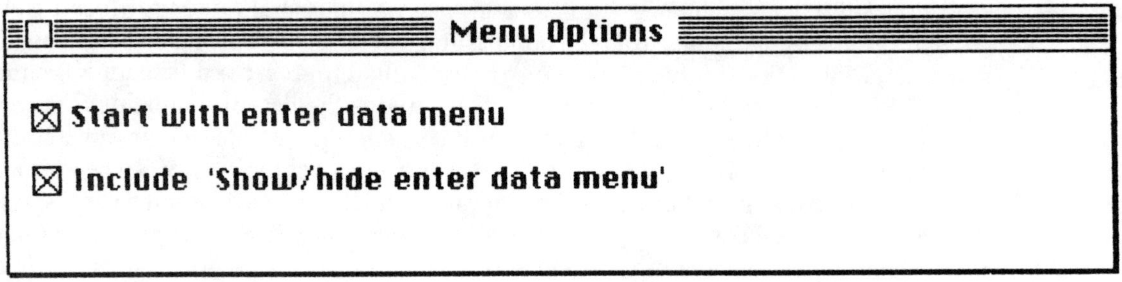

```
╔══════════════════════ Menu Options ══════════════════════╗
║                                                           ║
║  ☒ Start with enter data menu                             ║
║                                                           ║
║  ☒ Include 'Show/hide enter data menu'                    ║
║                                                           ║
║                                                           ║
╚═══════════════════════════════════════════════════════════╝
```

Fig. 5-8. Turning off the Enter data menu.

we'll leave this item out of our menu. The next time the user wants to enter
data with this Entry layout, he will not see Omnis 3's Enter data menu, so now
we have to build our own!

We'll start with the title of our new menu. The title is entered as Sequence
#1.

☐ Click on line 1.
☐ Type **Customers** like this:

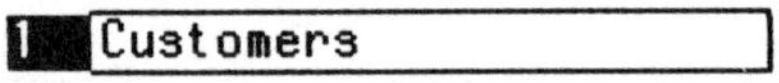

```
┌─┬─────────────────────────────────┐
│1│Customers                        │
└─┴─────────────────────────────────┘
```

We'll start slowly, and build a menu with just a few items in it. Let's set the
most commonly used command as the first item in this sequence menu.

☐ Click on line 2.
☐ Type **Add a customer**
☐ Click on the first line of the **Commands** area.
☐ Click **Edit/insert** in the **Command choices** area.
☐ Using Fig. 5-9 as your guide, set this command as:

   Prepare for Insert Enter data Update files

☐ Click on line 3.

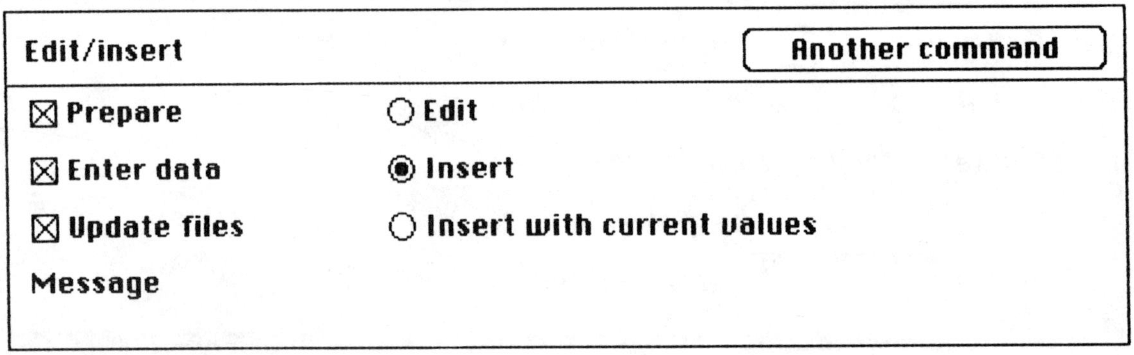

```
┌─────────────────────────────────────────────────────────────┐
│ Edit/insert                          ( Another command )     │
├─────────────────────────────────────────────────────────────┤
│ ☒ Prepare          ○ Edit                                    │
│                                                              │
│ ☒ Enter data       ◉ Insert                                  │
│                                                              │
│ ☒ Update files     ○ Insert with current values             │
│                                                              │
│ Message                                                      │
│                                                              │
└─────────────────────────────────────────────────────────────┘
```

Fig. 5-9. The first command of this sequence.

Here are the basic definitions of these commands. *Prepare for Insert* puts Omnis 3 in "Prepare mode," where you must be if you want to have access to any data in a Data file. *Enter data* is the sequence command that initiates the entire data entry process in Omnis 3. This puts the OK and Cancel buttons on the screen, and handles all user input until one of these buttons (or the Return or Shift-Return keys) is pressed. *Update files* must always be called to save any data that might have been input or changed. We'll talk about each of these commands in more detail, as well as the rest of the Omnis 3 sequences, in the next chapter.

An important footnote to the above is that it is entirely unnecessary to use Omnis 3's terminology in your own custom menus. For instance, if you prefer (as we did above) the word "add" instead of "insert," then it is fine to use that word in place of Omnis 3's word. However, be aware that another tenet of good program design is consistency. If you settle on a word, take care to use it throughout the application, or you will completely confuse the user.

The next command is very similar to the Insert command: the *Edit* command. The next item will use that command, and the subsequent items will be a blank line, then the Find command.

☐ *Click on line 3.*
☐ *Type **Edit a customer.***
☐ *Click on the first line of the **Commands** area.*
☐ *Click **Edit/insert** in the **Command choices** area.*
☐ *Set this command as:*

Prepare for Edit Enter data Update files

☐ *Click on line 5 (leaving line 4 blank).*
☐ *Type **Find.***
☐ *Click **Find/next/etc** in the **Command choices** area.*
☐ *Set this command as:*

◉ Find (prompted)

☐ *Close this window.*
☐ *Choose **Enter customers** from your **The Work Station** menu:*

```
┌─────────────────────────────┐
│ The Work Station            │
│ Enter customers             │
│·····························│
│ Print mail labels           │
│ Print salesperson list      │
│ Search System & Notes       │
└─────────────────────────────┘
```

The *Find (prompted)* command is the equivalent of pressing the Find button while in an Entry layout. Omnis 3 prompts the user for a field and data, then performs the operation when the user clicks the OK button (or equivalent). There is another type of Find command available from within a sequence: *Find*. This second type is for times when you know in advance what it is that you wish to find. For instance, you may always wish to find the record in a Parts database that has the largest part number. But remember, to use any Find command, you must be certain that you are using an indexed field. This command is similar to creating a simple Search format, since it is "hard wired" to find whatever data you enter in the form when the sequence is built.

Notice that Omnis 3 has automatically installed your new Menu on the menu bar.

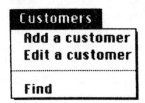

Try out the commands! If all worked as planned, we can move ahead, adding a few more commands to this menu.

This points to yet another tenet of good program design: *testing*. If we installed 10 or 15 different commands immediately, and one or more didn't work, how could we be certain which was causing the trouble? It is always best to work systematically. The most effective method is:

1) Design.
2) Build a little bit.
3) Test.
4) If step 3 works OK, continue with step 2.
   If step 3 doesn't work, return to 1!!

Now that we've had one successful run through step 3 above, let's build a bit more.

The next step is to add items to turn on (activate) and turn off (clear) the Search format SYSNOTE from within this layout. Of these two commands, turning on the Search is trivial, but turning it off will be trickier. As was noted in the Plan section, we'll have to "fake out" Omnis 3 for this to operate correctly. Let's first create our "fake" Search format.

☐ Choose **Search formats** from the Options menu.
☐ Create a **New** format named **ZERO**.
☐ Once the Search format window has appeared, close it (see Fig. 5-10).
☐ Choose **Sequences for 'CSTENTR'** from the Options menu.

When we closed the window, Omnis 3 saved that Search format in the Library file under the name ZERO. Whenever we activate ZERO, it will become

```
▦ ═══════════ Search format  ZERO ═══
   Field    Mode   Value/calculation
1            =
2
3
4
5
6
7
8
```

Fig. 5-10. Creating a blank Search format.

the current Search, deactivating the current one. But since it is empty this will effectively clear all Searches. We'll add the Search item first, then the Clear Search.

☐ Click on line 6 (below the Find sequence).
☐ Type **Search**
☐ Click on the first line of the **Commands** area.
☐ Click the **Select** command choice.
☐ Using Fig. 5-11 as a guide, set this command as:

Select Search name [SYSNOTE]

☐ Click on the second line of the **Commands** area (below the line which was just filled in).
☐ Click the **Find/next/etc** command choice.
☐ Set this command as:

Search

The Commands area should now appear as in Fig. 5-12.

```
Select                                    ( Another command )

○ Report name         ◉ Search name        ○ Printer

○ Report (prompted)   ○ Search (prompted)  ○ Screen

                      ○ Output (prompted)

Name
[SYSNOTE]
```

Fig. 5-11. Using the "Select search" command.

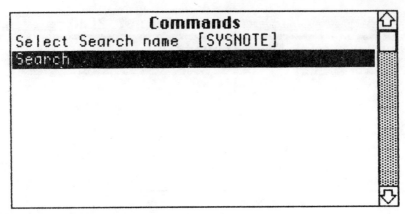

Fig. 5-12. The current appearance of the sequence.

☐ Click on line 7 (below the Search sequence).
☐ Type **Clear Search**
☐ Click on the first line of the **Commands** area.
☐ Set these commands as: (they must be on separate lines!)

Select Search name [ZERO]
Search

☐ Test the additions by choosing **Enter customers.**
☐ Choose the two new items and confirm that they work.

If all went well above and in the preceding chapters, the Search item should restrict all viewing and editing to those records that contain "Laser" in their NOTES or SYSTEM fields. When the Clear Search item is chosen, *all* records should be accessible. If for some reason you get an error message, or the system doesn't seem to be operating properly, verify that the Search formats ZERO and SYSNOTE have been entered correctly. If not, make the necessary repairs, and try again.

The last step in this particular set of sequences is to add the option for deleting a customer's record. We were asked to supply an appropriate warning to try to prevent accidental deletions. To do this, we can use one of Omnis 3's Message boxes, also known as a *Dialog* or *Alert* box. These boxes are available in varying levels of intensity depending on what your need. There are warning boxes that have only an OK button; ones that have both a YES and a NO button; and working boxes, which are the type Omnis 3 displays when it is in the process of printing.

In sequences, the Delete command has a built-in option to call on a message box. You can set a *Delete with confirmation* command, which automatically posts your message in a box requesting a YES or NO response. Once the user has made a decision, Omnis 3 handles the outcome automatically. We'll use this command here.

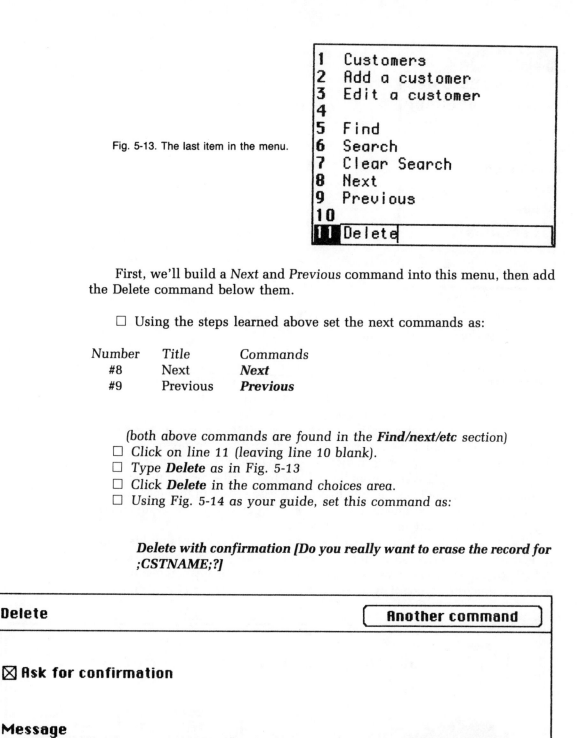

Fig. 5-13. The last item in the menu.

```
1  Customers
2  Add a customer
3  Edit a customer
4
5  Find
6  Search
7  Clear Search
8  Next
9  Previous
10
11 Delete
```

First, we'll build a *Next* and *Previous* command into this menu, then add the Delete command below them.

☐ Using the steps learned above set the next commands as:

Number	Title	Commands
#8	Next	**Next**
#9	Previous	**Previous**

*(both above commands are found in the **Find/next/etc** section)*
☐ *Click on line 11 (leaving line 10 blank).*
☐ *Type **Delete** as in Fig. 5-13*
☐ *Click **Delete** in the command choices area.*
☐ *Using Fig. 5-14 as your guide, set this command as:*

Delete with confirmation [Do you really want to erase the record for ;CSTNAME;?]

Delete   (**Another command**)

☒ **Ask for confirmation**

Message

```
Do you really want to erase the record for ;CSTNAME;?
```

Fig. 5-14. The 'Delete' command, along with the message for the confirmation box.

Fig. 5-15. The current appearance of the sequence .

☐ *Close this window once all items have been set.*
☐ *Test the new menu items.*

The menu should now look like Fig. 5-15. If not, go back and make sure the items are on the correct lines (see Fig. 5-13), and that the items are all spelled correctly. (The spelling is actually unimportant, because the sequence names are for your use only. Internally, Omnis 3 uses only the numbers.)

The Delete command is worth noting here. Notice the message that is entered in Fig. 5-14. The field name is surrounded by semicolons. In any message box, this is the way of telling Omnis to include a field from a record in that message. Importantly, the field is read from the current record, the record on the screen at that time. Any field can be included in a message box in this manner if its name is surrounded in semicolons. The resulting message (Fig. 5-16) appears if you use the Delete item in the *Customers* menu.

The last step for this chapter is the inclusion of ⌘ shortcuts in this menu. Just like "real" Macintosh menus, Omnis 3's menus can contain these shortcuts. If you open the Edit menu, you will see that the Copy command can be executed from the keyboard by pressing ⌘ . When building custom menus, you

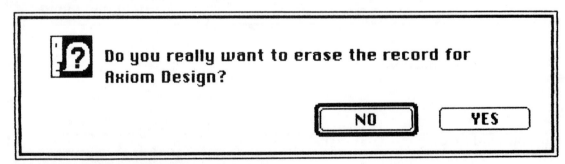

Fig. 5-16. The message that appears if you press "Delete."

```
Customers
Add a customer    ⌘A
Edit a customer   ⌘E
..............................
Find              ⌘F
Search            ⌘S
Clear Search
Next              ⌘N
Previous          ⌘P
..............................
Delete            ⌘D
```

Fig. 5-17. The menu with command-key equivalents added.

have access to these shortcuts as well. So let's assign keyboard shortcuts to the new menu.

You needn't assign shortcuts to all of the menu items, or even any at all. For those that are to receive them, you must decide what key you want to assign to which items. In this case, we want the menu to look like Fig. 5-17. In order to do this, you must add a slash (/) followed by the desired key. Let's add the shortcuts now.

☐ *Open the Sequences window again.*
☐ *Edit each of the items as shown in Fig. 5-18, until that area appears as in Fig. 5-19.*
☐ *Close the window and test the menu.*

Now most of these commands can be entered from either the keyboard or the custom menu.

Verify that all the options are operating properly before you move on. If

```
1   Customers
2   Add a customer/A
3   Edit a customer
4
5   Find
6   Search
7   Clear Search
8   Next
9   Previous
10
11  Delete
```

Fig. 5-18. Adding the "/A" that creates command-key equivalency.

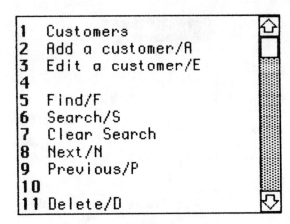

```
1   Customers
2   Add a customer/A
3   Edit a customer/E
4
5   Find/F
6   Search/S
7   Clear Search
8   Next/N
9   Previous/P
10
11  Delete/D
```

Fig. 5-19. The final appearance of the Sequences window.

anything went awry, fix it now before you compound it later! There *is* something amiss, and you might have noticed. Some of the on-screen buttons do not work exactly like the corresponding menu items. Even though we have a Delete in both, they work differently. Try them and observe the differences. The on-screen button version uses the ''generic'' Omnis 3 warning box, not the custom one we built. And the Search button does not work exactly like the Search menu item.

In the next chapter, we'll see how to ''coordinate'' the two, and we'll learn quite a bit more about sequences.

Omnis 3
The DataBasics
Useful Reports
Search Formats
Custom Menus
Sequences
More Sequences ⌘6

More Improvements

The Problem. In this chapter we will continue to work on the sequences developed in Chapter 5. In particular, we'll eliminate the "standard" on-screen buttons in favor of custom ones that we'll build, and we'll also build some "logical branching" into the existing sequences using some of the advanced sequence commands.

THE PLAN

In Chapter 5, we talked about the ability of sequences to do logical testing and then perform conditional "branching" based on the results of those tests. Conditional branching is the ability of a program to execute different instructions depending on the result of a logical calculation. In this chapter, we will try some simple logical expressions to demonstrate the use of Omnis 3's logical operators.

In CSTENTR's Entry layout sequences, there is no visual feedback to confirm that a customer's data has been entered correctly. This is not something normally built in to a database, but it is a relatively simple feature to add, and will serve as a good example of using Omnis 3's logical capabilities. If this feature becomes tiresome, it is quite easy to remove or modify. But for a beginning user of computers, visual feedback can be reassuring. We will also use two more types of message boxes: OK Messages, and Working Messages.

OK Messages are very simple in nature. They are commonly used simply to confirm that an action has taken place. For instance, if the user presses Cancel during an input operation, we can instruct Omnis 3 to display a message confirming that the customer's data was *NOT* entered in the file. OK Messages stay on the screen until the user presses Return or clicks the mouse on the OK button.

Working Messages are quite different from OK Messages, and are much more specialized. A Working Message is the type of Dialog box that Omnis 3 uses when it is printing a report or Sorting a file. These boxes can also be used by you within your sequences. In The Work Station's application, user entry of a new customer places a Working Message on the screen. This will be placed in the sequence before the *Update Files* command, so the user will be apprised of the progress of the operation. This is actually a rather trivial application for a Working Message, but it will serve to demonstrate how one works.

Working Messages are generally applied to more complex applications. For instance, an accounting application that is programmed in Omnis 3 to cycle through all the customers in a file, updating their balances once a month, can use one. This could be a time-consuming operation, and a message box can inform the user as the program proceeds.

As I mentioned at the end of the previous chapter, the sequences in the ''Customers'' menu do not react the same as the on-screen buttons in the CSTENTR Entry layout. If you use the ''Delete'' command in the Customers menu that you created, you are presented with the OK Message box shown in Fig. 6-1. This is one that you created by using the *Delete with confirmation* sequence command. If you click the onscreen Delete button, you are presented with the OK Message box shown in Fig. 6-2. This box is ''standard equipment'' with Omnis 3, but is abrupt and not very informative.

This is not acceptable in our application, because a program has to be consistent in order to be useful and easy to operate. We need to coordinate the onscreen buttons with the custom menu which we built. This can be done using the *Set Screen Information* command available in the *Amend sequences* menu. This command allows you to build various options into each of the 12 screens of an Entry layout. As you may remember, each screen is independent (in some respects) from the rest. Using this command, you can change the following information for each screen:

1) Give it a heading (the window's title).

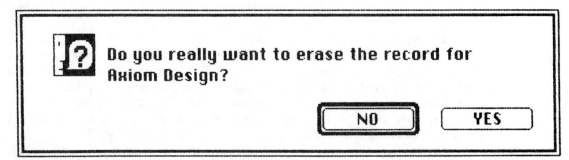

Fig. 6-1. Your ''Delete with confirmation'' message box.

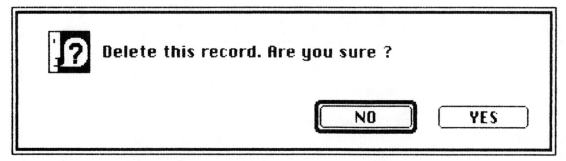

Fig. 6-2. Omnis 3's standard confirmation message box.

2) Set its on-screen buttons (up to 8 per screen).
3) Set the sequence which each button will initiate.
4) Determine whether the user will be allowed to use the scroll bar to access any secondary screens.

Because of the simplicity of this application at this time, there is no need to use any more than one screen, so we will not be using the fourth option above. However, we'll use the other three options to help improve the user interface of our application.

Window Headings

The first is quite simple. When entering data with this application, the Entry layout window is normally entitled "Entry layout CSTENTR." This certainly is no help to the casual user, and is actually too vague for almost all users. You can change that title by entering a more appropriate "Heading" for that screen. Each the 12 screens of the Entry layout can have its own title.

Buttons

Manipulating the on-screen buttons is slightly more complex than setting the window title. Each screen can have up to 8 buttons along the right side of the window. Omnis 3 supplies you with a default set of buttons that includes Next, Previous, etc. Most of these are acceptable, so our set of custom buttons will be very similar to the standard ones. The reason for assigning a new set of buttons, similar as they may be, is that Omnis 3 will assume that you want to use the default set if you don't assign any others. The buttons themselves are not the problem, though; the problem is the commands to which these buttons refer. If you use the default buttons, you also must use the default commands. Consequently, to coordinate the buttons with our menu and its sequences, the standard buttons will have to go in favor of a custom set.

Each button must be set to call a particular sequence. This is done by entering a sequence number along with a name for the button. In this application the numbers will simply be those of the matching Menu commands. If you wished to have a button that called a sequence *not* associated with any menu item, you would have to use a number greater than 20. Remember, the first 20 sequences are reserved for the menu; the first one is for the title, and the next 19 are for command choices in the menu. However, you have all the numbers greater than 20 to work with. You would simply have to build a sequence (#25, for instance), and enter that number along with the description of the button in the Screen Information window.

We should continue with the convention of using the term ''Add'' instead of Omnis 3's ''Insert'' (consistency!). The reason for this change is simply to illustrate just how easily you can change the program around to suit your needs. If you are more comfortable with Omnis 3's standard terminology, you may certainly use ''Insert'' instead.

THE STEPS

In this chapter, we'll add on-screen buttons to coordinate with the existing custom menu which was built using sequences in Chapter 5. But first, let's expand upon a couple of the sequences that we built.

☐ Recall the **Sequences for 'CSTENTR'** window.

The sequences in your window should be the same as Fig. 6-3.

Logic 101

We will be adding a conditional test here based on the ''Flag.'' The *Flag* is an internal Omnis 3 logical indicator. (Experienced programmers would call the Flag a ''global boolean variable.'') It can be used in sequences to determine the result of most operations that a user can perform, and to test conditions such as the results of a Search or Find. In this case we will use it to determine the result of the ''Enter data'' operation.

When Omnis 3 is running a sequence, it takes care of maintaining the Flag for you. It sets the Flag to True or False depending on the outcome of various operations.

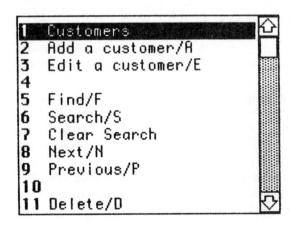

Fig. 6-3. The sequences as they should be at the end of the last chapter.

```
Prepare for Insert  Enter data  []
If Flag False
   OK message  [OK, customer was not added...]
Else
   Working message  [Adding customer to file...]
   Update files
End If
```

Fig. 6-4. A simple example of an If-Then-Else expression.

In this case, when Omnis 3 returns from the *Enter data* operation, it will do so in one of two ways: the user completed the entry of a new customer either by pressing Return (or clicking OK), or by cancelling the operation. At that point, Omnis 3 sets the Flag to True if the entry was completed successfully, or to False if the user cancelled. You can then set the line following the "Enter data" sequence command to say "IF Flag False" (see Fig. 6-4 for the complete sequence). This is the "test" part of a conditional expression. After reading this line, Omnis 3 processes the test, determining if in fact the Flag was True or False. It then continues reading the expression based on the result.

If the Flag ends up True (i.e., the "If" test failed, meaning that the user completed the operation), the part of the expression directly following the "If" is skipped, and Omnis 3 looks for an "Else" clause. In this case, it finds one, so the instructions there are executed until the "End If" is reached, which signals the end of this expression. However, if the Flag was True (i.e., the "If" test passed and the user did cancel) Omnis 3 will execute the instructions directly after the "If" test, then skip over any "Else" clause(s) directly to the end of the expression.

This is a very simple example of an If-Then-Else expression. In Omnis 3, as well as other programming languages, you can use an "Else If" test in place of an "Else" to string together multiple tests of similar conditions. Experienced programmers will note the lack of a "CASE" (Pascal) or "switch" (C) statement in Omnis 3; stringing together "Else If" statements is the recommended method to simulate a multiple-way branch.

Adding to Existing Sequences

Let's go ahead and use some of these logical tools to expand upon our existing sequence.

☐ Click on line 2, **Add a customer/A**
☐ Click on the second line of the sequence list (see Fig. 6-5).
☐ Click the **If/repeat/etc** command choice.
☐ Set this command (see Fig 6-6):
   If Flag False
☐ Click on the third line of the sequence list.
☐ Set this command (see Fig. 6-7):
   OK Message [This customer was not added.]

93

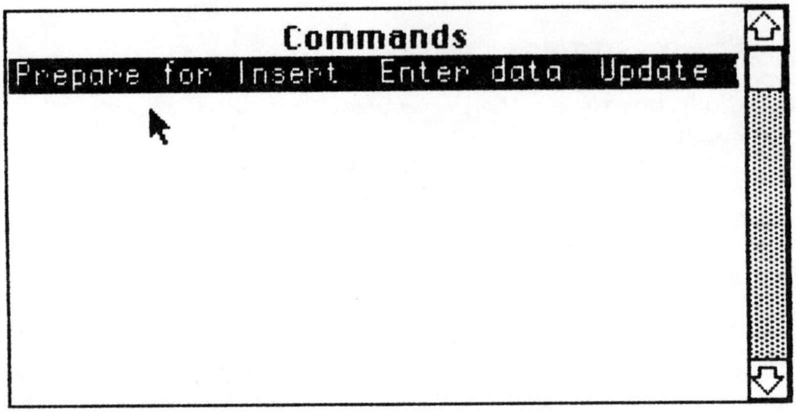

Fig. 6-5. Put the command on this line.

☐ Set the last three commands (Omnis 3 adds the indents):
Else
   Working Message [Adding new customer . . .]
End If

The sequences in your window should be the same as Fig. 6-8.

This sequence is almost complete. However, astute observers will notice a small glitch in the order of the commands. As you can see, the first command is "Prepare for Insert-Enter Data-Update files." This is not entirely what we had wished, as the user is to be apprised of the Update files command by the Working Message box as it is being done. Therefore, we need to edit the first line to remove the "Update files" statement, and then replace it farther down in the Sequence. Let's see how that is done.

☐ Click on the first line of your Sequence (as in Fig. 6-8).
☐ Clear the **Update files** command from the statement.
☐ Click on the line: **End if.**
☐ Insert a blank line by choosing **Insert line** from the **Amend sequences** menu (or press ⌘-I as in Fig. 6-9.

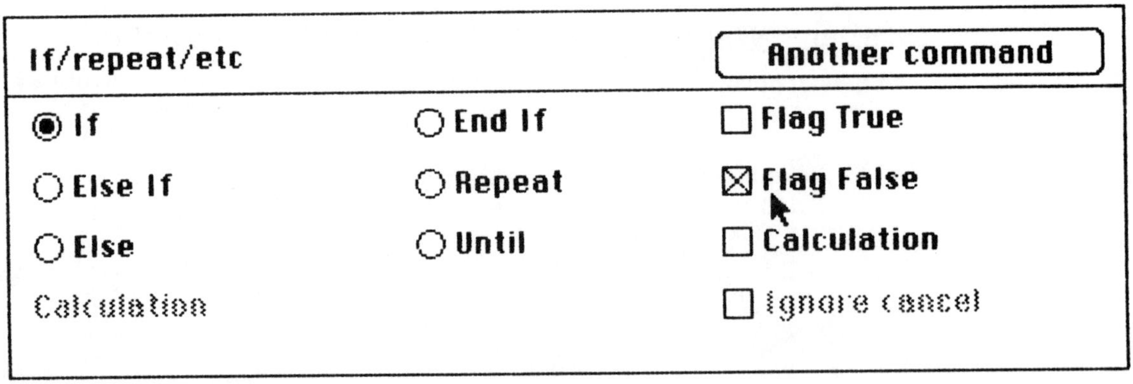

Fig. 6-6. The first part of the logical structure.

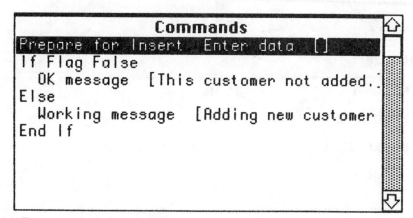

Message

◉ OK message   ○ Comment

○ YES/NO message

○ Working message

Message

This customer was not added.

Fig. 6-7. The second part of the logical structure.

☐ Set this command as: (use the Edit/insert choice)

Update files

Your screen should now look like Fig. 6-10. This last step was done to demonstrate just how simple it is to modify sequences, even after they are in place.

The Delete sequence on line 11 is similar to the "enter data" problem above. It would be best to confirm to the user if, in fact, a record actually has been deleted. Conversely, users should be reassured that cancelling the Delete operation preserved the record in the Customer file. Let's build a similar If-Then-Else expression into the Delete sequence.

☐ Click on line #11, **Delete/D**
☐ Set this sequence as shown below; see Fig. 6-11 for the final product).
  Delete w/confirmation [Do you really want to erase the record for ;CSTNAME;?]
  If Flag False
      OK message [OK, ;CSTNAME;'s records was not deleted . . .]

Commands

Prepare for Insert Enter data []
If Flag False
   OK message [This customer not added.]
Else
   Working message [Adding new customer
End If

Fig. 6-8. The current look of the logical structure.

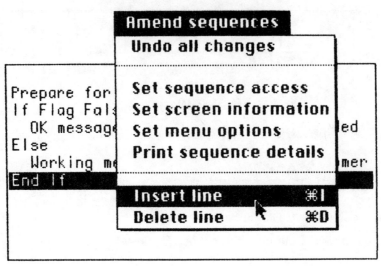

Fig. 6-9. The "Insert line" command.

> *Else*
> > *OK message [That customer has been deleted.]*
> *End If*

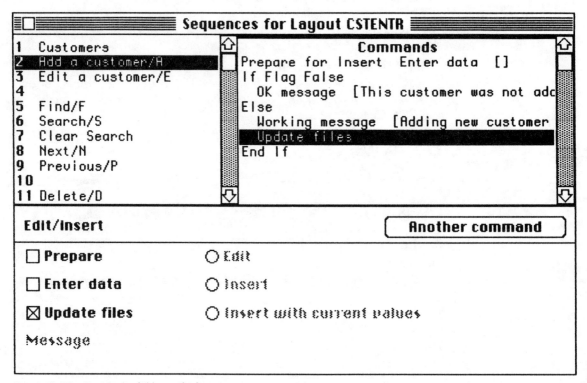

Fig. 6-10. The final look of this particular sequence.

```
┌─────────────────────────────────────────────────┐
│              Commands                          ⬆ │
│Delete with confirmation  [Do you really          │
│If Flag False                                    ▓ │
│   OK message  [OK, ;CSTNAME;'s record ho        ▓ │
│Else                                             ▓ │
│   OK message  [The customer has been del        ▓ │
│End If                                           ▓ │
│                                                   │
│                                                   │
│                                                 ⬇ │
└─────────────────────────────────────────────────┘
```

Fig. 6-11. The final product.

Go ahead and test these new sequences. As an example, use the Delete command in your Customers menu. It still asks you the same question as it did in the last chapter, but press the CANCEL button. The message box in Fig. 6-12 should be displayed. This is meant simply to comfort a user who might have strayed and wants confirmation that a customer's record has not accidentally been deleted.

Building On-Screen Buttons

A very important task of this chapter was to make our Customers menu coordinate with the on-screen buttons. As mentioned in the Plan section earlier, this can be done by using the *Set screen information* command. This command was discussed in depth before, so let's get on with it.

☐ Choose **Set screen information** as in Fig. 6-13. *This will call up the window shown in Fig. 6-14.*

This window is the one used to set the characteristics for each of the 12 screens of your Entry layouts. The window's three main areas are as follows.

The top area is the list of the 12 screens. To access the screen information for that screen, you simply click on its button. Each screen has a check box be-

Fig. 6-12. A message box confirming that this customer's record is still intact.

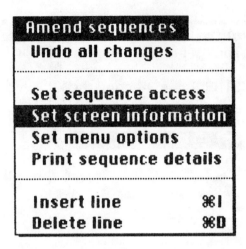

Amend sequences	
Undo all changes	
Set sequence access	
Set screen information	
Set menu options	
Print sequence details	
Insert line	⌘I
Delete line	⌘D

Fig. 6-13. The "Set screen information" command.

neath it to indicate if it is a primary screen or a secondary screen. A *secondary screen* is one that is simply an extension of another screen. One or more might be needed if there were too many fields in an Entry layout to fit in one screen. If you assign screen 2 as a secondary screen, the scroll bar would become accessible, allowing the user of that Entry layout to scroll back and forth between #1 and #2. A secondary screen has no function other than to be scrolled to, and relies on the sequences of the primary screen which called it.

The center section has two areas for entry: a *Heading* and an *Initialization*

Screen Information for CSTENTR

Screens ☐1 ☐2 ☐3 ☐4 ☐5 ☐6 ☐7 ☐8 ☐9 ☐10 ☐11 ☐12

Primary ☒ ☒ ☒ ☒ ☒ ☒ ☒ ☒ ☒ ☒ ☒ ☒

Heading

Initialization sequence

Button Definitions

	Text	Sequence		Text	Sequence
1			5		
2			6		
3			7		
4			8		

Fig. 6-14. Button definition form in the "Screen information" display.

sequence. The Heading is the window title which will be displayed when the selected screen becomes active. The Initialization sequence is the number of any sequence which you want Omnis 3 to execute automatically when the selected screen is activated. This affords you the opportunity to take some action immediately before the user is allowed to input any data. This is similar in theory to the STARTUP menu format which we created in Chapter 4. It is just one more way that Omnis 3 gives you a tight rein on users of your applications.

The lower section is the area that the on-screen button assignments are made. As you can see from Fig. 6-14, there are a total of eight possible buttons available for each screen. For each on-screen button, you must enter three pieces of information. The button's position on the screen is reflected by its number in the list: button 1 will appear at the top of the margin, with button 8 appearing at the bottom.

You must obviously give each of the buttons a name, but their size is limited, so about eight characters is all that will fit inside. The same rule applies here as in the sequence menus; the actual names are for your use only, and do not have to be the same as Omnis 3's names.

The last piece of information is the most crucial. Unlike the sequence menus, where the commands were directly attached to each command, there are no sequences visible here; you must enter a sequence by number. In this application, we only assigned the first handful of sequences. In a more complex application, there can be many more, and each can be simply referred to by its number in the list. For instance, the Delete sequence will be accessed by its number, 11.

Primary and secondary screens are inconsequential for this application, since the Entry layout is quite simple and needs no extra space. Let's set the buttons and the window heading now.

☐ *Set the Heading.*

Heading [The Work Station Customer Entry Form]

Initialization sequence

☐ *Tab to the first button's text box.*
☐ *Enter **Add** as the button's title.*
☐ *Enter **2** as the Sequence number:*

```
          Text        Sequence
    1     Add            2
```

Button Definitions

	Text	Sequence			Text	Sequence
1	Add	2		5	Search	6
2	Edit	3		6	Next	8
3	Find	5		7		
4				8	Delete	[11]

Fig. 6-15. The rest of the button information.

☐ *Enter the rest of the buttons' titles and sequence numbers as shown in Fig. 6-15.*

The actual order of the buttons on the screen is purely esthetic. However, in keeping with the tenets of good user interface design, whatever you choose should be consistent. It is best to group the most-often-used commands at the top of the margin.

The only thing left to do is to actually test the new configurations, but before we do that, a fine idea here is to quit Omnis 3 and make a backup of *all* your Library and Data files; what follows could be a disastrous testing procedure. Playing with sequences is like playing with fire: in the hands of a careful profes-

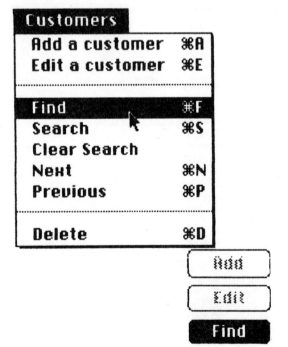

Fig. 6-16. The onscreen buttons coordinate with the menu items.

```
SEQUENCES FOR CSTENTR

1 Customers
- - - - - - - - - - -

2 Add a customer/A
- - - - - - - - - - - - - - - - - -
Prepare for Insert  Enter data []
If Flag False
   OK message [OK, customer was not added...]
Else
   Working message [Adding customer to file...]
   Update files
End If
* This is a comment, not a command.

3 Edit a customer/E
- - - - - - - - - - - - - - - - - -
Prepare for Edit  Enter data  Update files []

5 Find/F
- - - - - - - -
Find (prompted) []

6 Search/S
- - - - - - - - - -
Select Search name [SYSNOTE]
Search

7 Clear Search
- - - - - - - - - - - - -
Select Search name [ZERO]

8 Next/N
- - - - - - - -
Next

9 Previous/P
- - - - - - - - - - - -
Previous

11 Delete
- - - - - - - - -
Delete with confirmation [Do you really want to erase the record for ";CSTNAME;"?]
If Flag False
   OK message [OK, ";CSTNAME;"'s record was not deleted...]
Else
   OK message [That customer has been deleted.]
End If


Screen 1 (Customer entry screen) Primary
- - - - - - - - - - - - - - - - - - - - - - - - - - - - - - - - - - - - - -
Button 1 (Add) Sequence 2
Button 2 (Edit) Sequence 3
Button 3 (Find) Sequence 5
Button 4 (Search) Sequence 6
Button 6 (Next) Sequence 8
Button 8 (Delete) Sequence 11
```

Fig. 6-17. The listing of the sequences for this chapter.

sional, fire is an indispensable tool in many applications—but those of us who are less experienced are very likely to simply burn ourselves. It is quite easy to enter a just a few misplaced sequence commands that will end up deleting data, or even hopelessly scrambling your database!

When the new sequences are tested, and the buttons are used, something very interesting happens.

☐ *Choose **Find** from your Customers menu.*

Look at the Find button which you just created. When you choose a sequence menu item which has a corresponding on-screen button, that button is highlighted to further clarify which command the user just chose. See Fig. 6-16 for an example.

Figure 6-17 lists the sequence for our CSTENTR database.

What's Next?

We might say that the easy part is now over. Up to this point in the book, we've covered almost all of the elementary concepts and commands of Omnis 3. File formats, entry layouts, reports, simple menus, sequences, and on-screen buttons. From here on out, we will be moving at an accelerated pace, building upon what has been covered in these introductory chapters. You may have to strap on your thinking cap, as the new ideas and commands will be coming fast and furious. But now this all gets even more fascinating, as we begin to uncover the true powers of Omnis 3!

```
Omnis 3
   The DataBasics
   Useful Reports
   Search Formats
   Custom Menus
   Sequences
   More Sequences
 Expansion        ⌘7
```

Starting the
Inventory System

The Problem: The Work Station's management would like to have an inventory control mechanism added to their system. This new addition should be able to track their merchandise by part number, as well as carrying a description, wholesale and retail price, and the number of units in stock. They would like to see a printout of all this information accompanied by a calculation of the gross profit and profit margin for each item.

This latest addition will become the second subsystem in the developing package. (The first was the Customer database.) The Work Station's management would like this inventory database to be used in the future to look up prices and descriptions for purchase invoices. Therefore we will design with that need in mind, but we'll leave the other subsystems for subsequent chapters.

THE PLAN

With most conventional database management software, we would proceed to build a completely different database for the inventory file. However, Omnis 3 is more flexible than that. The Library file that Omnis 3 uses to store the File formats, Entry layouts, Reports, and other formats can actually hold up to 12 independent database File formats. This is a unique and very flexible capability, one which allows your database files to share a common menu format, among other things. This menu (most likely the STARTUP menu) can have selections that lead you off in different directions within that Library. Once you get to a different Entry layout (and its corresponding File format), that layout's sequences can take over and guide you during your work with that file. As we saw in preceding chapters, each Entry layout can have its own menu and up to 12 input screens, each with its own appropriate functionality. Keep in mind that you are not limited to only one file format per Entry layout. When you add the capacity of 120 fields per File format, this becomes an incredible capacity indeed!

The File Format

First we need to create a new File format. There is no need to "relate" any of the fields of this new file to any of the fields in any other file, because Omnis 3 can draw relationships between seemingly unrelated files. (They must be in the same Library, though; more on this later.) The new File format is relatively undistinguished in construction. We have a very simple application for it right now: simply looking up stock levels and prices in the Work Station's inventory. We will probably see more data that must be tracked later in building the total system, but recall Omnis 3's unique ability to rearrange a database file after a change has been made in a File format. The *Reorganize data* command allows you to add fields or change existing ones at any time, even after data has been entered and saved using the existing format.

The fields we will track are common ones for an inventory system: part code, part description, date of last change, wholesale and retail prices, and the current quantity of the item in stock.

The part code field will be set as *indexed* to allow use of the Find command to look up items in inventory. The index will also allow this database file to be used in an eventual connection with an Invoicing database file. This field will be the "key" into the Inventory file, but there is nothing special that needs to be done to facilitate this capability. Simply by indexing this field, you make this eventual connection possible.

The *Description* field, because of its length, will not be indexed. This conserves space in the data file. We can index the *Retail price* field to allow simple listings ordered by price for the salespeople. The *Last updated* field can also be indexed to facilitate simple reports based on inventory movements. Needless to say, the price fields (as well as the *Stock on hand* field) will be Numeric, with the *Last updated* field being a new type: Date. The Date field type is just as it seems: it displays a date in whatever format is appropriate for your country. The *Part code* and *Description* fields are Character fields. The reason for making the *Part code* Character, as opposed to Numeric, is that many manufacturers use letters in their codes along with the numerals.

The lack of indexing of the *Description* field merits some discussion. This will necessitate the use of a Search command if data is to be looked up based on a description alone—as opposed to the above example of the *Part code* field. For instance, if we needed to look up the price of Apple's MacWrite software package, we would have two ways of doing so. If we didn't know the part code but knew that the name was MacWrite, we could use a Search format that looked through all of the *Description* fields and checked if they contain "MacWrite." Given the speed of Omnis 3, a search is a very fast process, even if there are hundreds or thousands of parts in inventory. On the other hand, if you know the part code of the item, or at least the first few characters of it, you can use the Find command. This command can only work on indexed fields, but is much faster than a search.

Another advantage of the Find command is that it can be executed directly from the Entry layout, whereas the Search format uses a different window. The Find command is more practical for the above type single-keyed lookup. However, suppose that all you knew was that the program was named MacSomething, but you were also sure that it was priced at $195. A Search format would be more practical because of its ability to use logical operators. You can build a Search that says, in effect, "Look up all parts whose names start with 'Mac' AND whose price is $195." Using Find is much more awkward for this kind of lookup.

There are always trade-offs in building anything. If we all had our way, we'd have the finest possible copper, brass, hardwood, and stainless steel hardware in our homes. Because of financial considerations, however, we generally use plastic and linoleum in their places. Nevertheless, these less-expensive alternatives sometimes actually perform better than their more esthetic counterparts. The same kind of trade-offs are involved in database design. Some factors to consider are:

—Ease of use
—Ease of development (that's *your* time!)
—Cost of development
—Ease of modification and maintenance
—Effectiveness for each of its purposes
—Overall effectiveness
—Overall cost

Each of these factors has a different weight depending on the nature of the application.

For instance, if you are developing an in-house application for personal use, "ease of use" might not carry too much weight. If you are the sole user of the database, it sometimes pays to keep it "stripped" of any extraneous features such as help screens, verbose menus, or complicated sequences for error checking. On the other hand, you may be developing an application under contract for another person or company, and may even be selling it as a turn-key system. "Turn-key" generally refers to a system that needs little or no maintenance, and is fully documented and supported. For this type of application, there is certainly a different ordering of priorities, with financial ones certainly becoming more important.

There are no hard-and-fast rules governing this type of decision-making process; just acknowledge each of the factors, and try to determine its relative weight. Then develop away!

Getting back to the task at hand, the File format is fairly straightforward here. Once the File format is completed, however, it is best to use the *Reorganize data* command to check if the data file is in need of repairs. Simply adding a new file format to an existing Library file will not cause Omnis to scramble the data in the Data file, but it doesn't hurt to check.

Remember, the Library file is only one of the two files which make up a database on your disk. The Data file is an equally important part of the overall picture. Internally, Omnis 3 usually reserves quite a bit of room in the Data file that you create. The data for the new File format which you will be creating will be kept in the same data file by default. However, Omnis 3 maintains the Data files with room for more than one File format's data. Recalling an analogy from Chapter 1 (the File format is like the foundation of a house), simply adding new File formats to a Library file is like adding on a simple garage or a porch to your home; there is no need to make major changes to the house itself. It is only when you make changes to an existing File format that the *Reorganize data* command is needed.

The Entry Layout

We are creating a new layout for a simple reason. We could use a different screen of an existing layout, but we would not be able to have a unique sequence menu for that layout. The requirements for this Entry layout are somewhat similar to the CSTENTR layout from the previous chapters, but there are a few new wrinkles. One difference is that we need to prevent users from deleting parts from inventory. This is a fairly common requirement in this type of system. One of the future applications for this system is the invoicing file. It would be quite a problem if a part were deleted from the parts file after an invoice was written. There are very complicated ways around this, but for now, we'll simplify things for ourselves (and The Work Station) if we lock the users out from the Delete command. We will, however, allow them to Edit records.

As I mentioned in the Problem section, the management requested a calculation be done automatically for the gross profit and profit margin for each item in inventory. This gives us the chance to play with two new field types on the Entry layout, local fields and calculated fields.

Calculated and Temporary Fields

Calculated fields are similar to their namesakes in the Reports we've already built. In an Entry layout, they cannot be altered directly by the user, but their value is derived from a calculation. There are two kinds of calculated fields, both sharing this characteristic. However, there the similarity ends.

Any regular field within an Entry layout can be calculated if the user is prohibited from entering data therein. An example of such a situation will be demonstrated in this chapter's exercises, the *Last updated* field. The reason for having this field is to record when the last change was made to the part record. Omnis 3 can do this for you, by specifying the field as *Calculated*. This particular calculation takes advantage of one of the features of Omnis 3, its *constants*. Certain pieces of information, such as the date, are always available in constant form. In order to reference the current date, you need only use the constant #D. The calculation for this field will simply be #D. This way, whenever the record is written to the file, Omnis 3 will know to update this field with today's date.

There is another field type which is used as a calculated field. In reports, you have used temporary (#S) string field to glue text together. This string field is the very useful for working with character-type fields, and is even of some use in working with numeric fields. But often calculations are needed that are not text-related, such as calculating a profit margin. The tool we can use for these is Omnis 3's *temporary numeric fields*. These fields are simply storage areas used to hold on to numbers; programmers will recognize them as *variables*.

Omnis 3 makes 60 of these temporary fields available to you, referring to them by the names #1, #2, #3, and so on up to #60. These fields can hold any number that Omnis 3 can work with, including the result of a function, but they can't remember the function itself (like a spreadsheet can). They are available from any location where you are working with data, such as reports, entry layouts, and sequences. Because they are temporary, they're never saved to the disk; they aren't part of any file, record, or field.

Temporary numeric fields are commonly used on the Entry layout to display the result of a calculation. It would be senseless to take up space in the Data file with fields for margin percentage and gross profit, since it is trivial to calculate these whenever the record is displayed or edited. Calculated fields can even use logical and relational calculations. For instance, we will have a calculation in our new Entry layout to display the profit margin. This will be a temporary field for reasons outlined above. The traditional formula for profit margin is:

(RetailPrice − WholesalePrice) / RetailPrice

Consider this when you call up this Entry layout to work with it: Omnis 3 always defaults to displaying a blank record when you start an Entry layout. When Omnis 3 calculates this temporary field for the blank record (it always calculates temporary fields), the result will be undefined. You are dividing by zero, which is not allowed in regular math. Therefore, to keep an unsightly error from appearing on the Entry layout, we'll have to build a formula that can do a bit of detective work for us.

Typical relational operators are greater than (>), less than (<), less than or equal to (< =), etc.. Using them in formulas or functions is quite simple. Every logical statement evaluates to 1 if True or 0 if False. For instance, for the blank record mentioned above, the statement:

RetailPrice = 0

evaluates to True. We can then "trick" Omnis 3 into avoiding the error condition detailed above by constructing the formula like this:

(RetailPrice − WholesalePrice) / (RetailPrice + (RetailPrice = 0))

Note the obvious difference. In the two possible situations, this addition will solve the problem. When correct data is being displayed on the form, this formula is not affected because the logical relation (RetailPrice = 0) is evaluated to 0 (False). When there is a blank record present, the expression evaluates to 1 (True), making the overall formula return 0, instead of an error. The (RetailPrice – WholesalePrice) part of the expression will have evaluated to zero as well.

This temporary field will also have to be declared as Local in the field attributes box. Local fields are most often used to hold temporary values resulting from calculations. This is because the definition of a Local field is one that "belongs to" another field on the Entry layout. Every field on the Entry layout is given a number starting from the first field that was added to the layout (1). Not coincidentally, this number determines the order in which you "tab" through the fields on the screen. (The placement of the fields is not as critical as it may seem; field numbers can be changed at any time.)

A Local field belongs to the preceding nonlocal (normal) field, and its value is recalculated whenever the nonlocal field's value changes. In this case, the *Margin* and *Profit* fields must come after the *Retail* and *Wholesale* price fields (field number order) in the Entry layout. Therefore, when the user enters a value in (or even just tabs through) the price fields, the calculated fields will be updated automatically.

Message Fields

Another new type of field will be introduced this time through: the Message field. This is a special field for use in Entry layouts. In the field attributes box, when you check *Message*, you need only specify the justification (right, left, center), the length, and an optional default Message. This is a text field, but it has some important differences. First of all, Omnis 3 displays whatever text is entered here in Chicago font, the same proportional font used in the Macintosh's menus and dialog boxes. This alone makes them worth using, but they have another neat feature. When a sequence is defined, the "Insert," "Edit," and "Find" sequence commands have an optional message that can be displayed when the command is initiated. If there is a message field on your Entry layout, the message is displayed there. When the command is completed, the default message is restored. If there isn't a default message (i.e., you left the *default Message* box blank), the existing message is erased from the screen.

Message fields cannot fully replace Message boxes, but are a useful alternative to them. Message boxes tend to interrupt the work flow by obstructing the screen and demanding user intervention. Message fields are more subtle and are recommended for gentle reminders. For instance, you might use a message that says "Entering new part . . . " when the user chooses the appropriate command. However, you should still use Message boxes to report errors or warn of impending doom (e.g., "Are you sure you want to DELETE this record?").

Two more minor features we'll take advantage of in this chapter are the *Unique indexed* and *Upper case only* field attributes. It is crucial to the utility of this database that each Part in the file has a unique part code, or mayhem would result when the Invoicing system is finally complete. After all, the goal is to use the Part code as a key into the Inventory database; if there were duplicate Part codes, there would be no way of differentiating them. We will set the *Unique indexed* field attribute for the Part code on this Entry layout. Therefore, when the user enters a value in the field, Omnis 3 checks all the other entries in the database to verify that there are no identical entries. There is one requirement for this attribute: the desired field must be Indexed in the File format to make this option available. Also, this attribute *does not* apply to other copies of this field elsewhere in the layout, or in other layouts.

The other option we'll use for the first time is *Upper case only*. This one is rather obvious: it converts all input to the upper case. But there is a hidden significance in this command relating to the *Unique indexed* option. Because of the way computers store data, they differentiate between upper- and lower-case characters. By default, the word ''omnis'' is not equivalent to the word ''OMNIS'' because of the obvious difference in case. Therefore, it is generally necessary to force input into all one case in order to guarantee that duplicate values are never entered, even with *Unique index* set. The part number ''m2503'' might be inadvertently entered after ''M2503'' was input in another record, and Omnis 3 wouldn't catch the error unless you had forced all input into upper-case letters.

More Sequences

The adventure into Omnis 3's sequences continues in this chapter. This installment concerns three new areas. Of the areas we'll work with, perhaps the most useful is the ability of sequences to branch off to other sequence ''subroutines.''

Here's a scenario: We have a new Entry layout that will be used to input all the Inventory items using the STOCK File format. We'll certainly build our own version of the Enter data menu for use here, since it is very easy and rewarding to do. Two of the items in the menu will be an ''Add a part'' command and an ''Edit this part'' command. Because of strict requirements relating to cost information, we will have a simple set of commands within the sequences that check the values of some of the fields. All that this simple test will do is verify that the input data is correct. Based on the results of this test, you'll know whether to issue the *Update files* command, or reject the data and force the user to reenter it correctly. This test must be done in both Editing and Inserting records. Certainly the commands could be entered twice; once in each sequence. However, think back to one of the tenets of good programming from Chapter 5, working systematically and stepwise. If the same set of commands were entered in two different places, then any enhancement or modification to your set of commands would need to be entered twice.

The idea here is that there is no reason to duplicate commands in similar sequences. It is far more practical to build a third sequence which is *called* by each of the first two at the appropriate time. This way, you only have one set of commands to ''debug,'' not two. This mini-sequence is referred to as a *subroutine* in conventional programming.

There aren't any special instructions needed to make a subroutine a subroutine. It is constructed just as a normal Omnis 3 sequence. As is the case in the scenario above, however, you will often want to simply "branch" off temporarily to this subroutine. Therefore, there is a new Omnis 3 sequence command you will use here, the *Quit sequence* command. This command restores control to the sequence which "called" it originally. This way, a subroutine can be used by different sequences without caring which one called it. The Quit Sequence command is very different from the *Call Sequence #* command; the latter must refer to a specific sequence, but the former can return to any sequence.

Using the Flag

There is another problem in the above example that has cropped up now that we've discovered subroutines. The new predicament is this: How can a subroutine "report back" on the results of its testing?

Let's assume for a moment that our subroutine is evaluating a relational condition:

RetailPrice > 0

Obviously, there are only two possible answers to this question. But we have to have some means with which to report this result back to the calling program. No problem! Remember from the last chapter that the *Flag* is Omnis 3's global logical indicator. In most operations, Omnis 3 itself sets (True) or clears (False) the Flag to indicate the result of the operation. In the Enter data command, The Flag is set if the user clicks OK, and cleared if the user clicks Cancel. But the Flag is also available directly to you. Built into the *Quit sequence* command is the option to either *Set* or *Clear* the Flag. This way, your sequence can do the operations shown in Fig. 7-1.

```
Sequence 2
   Repeat
      Enter data
      Call Sequence 21
   Until Flag True

   . . . .

   . . . .
Sequence 21
   (RetailPrice > 0)
   If Flag True
      Quit sequence  Set Flag
   Else
      Quit sequence  Clear Flag
   End if
```

Fig. 7-1. A Repeat-Until structure using the Flag in a sequence.

```
(Retail > Wholesale) & (Wholesale > 0)
If Flag True
     Quit sequence  Set Flag
Else
     Quit sequence  Clear Flag
End if
```

Fig. 7-2. A useful mix of relational and logical operators.

In this instance, once the *Enter data* command in Sequence 2 was executed, Omnis 3 would immediately branch to Sequence 21 and begin executing the instructions there. Once it evaluated the condition there, it would Quit Sequence 21 with the Flag either Set or Cleared. When Omnis 3 encounters the *Quit sequence* command, it recalls who it was that called this one, and what line within that sequence originated the Call instruction. It then jumps right back to the line below the one with the Call instruction, and continues executing instructions on that line. Now, however, that calling sequence has had the Flag set for it by the subroutine, so it can determine the appropriate action to take.

Another fascinating feature of Omnis 3 is the ability to use logical operators in conjunction with relational operators. The test mentioned above for Sequence 21 is actually only half the story. Actually, we need to test both the Retail and Wholesale prices, and make sure that the Wholesale is greater than 0, and that the Retail is greater than the Wholesale. There is a very convenient way to build sophisticated logical equations using a logical AND and OR. *And* is entered as an ampersand (&), and *Or* is entered as an exclamation point (!). (There isn't any easy way to remember Or, except keeping your Omnis 3 Pocket Reference Guide handy at all times!) To use these operators, let's use the Retail and Wholesale example. To build this expression we'll rewrite Sequence 21 to use the test shown in Fig. 7-2.

Because of the & operator, the expression requires *both* sides to be True in order for the overall result to be True. If we rewrote the expression like this:

(Retail > Wholesale) ! (Wholesale > 0)

what would be the result? If either side of the expression were True, the entire expression would end up True. This demonstrates how the Or expression translates into "either (this) or (that)."

This use of mathematical, relational, and logical operators can be expanded when parentheses are used. The parentheses are evaluated from the innermost set outwards, just like in regular math. Here's an example of how the placement of parentheses can have a tremendous effect on the outcome of an expression such as:

$$20 - 3*5$$

For those of you who are sweeping away the cobwebs searching for the answer, it is 5. Why? Mathematical operations must respect a basic law of math called the *precedence of operators* (see Fig. 7-3). That is just formal terminology for the rule that certain math operations take precedence over others. Among the rules is that multiplication and division are done before addition or subtraction. If there is a tie, then you read from left to right through the equation.

Now, if you thought the answer above should have been 85 instead of 5, consider this expression:

$$(20 - 3)*5$$

This one evaluates to 85 because of the placement of the parentheses. These take precedence over all other operators. In the case of multiple sets of parentheses within each other, the calculation starts with the innermost set and works outward.

Here are some popular conventions followed with respect to subroutines (and programming in general). First of all, remember that Omnis 3 reserves the first 20 sequences for use with the Sequence menu. Therefore your subroutines will need to be entered in the numbers greater that 20; otherwise, they may end up listed in the Menu! Omnis 3 also can insert comment lines within sequences. These are lines, preceded by an asterisk (*), that are ignored when Omnis 3 runs a sequence. They are simply there for your information. This capability is implemented in all programming languages in order to make programs readable once the author has forgotten the actual reason for his logic. Omnis 3's language is very readable, but there is still a need to document things like this subroutine. Writing programs is such an inexact science, programmers invariably forget exactly why they did certain things where they did them. Therefore, another tenet of good programming is:

Comment your programs clearly.

The time you save may very well be your own!

Yet Another New Report

The report for this chapter is fairly straightforward, since it simply builds upon what has been done in the previous chapters. However, a new wrinkle in this one is that we will build the command for it into the Sequence menu rather than in the STARTUP menu.

The reason for putting the Report command into the Sequence menu is we should now start to make this system more modular. *Modular* here refers to the program being segmented into appropriate areas. The command will be hardwired to simply spit out a report to the screen, then automatically return to the Entry layout. The limitation of using the STARTUP menu is that when the Re-

Precedence of Operators in Omnis 3 Expressions

Mathematical	_Logical_	_Relational_
/ *	&	< > <= >= <> =
+ -	!	(all have equal precedence)

Overall Precedence
(parentheses)
Mathematical
Logical
Relational

Operators at the TOP of each
list are evaluated FIRST...

(Ties are broken by reading from
left to right across the equation.)

Fig. 7-3. Omnis 3's precedence of operators.

port commands installed there terminate, all sequences also terminate. By leaving the Report command in the Sequence menu, you preserve the modularity: Omnis 3 will redisplay the Entry layout after the report finishes printing.

This Report will make use of the temporary fields that were detailed above. It is important to reiterate that these fields can be used anywhere within Omnis 3 for calculations. We'll use formulas similar to the ones that were built in the Entry layout, because the printout will also list profit margin and gross profit for each item in inventory. One extra wrinkle that we'll add is totals at the end of the report.

Recall that Omnis 3 Reports are divided into sections. We've worked previously with the Heading and Detail sections. We'll be using the Totals section for this report. Most of the hard work is done for you by Omnis 3. There

113

is a new field attribute specific to Reports: *Totaled*. If a field in the Detail section is set to be Totaled, Omnis 3 keeps a running total of the values of that field. Then, if that field appears in the Totals section, the value of that field will be the running total.

There is another constant available in reports, #R, which holds the total number of records printed for this report. This enables you to do additional calculations based on the totals above. Let's say, for instance, that you have defined #1 as a temporary, calculated Numeric field in the Detail section. Its formula will calculate and list the gross profit for each item in the report. All you need to do is place another copy of #1 in the Totals section, and Omnis 3 will print the total of all #1s from the Detail section. Furthermore, you might define another temporary field (#2) in the Totals section to be this calculation:

#1/#R

Can you figure out what this will calculate? If you guessed the average of all #1s, you are right! As you will see, using the Totals section is really quite simple.

Figure 7-4 lists all of the basic operators available to you for your calculations in Omnis 3.

THE STEPS

Are you ready for another adventure with Omnis 3? Let's go.

Omnis 3 Operators		

Mathematical	*Logical*	*Relational*
+ Addition **–** Subtraction **✱** Multiplication **/** Division	**&** Logical And **!** Logical Or	**=** Equal to **<>** Not Equal to **>** Greater than **<** Less than **>=** Greater than or Equal to **<=** Less than or Equal to

Fig. 7-4. Omnis 3's operators.

For this chapter, as with the previous ones, make sure that you're working with a relatively unadulterated version of last chapter's database. If you have made any major changes, the results might not match our goals here.

We must assume by this stage in your work with Omnis 3 that you have a solid understanding of the basics: File formats, Fields, Records, Entry layouts, and Reports. Therefore, this chapter will follow the trend established earlier, i.e., less actual "hand-holding" will be presented in the Steps here. In the previous chapters you were typically instructed to "Choose File formats from the Options menu," "Click New," "Type 'AFILE'," etc. From this point on, this type of instruction will be consolidated to read: "Create a new File format named AFILE." If a review is necessary, you can read through the appropriate chapters before tackling the exercises here.

A New File Format

Before any work can be done in the Inventory system, a new File format must be created. This is because the Inventory data that will be entered bears no direct relationship to the data that already exists in the CUSTS File format (can you remember that far back?). Omnis 3 Libraries, which store the details and descriptions of File formats, can hold up to 60 such descriptions per Library. In Omnis 3, the Library file is the "universe" in which you do your work. There is no direct way of working with files in different Libraries. The only way to do this is to use the *Utilities* program (more on that later in the book).

Let's go ahead and create a new File format.

☐ *Verify that you are using the WorkStation Library file. (If you aren't, use the **Select Library** command)*
☐ *Create a new File format named **STOCK***

Omnis 3 has presented you with a blank list of fields and characteristics. This new File format is being defined to contain the data for the Inventory control portion of the database system. There are six actual fields to be defined at this point. As mentioned in the Plan section, we can grow the number of fields in this File format later. As a matter of fact, we probably will, but we'll keep this file as-is for now.

The actual steps involved in inputting the field characteristics should be recalled from Chapter 1. Let's build the format.

☐ *Using Fig. 7-5 as a guide, set up each of the six fields of this File format.*

Once all six fields have been filled in correctly, we can verify that the database hasn't been "polluted" by this change in the File Library. This command is the key to your ability to make significant changes to a File format as you develop a database system.

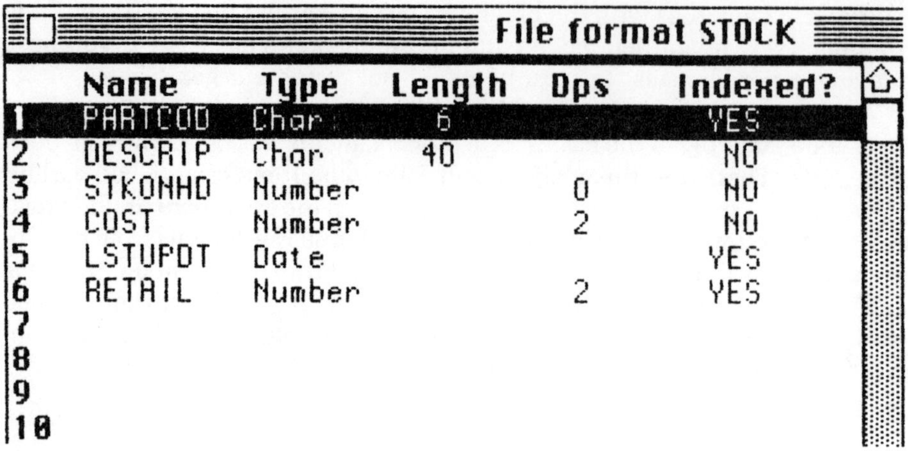

Fig. 7-5. The fields for the File format STOCK.

☐ *Choose the Reorganize data command.*

Note that Omnis 3 is verifying the assumption that you've probably made already: the data needs no further reorganization (Fig. 7-6).

☐ *Click **Cancel**.*
☐ *Close the **File format STOCK** window to save it.*

The reason for this condition is that you didn't actually make any changes that would affect the Data file's structure. Now that the File format has been stored, however, any subsequent changes to this File format once data is entered using it, would require the use of the *Reorganize data* command.

The Inventory Entry Layout

The actual data requirements for this Entry layout are quite simple. The Work

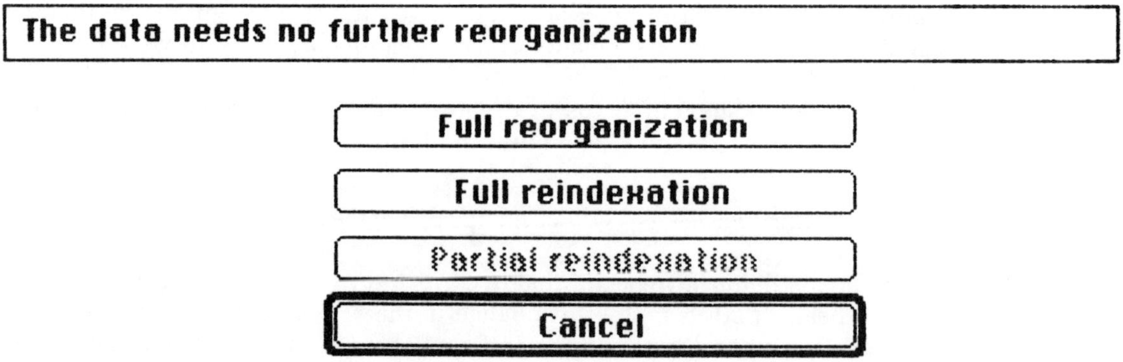

Fig. 7-6. The "Reorganize data" command.

Station will use this entry form to input a record for each of the items they sell. Each will be input along with the data that was set in the File format. Because there are only six pieces of data, the layout will be simple visually.

But remember that The Work Station requested a few more amenities. First, they want a calculation done to display the gross profit and profit margin on the Entry layout alongside the pricing figures. This can be done on the Entry layout with the use of temporary calculated fields. It would be preferable for the LSTUPDT field for each record entered to be filled in with the current date automatically by Omnis 3. Also, if the record is modified in any way at a later date, this field should be changed to that new date.

We'll add the sequences later, after the layout is visually complete. This time around, we'll work from the printout that Omnis 3 produces when you use the *Print layout details* command. This way, you can use that command to compare your layout with this one, and track down mistakes more easily. Input the fields in the order they appear on the list. Some points to note before running off to build the layout are:

1) Field #1 is a Message field, so it needs no field name.
2) Take care to assign all the attributes listed in the printout.
3) The field positions on the Entry layout are not critical, but their order is.
4) The formulas used in the two #S fields were covered in the PLAN section. The reason for using the CON() function is that the $ and % characters should be added on to the resultant numbers, and CON() is the simplest way of doing so.

Let's go ahead and build the basic Entry layout.

☐ *Create a new Entry layout named* **STKENTR**
☐ *Build the layout, using Figs. 7-7 and 7-8 as your guide.*
☐ *When you finish, choose* **Print layout details***. Compare your work with Fig. 7-7.*

Notice that there are some simple graphics included on the layout in Fig. 7-8. There are two types: rectangles and lines. Below are the steps to draw these graphics.

☐ *To draw a rectangle on the Entry layout:*
   1) *Click and drag to highlight the area for the rectangle.*
   2) *Keep clicking the* **Rectangle** *button until the desired rectangle is displayed (Omnis 3 will cycle through each of the available types).*
   3) *Click anywhere else on the layout to preserve the new rectangle.*

☐ *To draw a line on the Entry layout:*
   1) *Click and drag to highlight the area for the line. It must be only one character wide (for vertical lines) or one line high (for horizontal lines), or else you'll end up with a rectangle.*

```
ENTRY LAYOUT STKENTR

            FILE      FIELD    VERTICAL  HORIZONTAL  ATTRIBUTES    LENGTH     JUST
----------------------------------------------------------------------------------
1                               2         10          MV            45       Center
Message    The Work Station's Inventory Adjustment Form
2          STOCK     LSTUPDT   5         17          +DV           9         Left
Formula    *D
3          STOCK     PARTCOD   7         17          JUV           6         Left
4          STOCK     DESCRIP   9         17          V             40        Left
5          STOCK     STKONHD   12        17                        4         Left
6          STOCK     COST      13        28                        11        Left
7          STOCK     RETAIL    13        44          V             11        Left
8                    *S        16        28          +LDV          11        Right
Formula    CON('$',RETAIL-COST)
9                    *S        16        47          +LDV          5         Right
Formula    CON(INT(((RETAIL-COST)*100)/((RETAIL=0)+RETAIL)),'%')


List of attribute codes:
       +    Calculated            I    Invisible
       M    Message field         D    Display only
       F    Automatic find        U    Upper case
       J    Unique indexed        V    Negative values allowed
       L    Local                 E    Zeros shown as empty
       P    Delete protected
```

Fig. 7-7. The printed details of the Entry layout STKENTR.

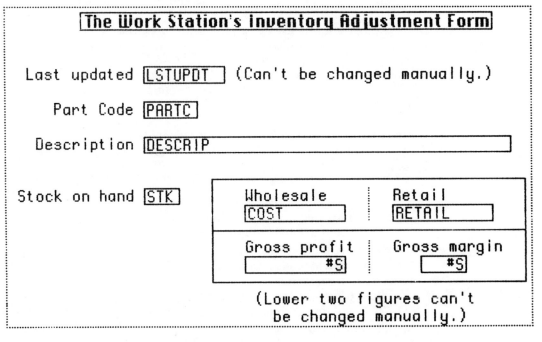

Fig. 7-8. The appearance of the Entry layout STKENTR.

2) *Keep clicking the* **Rectangle** *button, until the desired line is displayed.*

Now that the layout is completed, remember that we had some other requirements. To satisfy these, we'll now move forward and build the sequences for this layout.

The Inventory Sequences

The first request was that there be no Delete option available from the layout. By creating our own customized version of Omnis 3's "standard" Enter data menu (as was done in Chapter 6), we can completely control what options are available. Moreover, we can control the exact actions that each of the available commands takes by building sequences to support them.

This leads to the other, less obvious, consideration. Because of the nature of the database, we will build some error-checking and input "filtering" into this layout. We don't want the user to be allowed to enter inventory items with no prices, so we must check that the prices input are greater than zero. We can also do a rudimentary check that the prices are valid by verifying that the retail price (RETAIL) entered is greater than the wholesale price (COST). This may not be a permanent solution, nor the most elegant way of accomplishing the desired result, but we'll leave that for later. You should always concentrate on making sequences work before you waste too much time optimizing them!

You'll again be working from an Omnis 3 printout in this exercise. This is the listing which results from the *Print sequence details* command. The listing in Fig. 7-9 was actually printed to a File, which was then opened and "spruced up" in MacWrite and printed from there. The boldface is just for emphasis. Here are some points to note before you dive in:

1) Sequence #8 is optional.
2) You'll need to use the Set screen information command to set the on-screen buttons listed at the end of the printout.
3) Don't forget to take advantage of the command-key equivalents by adding a slash to the end of the sequence name, followed by the desired character.

☐ *Build the sequences, using Fig. 7-9 as your guide.*
☐ *Use* **Set menu options** *to turn off both the* **Enter data** *menu and the* **Show/Hide Enter data menu** *items from being displayed.*

After all this anticipation, you're probably dying to jump in and try out this layout. Therefore, Fig. 7-10 is a preliminary list of The Work Station's inventory. Obviously, there is no need to enter *all* the items listed. But it will help you to have some real data entered when you produce a new report format later. Remember, you aren't allowed to Delete items, so use the Edit command to patch

SEQUENCES FOR STKENTR

1 Inventory

Set main file to **STOCK**
Clear: Main file Connected files Other files # fields from 1 to 10 Temporary string fields

2 Add new items/A

Prepare for Insert
Repeat
    Enter data [Adding new inventory item...]
    If Flag **False**
        Quit sequence
    End If
    Call sequence **21**
    * **Test if costs are OK (this is a comment...)**
Until Flag **True**
Update files

3 Edit existing item/E

Prepare for Edit
Repeat
    Enter data [Editing part record...]
    If Flag **False**
        Quit sequence
    End If
    Call sequence **21**
Until Flag **True**
Update files

5 Next/N

Next

6 Find/F

Find (prompted) [Enter the desired Find parameter...]

8 Sorry, no delete!

OK message [I told you there was no 'Delete' command. ;PARTCOD; still intact...]

Fig. 7-9. The sequences for STKENTR.

```
21 verify costs (OK yet?)
-------------------------
If (RETAIL>COST)&(COST>0)
    Quit sequence Set flag
Else
    OK message [Wholesale and Retail of ;PARTCOD; must be MORE THAN zero. Try again...]
    Quit sequence Clear flag
End If


Screen 1 (The Work Station) Primary
-----------------------------------
Initialisation sequence 1
Button 1 (Add) Sequence 2
Button 2 (Edit) Sequence 3
Button 4 (Next) Sequence 5
Button 5 (Find) Sequence 6
```

up mistakes. There is no need to enter the Date, since you set the field to default to today's date.

☐ *Try out your new creation by entering the inventory items listed in Fig. 7-10.*

Try to enter a new part number with either the RETAIL or COST fields entered as $0.00. Note that the message box in Fig. 7-11 appears with an informative message. This is a result of Sequence #21's logical test having failed to validate the input. But what if something went wrong? Don't panic! Here, in no particular order, are some likely snafus with an Entry layout of this type, accompanied by some suggested fixes:

1) *The Calculated fields for Margin and Profit aren't calculating properly.* Check that you have set these fields' attributes as Calculated, Display only, and Local.
2) *The on-screen buttons don't seem to be coordinating properly with the sequence commands.* Check that you have put the correct sequence numbers next to the button texts (Set screen information window).
3) *The "Last updated" field isn't working properly.* Check the field attributes (Calculated and Display only) and calculation itself (#D, the current Omnis 3 date).
4) *There's garbage on the screen when it first appears.* Make sure that your Initialization sequence is set to 1 (use the Set screen information window). Sequence #1 calls the *Clear data* sequence command.
5) *If all else fails.* Simply print out all of the details of the layout and its sequences, and then compare them line by line with the examples.

```
The Work Station's                                    Wholesale   Margin %
Inventory Report                                        Retail     Profit
----------------------------------------------------------------------------
M0131  Macintosh 800K ext. drive                         320.00      35%
       last updated FEB 4 86          5 in stock         499.00      179
----------------------------------------------------------------------------
M0160  LaserWriter w/Accessory pack                    3,800.00      36%
       last updated FEB 5 86          1 in stock       5,995.00     2,195
----------------------------------------------------------------------------
M0200  Macintosh carrying case                            55.00      42%
       last updated FEB 3 86          2 in stock          95.00      40
----------------------------------------------------------------------------
M0500  10/Apple 3.5 inch disks                            29.00      40%
       last updated FEB 3 86         51 in stock          49.00      20
----------------------------------------------------------------------------
M0524  68000 Development System                          115.00      41%
       last updated FEB 3 86          2 in stock         195.00      80
----------------------------------------------------------------------------
M2503  Macintosh Plus CPU                              1,648.00      38%
       last updated FEB 3 86          8 in stock       2,699.00     1,051
----------------------------------------------------------------------------
M2512  Macintosh 512K CPU                              1,100.00      38%
       last updated FEB 3 86         11 in stock       1,795.00      695
----------------------------------------------------------------------------
M2519  Macintosh Plus Keyboard                            90.00      30%
       last updated FEB 4 86          7 in stock         129.00      39
----------------------------------------------------------------------------
M2554  Apple Personal Modem                              300.00      31%
       last updated FEB 3 86         15 in stock         439.00      139
----------------------------------------------------------------------------
M2555  ImageWriter 2                                     398.00      33%
       last updated FEB 3 86          5 in stock         595.00      197
----------------------------------------------------------------------------
M2600  Macintosh Hard Disk 20                            903.00      39%
       last updated FEB 3 86          3 in stock       1,499.00      596
----------------------------------------------------------------------------
MDRW1  MacDraw                                           105.00      46%
       last updated FEB 3 86          4 in stock         195.00      90
----------------------------------------------------------------------------
MPAS1  Macintosh Pascal                                   75.00      40%
       last updated FEB 3 86          2 in stock         125.00      50
----------------------------------------------------------------------------
MPNT2  MacPaint                                           75.00      40%
       last updated FEB 3 86          8 in stock         125.00      50
----------------------------------------------------------------------------
MPRJ2  MacProject                                        120.00      38%
       last updated FEB 3 86          3 in stock         195.00      75
----------------------------------------------------------------------------
MSWT4  Switcher 4.6                                       12.00      39%
       last updated FEB 3 86          5 in stock          19.95       8
----------------------------------------------------------------------------
MTRM2  MacTerminal 2.0                                    75.00      40%
       last updated FEB 3 86          5 in stock         125.00      50
----------------------------------------------------------------------------
MWRT2  MacWrite                                           75.00      40%
       last updated FEB 3 86          9 in stock         125.00      50
----------------------------------------------------------------------------
                          Total Wholesale    44,972.00
                             Total Retail    72,330.75
                           Average Retail       827.72
                             Total Margin          37%
                               Total G.P.    27,358.75
```

Fig. 7-10. The Work Station's inventory list.

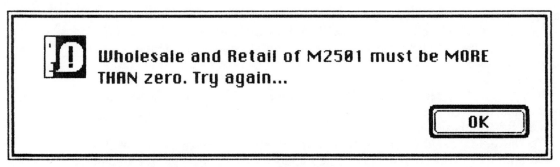

Fig. 7-11. The error message which you built into the sequences.

Good luck with your first debugging adventure! If all went well, however, you should now have a number of items in your new Inventory file. The next step is to build a Report format to allow you to see an informative printout of the contents of the Inventory file.

Yet Another Report Format

This chapter's report will pull together many of the tools that you have worked with in previous chapters. You will also work with a new feature of reports: Totals. This new capability opens up Reports significantly, because it adds to the informative content of Omnis 3 reports. This particular report is basically a listing of the items in inventory. However, it would be preferable to have some cumulative information at the end of the report, such as the total wholesale and retail value of the Inventory, profit margin, and so on.

As was detailed in the plan, adding totals to a report is straightforward. Basically, you need only set the Totaled attribute in the field attributes box for the fields which you want to be totaled.

☒ Totaled

Then, if an entry for that Detail section field appears again in the Totals section, it will print the sum of that item. The copy of that field that appears in the Totals section can simply be set as though it were a Normal field, and Omnis is smart enough to assume that, since it is a copy of a totaled field and it is in the Totals section, it should display the total there. From that point it is simple to calculate averages, differences, and other meaningful data using calculated fields in the Totals section.

Using the Heading section of a report, you can print a page number at the top of each page of your report. This involves the use of another of Omnis 3's built-in constants, #P. During a report, this one holds the current page number. We'll be using this constant in the report, as well as #R, which stores the total number of records printed during the current report.

The last new feature in this report is the use of two *Invisible* fields. These fields will be used to calculate the total Wholesale and Retail value of the inventory at the end of the report. This will be done by multiplying each of the two prices by the STKONHD field's value. It's not necessary to see these individual numbers for each inventory item, but we can't wait until the end of the report to calculate the individual numbers, or else we'd be faced with a difficult math problem. Therefore, we'll set the two fields in the Detail section to be Invisible, Totaled, and Calculated, so we will have access to their running totals in the Totals section.

As above, in the building of the Entry layout and the sequences, you'll work from a printout of the actual details of the Report format, as printed by Omnis 3 using the *Print report details* command. The final format will be wider than the display screen, so you'll have to use the horizontal scroll bar in the window to access the rest of the fields. The first area of the screen should look like Fig. 7-12. After you scroll over a bit, you can add the fields shown in Fig. 7-13.

A handy tool can be utilized here, the Copy and Paste features in the *Edit* menu. The #3 and #4 fields are going to be almost identical in the Detail and Totals section, so you can build the first two and then Copy and Paste them to the other section. After they are situated, you can set their attributes, which will be slightly different from their Detail section counterparts.

☐ *Create new Report INVENT*
☐ *Build the Report format, using the pictures in Figs. 7-12 and 7-13, and the listing in Fig. 7-14.*

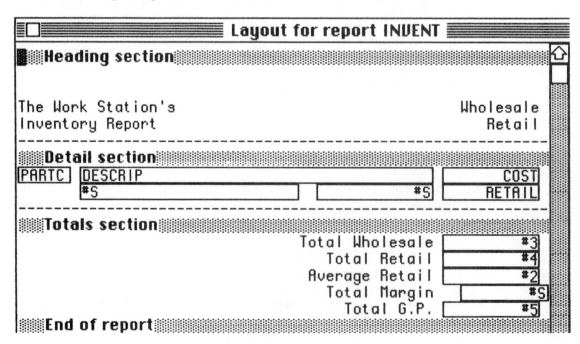

Fig. 7-12. The first view of the Report format INVENT.

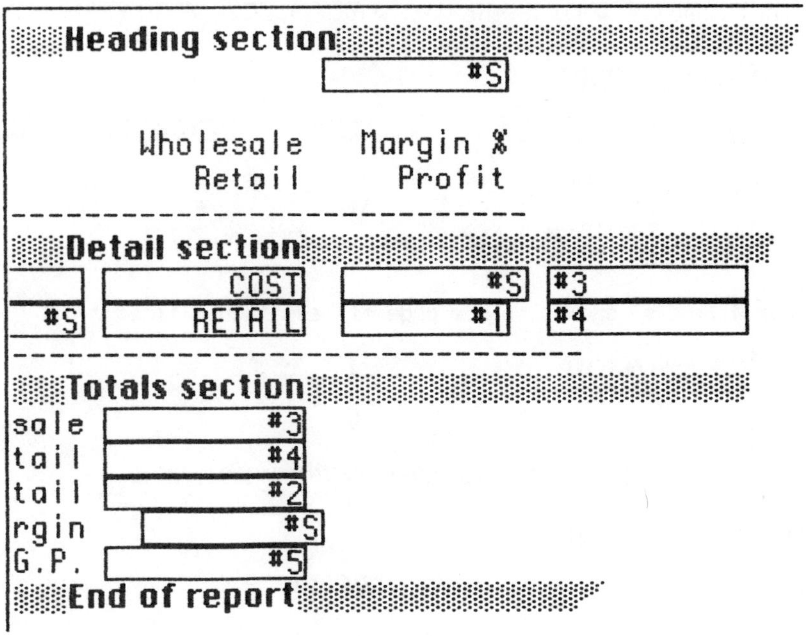

Fig. 7-13. The view of INVENT after scrolling to the right a bit.

One more detail should be set to make the Report appear properly. You might have missed it, but the Detail section needs to have its parameters set. Omnis 3 normally prints one page of the report at a time. When it reaches the bottom of the page, it skips to the top of the next page, prints another copy of the Heading section, and continues the reporting. However, it is quite common to have a record's Detail section split between pages. Not only is this unsightly, it can lead to confusion and misinformation as well. The mechanism to safeguard this is contained in the sections window.

If you double-click on the bar which says *Detail section*, this window reappears. In the lower half is an area where parameters of that particular section can be set. The one which needs to be set is shown in Fig. 7-15. Because the Detail section in this report is three lines long, this setting tells Omnis 3 to check before printing any record and make sure there are three or more lines left on the page. You can also use this setting to force Omnis 3 to skip a space between each of your Detail sections by adding a 1 where there is a 0 now. Various other options are available here, including printing only one record per page, and the default, which is single spacing with no special parameters. Line spacing can be set using the Report parameters command.

☐ *Verify that the Detail section's parameters are set as shown in Fig. 7-15.*
☐ *Go ahead and print the Report using the Options menu.*

Again, what happens if it doesn't work the first time? (If it *ever* works the

REPORT FORMAT INVENT

FILE	FIELD	LINE	POSITION	ATTRIBUTES	LENGTH	JUST

Heading

| | #S | 1 | 61 | + | 10 | Right |
| Formula | CON('Page ',#P) | | | | | |

Detail
Leave 0 line(s) and start new page if less than 3 lines available

STOCK	PARTCOD	1	1		6	Left
STOCK	DESCRIP	1	8		40	Left
STOCK	COST	1	49	T,	11	Right
	#S	1	62	+	10	Right
Formula	CON(INT(((RETAIL-COST)/RETAIL)*100),'%')					
	#3	1	73	+TI2	11	Left
Formula	COST*STKONHD					
	#S	2	8	+	25	Left
Formula	CON('last updated ',LSTUPDT)					
	#S	2	35	+	13	Right
Formula	CON(STKONHD,' in stock')					
STOCK	RETAIL	2	49	T,	11	Right
	#1	2	62	+,	9	Right
Formula	RETAIL-COST					
	#4	2	73	+TI2	11	Left
Formula	RETAIL*STKONHD					

Subtotals #1 to #9 and Final Totals
Leave no blank lines

	#3	1	49	,2	11	Right
	#4	2	49	,2	11	Right
	#2	3	49	+,2	11	Right
Formula	RETAIL/#R					
	#S	4	51	+	10	Right
Formula	CON(INT(((#4-#3)/#4)*100),'%')					
	#5	5	49	+,2	11	Right
Formula	#4-#3					

List of attribute codes:

+	Calculated	B	Duplicate values blank
C	Control character	I	Invisible
F	Automatic find	E	Zeros shown as empty
T	Totaled	(	Shown like (123.4)
X	No line if field empty	,	Shown like 1,234.5

Fig. 7-14. The printed details of INVENT.

○ **Leave no blank lines**

○ **Leave** 2 **blank line(s)**

◉ **Leave** 0 **line(s) and start new page if less than** ▓ **lines available**

○ **Start new page**

○ **Start** 3 **line(s) from the bottom margin**

Fig. 7-15. The report parameters for INVENT.

first time, you're probably not human!) Here's some possible problems, listed in no particular order along with probable solutions:

1) *Some fields end up only partially displayed.* Check that you have set the field lengths correctly.
2) *The text is not lining up properly.* Are you printing with Fonts? If so, turn off that option. We'll demonstrate some work-arounds later in the book.
3) *The data is completely scrambled.* Try opening up the STOCK File format, and choosing *Reorganize data.* You might have made a change to the File format, and inadvertently forgot to reorganize the Data file.
4) *All else fails.* Simply print out all of the details of the Report, then compare them line by line with the examples.

If all went well, you should end up with the same printout you used to enter the data originally, Fig. 7-10! If the report was printed to the screen, the last screen should appear as shown in Fig. 7-16. If you entered all the data exactly as it appeared in Fig. 7-10, your totals will match the ones above. If you made up your own data, you should probably use a calculator to check the answers. Never trust results just because they came from a computer!

Some Finishing Touches

In order to make this module of the system more complete cosmetically, we can make some additions to the menus that we've been using. The first is the STKENTR menu. Omnis 3's sequences can run almost any feature of the program, so it would be nice to be able to get a printout of the Inventory list right from the Entry layout, and then return to entering data.

If you remember our work earlier in this chapter, Sequence #8 in the STKENTR menu was left with a nonsense command in it; now we can replace that with this command. But consider yourself warned! If you have one of the numbered sequences highlighted, you should *never* use the *Insert line* or *Delete line* commands in the *Amend sequences* menu. For instance, if you use the *Delete line* command, Omnis 3 will delete that line, and move all the sequences below it on the list up one line. This will cause big problems if you have used any of the numbers below the deleted line for subroutines (we used #21) because their numbers will change. Unlike a spreadsheet, Omnis 3 can't automatically make these kinds of adjustments for you.

The correct way to do this is listed below. Go ahead and add this item to your menu:

☐ *Call up the Sequences for* **STKENTR.**
☐ *Click on Line #8. (If you didn't enter anything for #8, you can skip the next step.)*
☐ *Select this line's text, and press Backspace to clear it.*
☐ *Type* **Print list**
☐ *Click on the first line in the* **Commands** *window. (If you didn't enter anything for #8, you can skip the next step again.)*
☐ *Use the* **Delete line** *command to erase any commands that may have been entered for #8. (**Delete line** is OK on this side of the window.)*
☐ *Enter the sequences shown in Fig. 7-17.*

Feel free to make changes to this sequence if you'd rather have the report go directly to the printer, or you'd rather have Omnis 3 ask you with the familiar "File, Clipboard, Printer, Screen" prompt. You will find all these variations in the Select command choice.

```
 ⌘  File  Edit  Options  The Work Station
                                                        Page 5

   The Work Station's                      Wholesale   Margin %
   Inventory Report                          Retail     Profit
   ---------------------------------------------------------------
   MTRM2  MacTerminal 2.0                      75.00        40%
          last updated FEB 3 86    5 in stock  125.00        50
   ---------------------------------------------------------------
   MWRT2  MacWrite                             75.00        40%
          last updated FEB 3 86    9 in stock  125.00        50
   ---------------------------------------------------------------
                          Total Wholesale   44,972.00
                             Total Retail   72,330.75
                           Average Retail      827.72
                             Total Margin        37%
                              Total G.P.    27,358.75


   ◁ ▭                                                        ▷

      [   Finish   ]    [  Prev page  ]    [  Next page  ]
```

Fig. 7-16. The appearance of INVENT if printed to the screen.

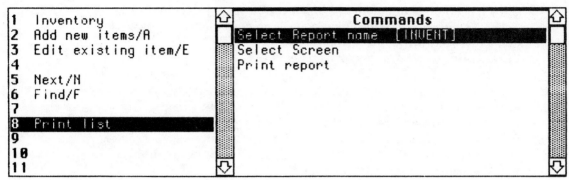

Fig. 7-17. Adding to the sequences.

☐ *Close the window.*
☐ *Choose **Enter data using 'STKENTR'** from the Options menu.*

Note that the new menu item has been installed in your Inventory menu. When you try it, you'll notice that the sequence automatically returns you to the Entry layout when the report has finished printing.

The last change for this chapter is to add an appropriate entry to the STARTUP menu. Remember, this is to be a modular program, so it would be nice to have a *Maintain Inventory* command in the system's main menu. This is almost trivial to accomplish, as Omnis 3's tremendous flexibility enables you to leap large databases in a single bound!

The sequences and associated menu for the STKENTR layout automatically become active when that Entry layout is displayed. Therefore, the only command necessary is *Enter data using STKENTR*, just like in the *Options* menu. We'll insert it just below the Enter customers command in the STARTUP menu. There is no problem using *Insert line* or *Delete line* in the menu formats, because the commands are not numbered. Let's add it now.

☐ *Call up the STARTUP Menu format.*
☐ *Click on the blank line below the **Enter customers** command.*
☐ *Use the Insert line command to add a blank line there.*
☐ *Type **Maintain inventory***

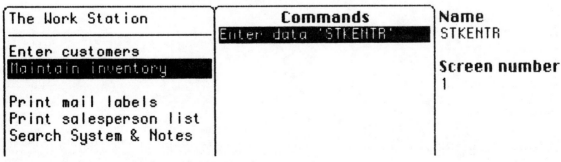

Fig. 7-18. Adding this new module to the STARTUP menu.

□ Click the **Enter data** command in the lower part of the window.
□ Tab to **Name**, and enter the Entry layout's name (as shown in Fig. 7-18).
□ Close the window.
□ Click **Install** to make this new version active.

You can now use The Work Station menu to go directly to the Inventory module of the database, and can even print the Inventory list from there. Congratulations!

You should spend time practicing the areas of the program we worked on in this chapter. A lot of material was presented here, and subsequent chapters will draw heavily on this information. There is only one way to build proficiency and, ultimately, expertise with Omnis 3:

Practice, Practice, Practice!

Onwards and upwards!

Omnis 3

The DataBasics
Useful Reports
Search Formats
Custom Menus
Sequences
More Sequences
Expansion
Connections   ⌘8

Adding to the Inventory Control System

The Problem: The Work Station's management continues to press on with plans for expansion of both their business and our growing Omnis 3 system. Expecting the opening of a new store, among other things, they are interested in adding to the Inventory Control system described in the last chapter.

Obviously, we will soon be adding an invoicing system (next chapter), but for now the management will be content with a system that allows them to debit or credit their Inventory when merchandise enters or leaves the store. This will be implemented with a system of inventory transfers, and the creation of yet another database. They also want to implement a modest auditing capability, by recording the store's inventory level for the part at the time of the transfer. Additionally, they would like to be able to delete transfers, but only on the day that they're executed. Last but not least, the outgoing inventory transfers must be checked against available inventory and invalidated before they're printed if the level is insufficient to fill the order.

It's a tall order, but no problem for you and Omnis 3!

THE PLAN

This chapter draws on the database that we built in the last chapter, the STOCK File format. Without that file, and some appropriate data entered into it, this chapter's exercises will be pointless; make sure your Library file is in the state we left it at the end of Chapter 7. Once that is done, you can press on!

The main goal here is to tackle the problem of the inventory transfer scheme,

131

but the larger purpose is to introduce the idea of connecting disparate files and somehow making them communicate. In this chapter's example, we will be using the second File format created, the STOCK file. However, to accomplish the desired objective, we will have to build yet another file, which we'll call XFER. This is because the inventory transfers described above will be kept in their own file. In Chapter 7, we built the STOCK file because the Inventory database had no direct relationship to the CUSTS file. In principle, the same holds true here. The XFER file will hold different information than does the STOCK file: transfer date, shipping company, etc. But there the similarity ends.

Although there is no direct relationship between Transfers and Inventory, there is an indirect relationship. A direct relationship would be of the type demonstrated in an earlier chapter when we added a NOTES field to the CUSTS database to track freehand notes on individual customers. For that application it was fairly simple to add the new field to the existing file. However, there is a more convoluted picture here.

For our purposes in this chapter, we will limit the transfers to one item per record. The indirect relationship comes into play in the fact that any item in inventory can possibly appear in an inventory transfer record. And the reverse is true as well: any inventory transfer record can refer to any item in inventory. So, as you can see, there is a loosely defined relationship between the files.

We could simplify this situation immensely if we backed down and stored the actual inventory information (part code, description, etc.) for each transfer in the XFER file. But why duplicate our efforts? Remember, all that information is already stored in the STOCK file—and if we don't use the STOCK file, how can we control the inventory? Therefore, we need to design a way for the XFER file to "look up" parts in the STOCK file, and store some sort of indicator as to which part was involved in the transfer. Having access to this record will also enable the XFER file to "check" the "Stock on hand" figure to verify that the transfer request can be filled, and then actually adjust it according to the nature of the transfer.

You are probably envisioning the need for hideously involved sequences, Entry layouts, and ugly, all-night programming sessions. Don't panic! Omnis 3 has a phenomenal built-in mechanism for drawing relationships between files in the same Library: *File Connections*. It is certainly not trivial to understand (or explain!), so this chapter is totally devoted to outlining, explaining, and demonstrating this capability. Sit up straight, put on your thinking cap, and let's explore Connected files!

The Transfers File Format

The first step we'll take in expanding this system is to create a new File format (XFER) to hold the data which will be recorded for the Inventory Transfer records. This file will contain the following fields: *Transfer Date, Trucked By, Received By, Incoming, Quantity Moved,* and *Stock Level* (at the time of the transfer). Of these fields, the Trucked By and Received By fields are Character fields, Quantity Moved and Stock Level are both Numeric, and Transfer Date is obviously a Date field. The Incoming field is a new type: Boolean. This is a logical field (similar to the Omnis 3 Flag) which can hold only a Boolean truth value. This field accepts only "YES" or "NO" (or their first letters) or "1" or "0", as input. In this application we'll use this field to make a determination as to whether the inventory item being transferred is coming into the store or going out.

Conspicuously absent in the above list is any reference to the inventory item itself. This is not an oversight. After all, we already have all the inventory items stored in a separate file, STOCK; we have to find a way to access that file without taking up precious disk space in the XFER file.

What's the Connection?

Omnis 3 allows you to create a relationship where the data in one file can "look up" information in another file and then make use of it in a variety of ways. The process of creating one of these relationships is certainly not trivial, but it is straightforward. What follows is a synopsis of the schemes involved in Connected files using Omnis 3. If this is not absolutely clear, *don't panic!* The main goal of this chapter's Steps is a succinct demonstration of how this all works. A clear and contextual example often can be more useful than 50 pages of the clearest and most detailed explanations.

As you saw in the very first File format we constructed, Omnis 3 maintains a special field along with every file created: the Sequence field (which is an unfortunate choice of words because this has nothing to do with the sequences you have used to program Omnis 3). Do you remember that far back? To refresh your memory, you can use them as an Indexed field in your file formats, but regardless of whether or not *you* use them, Omnis 3 always uses them. If you don't explicitly include it in your File format, it is still there, but is invisible to you. The most important piece of information about Sequence fields is that once a particular number is assigned, it is never reassigned, even if that record is deleted. And it can never be changed. This field is the key to making connections work.

In our example we will set the STOCK file as a connected file *for* the XFER file. This is because connections are the based on a "one-to-many" relationship. Let's call XFER the *primary file*, and STOCK the *connected file*. Using these more general names, this type of relationship can be characterized by the following rules:

1) Each record in the primary file is connected to *only one* record in the connected file.
2) Each record in the connected file can be connected to *many* of the records in the primary file.

In designing our file format, we must decide the "direction" of the connection. In this case, let's substitute our actual file names into the above rules and see if it makes sense:

1) Each transfer in the XFER file can be connected to *only one* inventory item in the STOCK file.

2) Each inventory item in the STOCK file can be connected to *many* of
the transfers in the XFER file.

Translated into more familiar English, this means that each of the transfers will
be for exactly one inventory item, but that doesn't preclude inventory items from
appearing on more than one transfer. This makes sense as the logical way to
make our connection. If you reverse the order, you'll see that it doesn't make
sense for this application.

1) Each inventory item in the STOCK file can be connected to *only one*
transfer in the XFER file.
2) Each transfer in the XFER file can be connected to *many* of the inventory items in the STOCK file.

And there is a third rule which can come into play in more complex database
systems:

3) Connections cannot be *circular* (two or more files all connected to each
other).

The actual mechanism Omnis 3 uses to maintain connections is fairly complex, but examining what happens behind the scenes when one file becomes
connected to another can help your understanding. In this case, we designated
STOCK as a connected file for XFER. By doing so, we create what amounts to
an invisible field in the XFER file. When you enter a transfer using the XFER
file, you create a new record (let's call it TransferOne), just as with every previous
file with which you've worked.

But there is a difference here: Omnis 3 proceeds to "connect" that record
to a particular record (let's call it PartOne) in the STOCK file. It does this by
saving the sequence number of PartOne in the invisible field of TransferOne.
Using this "pointer" field, TransferOne always knows exactly where to look
in STOCK file to find PartOne's data. The reason that Omnis 3 never changes
sequence numbers around suddenly becomes apparent; we see that the Sequence
number is the means of connecting records from different files. (Those of you
who are familiar with database terminology will recognize this concept as the
linked list.)

You might say at this point, "How does Omnis 3 know which part from
the STOCK file to use in the connection?" The answer lies in the new Entry
layout which we will build here. In the previous chapter you probably noticed
that, after the STOCK File format was created, the ubiquitous *Automatic names
window* displayed the names of all of the fields from both files. Omnis 3 allows
fields from more than one file to be built into an Entry layout. This is the way
we can reference parts from the STOCK file, even though the main file for this
Entry layout will be the XFER file.

As an example, we can simply include PARTCOD (from the STOCK file)
on the Entry layout, and use it to enter the code for the part to be transferred.

But how will Omnis 3 know the sequence number of this part? The key to this lies in setting PARTCOD with a new field attribute: *Auto find*. This type of field on an Entry layout actually "looks up" the value entered into it in the file where it came from. The only requirement for an *Auto find* field is that it must be an indexed field in the originating File format.

If we entered "M2503" into the PARTCOD field, for example, Omnis 3 would look for that value in the STOCK file's PARTCOD's. Once the correct record is found, it is connected to the record being entered at the time. Fortunately, an error message is displayed if Omnis 3 is unable to find an exact match for the value. Unlike a regular Find command, which defaults to picking the record closest to the entered value, *Auto find* fields only perform "exact match" finds. (Do you see the value of the *Unique indexed* attribute here?) Once the *Auto find* field has done it's thing, you can display other fields on the Entry layout from the connected record; you can display other fields on the Entry layout from the connected record; we could bring up the DESCRIP or STKONHD fields to appear on the transfer form if we wished.

But wait! What if we don't want the user to be able to make changes to the fields from the STOCK file? After all, the data will be right there. No problem. First, Omnis 3 never uses the Auto find fields as actual data input fields. Although they appear on the Entry layout, like any other field, the actual values entered therein are used only in the Find operation.

But what of the DESCRIP or the STKONHD fields? If these fields are to be used for display purposes only, as they are here, they can be assigned two attributes (one of them new): *Display only* and *Local*. Display only has been used before (in the STKENTR Entry layout) to prevent the user from entering a date. Local is a new attribute which tells Omnis 3, "This field is for internal use only, and is dependent on the first previous *non-local* field for its data." In this case the field will actually be read in from the STOCK file. You don't want the user to be able to update the Inventory information (such as part codes or prices) from the Transfer form; setting the field as *Local* (and *Display only*) will prevent that from happening.

When an *Auto find* field is used in and Entry layout, Omnis 3 performs an Exact match Find on the contents of that field. Once it validates the value entered by connecting with the record of choice, that record in the connected file is actually read into the Macintosh memory. As we've seen above, the data is then available to the Entry layout for display. But the Entry layout can also make changes to the record from the connected file, just as with the input to the primary file.

Our Entry layout will eventually look like Fig. 8-1. Using this screen as a guide, the chain of events for data entry will be as shown in Fig. 8-2. As you can see, well-designed sequences can greatly increase the power of connected files by controlling the updating of fields from connected files.

This Chapter's Enhancements

According to The Work Station's requests, we will build the Inventory Transfer system in this chapter. The fundamentals of using Connected files and

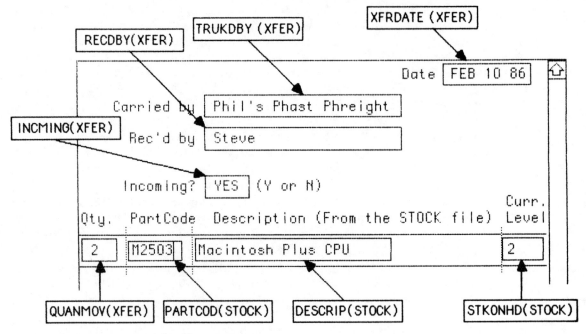

XFRDATE (XFER)

TRUKDBY (XFER)

RECDBY(XFER)

INCMING(XFER)

Date | FEB 10 86 |

Carried by | Phil's Phast Phreight |

Rec'd by | Steve |

Incoming? | YES | (Y or N)

Qty.   PartCode   Description (From the STOCK file)   Curr. Level

| 2 | | M2503 | | Macintosh Plus CPU | | 2 |

QUANMOV(XFER)   PARTCOD(STOCK)   DESCRIP(STOCK)   STKONHD(STOCK)

Fig. 8-1. The eventual look of this chapter's Entry layout.

Auto find fields were covered above, because they are integral to the success of this component of the system. In addition to the features that were discussed earlier, a few more will be included by the end of the chapter.

The system is designed to log all inventory transfers other than invoices. After verifying sufficient quantity first, it will be responsible for updating the inventory. If there aren't enough of the requested part available, it will prevent the transfer from being issued and display a message. It will be responsible for the handling of incoming and outgoing merchandise, debiting or crediting inventory as appropriate. Although you can enter the number of parts transferred, the system will be able to handle only one inventory item per transfer. (A solution to this situation won't be available until the next chapter. Stay tuned.)

We will include a field called CURRLVL to hold the stock level of the requested part at the time of the transfer. Consider this scenario: three ImageWriters II's are transferred out today. Before they were transferred out, there were five in stock. Obviously, there are now two left. Pretty simple, huh? You might first think to directly reference the STKONHD field from the STOCK file. Unfortunately, this would produce undefined results when this record is printed two weeks from now—the connected record would simply report the number of items in inventory on the day of the report, instead of on the day of the transfer. Therefore, we'll make a point of explicitly recording the stock level in the CURRLVL field, along with the rest of the transfers data.

The sequences in this chapter will again build in complexity, as they have in the past. This time around they will be used to manipulate data in the involved files, and also to do some rather sophisticated error detection and error

---

1) The user chooses to "Log transactions".

2) The user enters the first few Normal fields from XFER.

3) The user enters a part code (the Auto find field).

4) Omnis 3 "looks up" that PARTCOD in the STOCK file.

      (If the Part code is found, continue to step 5; otherwise, display an error message, and go back to step 3.)

5) Read that record into memory, and fill in the Local fields on the Entry layout.

      (more fields entered if necessary...)

6) The user clicks OK to save the Transfer.

7) A Sequence takes over which subtracts the Quantity of items transferred from the number of items currently in inventory (STKONHD).

8) The Sequence issues the "Update files" command, which writes out XFER's new record, as well as the modified STOCK record.

Fig. 8-2. The chain of events for data entry.

reporting. For instance, when a transfer is entered, it is very important that there be a sufficient stock level of that item to supply the transfer. If there isn't, the inventory of that item would go into the red, creating at best an accounting headache.

According to management's wishes, the transfers can be entered as either incoming or outgoing. There is obviously a very different situation in each of these two cases. Incoming inventory needs no checking, since it is simply adding to existing inventory. So we need a reliable method of determining the direction of the transfer. We will use the Boolean field, INCOMNG.

Boolean fields are distinguished by the fact that they can hold only one of two values: True or False. (Remember the similarity to the Omnis 3 Flag used in your sequences?) Unlike the Flag, however, Boolean fields store data permanently in a file just like all the other field types. But how is the data stored? As the words "Yes" and "No"? Not exactly. Omnis 3 will recognize these words as valid input, but it would not be space-efficient to store a two- or three-letter character variable when there are only two possibilities that can ever be input and saved. Omnis 3 actually stores Boolean fields as a 0 (False) or a 1 (True) value, reserving only one byte (character) of storage space for that field in a File format. (It could theoretically reduce that even further, to only a single bit!)

Using the Boolean INCOMNG field, we can build a sequence that after data is entered, asks the question:

If INCMING = 1

If you remember our discussion of relational operators and logical expressions in the last chapter, you will recall that these expressions always evaluate to True or False. But we can use these truth values in equations, because Omnis 3 interprets these truth values as actual numbers: 0 (False) or 1 (True), the same as above. In essence, we are asking "Is INCOMNG = True?"

All of the testing above will be performed in our sequence before issuing the *Update files* command. This is to take into account three possible scenarios. In the first, INCOMNG equals one (it is true, meaning that the transfer is incoming), and we won't do any checking. However, we do need to do some math before we update the files. In order to increment the inventory correctly, we must perform two calculations. The first one calculates the new STKONHD figure for the STOCK file:

Calculate STKONHD as QUANMOV + STKONHD

The second equation actually sets the CURRLVL field as equal to the STKONHD figure's new value, which we just calculated above:

Calculate CURRLVL as STKONHD

Note that we nonchalantly altered the value of a field from a different file (STOCK). Remember, once an *Auto find* has read in a record from another file, you can assume that you have access to those fields, as well as the fields from your primary file.

The other two scenarios are related to each other, as both are possible if the INCOMNG field is equal to 0 (false, i.e., the transfer is Outgoing). It is here that we must proceed with caution, as we have the possibility of a problem. The worst case is where there is insufficient level in inventory for a successful transfer. In order to determine this, we have to test the values in a couple of the available fields. This can be done using the following relational test:

Else If STKONHD < QUANMOV

In this instance, the sequence will post an informative error message, then proceed to call the *Quit Sequence* command. This will prevent the *Update files* command from ever being issued for the data on the screen, and the file will remain as it was before.

However, assuming that the employees are generally safer than that, we will usually see the case where the level is sufficient. We can then do a similar calculation to the one used above to increment the inventory:

Calculate STKONHD as STKONHD - QUANMOV
Calculate CURRL VL as STKONHD

Notice that the QUANMOV field was subtracted here instead of added.

Putting the three scenarios together, we can see an extension of the familiar If-Then-Else control structure in Fig. 8-3. The addition here is the *Else If* statement. The rule to follow in the reading of these types of complex expressions is: Read down the list of If and Else If statements until you reach a True statement; skip beyond the first End If statement that you reach, then continue on with the sequence. The Else If statement is very useful if more than two possible results must be tested, as is the case with our three scenarios above.

The last order of business for these sequences is handling a requested deletion of a transfer. As was mentioned earlier, the management has asked that legal deletions be limited to current-day transfers. This is quite simple to im-

```
If INCMING = 1
   Calculate STKONHD as QUANMOV + STKONHD
   Calculate CURRLVL as STKONHD
Else If STKONHD < QUANMOV
   OK message Bell [There aren't enough ;DESCRIP ;'s for the Transfer ( ;STKONHD;).]
   Quit sequence
Else
   Calculate STKONHD as STKONHD - QUANMOV
   Calculate CURRLVL as STKONHD
End If
Update files
```

Fig. 8-3. Using the "Else if" statement.

```
If XFRDATE = #D
  If INCMING = 1
    * REMOVE the items from inventory
    Calculate STKONHD as STKONHD-QUANMOV
  Else
    * ADD the items back into inventory
    Calculate STKONHD as STKONHD+QUANMOV
  End If
  Delete
End If
```

Fig. 8-4. Deletion sequence.

plement, by building a logical test that must be passed before the data can be erased from the file:

If XFRDATE = #D

The #D represents Omnis 3's internal calendar's date, and the equal sign means just what it says. Once this test passes, meaning that it is OK to actually delete the record, we have to do some fancy footwork. Deleting a transfer means that its net effect on inventory has to be reversed. In other words, if the transfer was originally an incoming transfer of two ImageWriter II's, the inventory has been incremented by two. The inventory figure in the STOCK file would then have to be decremented because of the voiding of the transfer. The sequence that handles the deletion is listed in Fig. 8-4.

The Transfer Log Report

As complex as it seemed to implement the Entry layout for our connection scheme, it is that simple to create a report to display the "log" of transfers. Once Omnis 3 has created a connection between records in different files, they are joined until one of them is deleted, or the connection is explicitly changed or altered in some other way. (Doesn't that sound a lot like marriage?) Producing a report is as simple as laying out all the fields that you want to have appear on the report, and then simply printing the report.

The only possible catch is the setting of the Main file. This must be set to the primary file, so that Omnis 3 can manage its connections properly. The setting of the Main file is accomplished in the *Sort fields* window. Omnis 3's default for the Main file in a report is the file from which the first detail section field on the report originates. Therefore, it is possible to foul up a report by entering a field from a connected file as the first on a report screen, then forgetting to set the Main file. But if you remember to do that, you are 95 percent on your way to producing meaningful reports from your connected files.

Enough preparation! Let's get started.

THE STEPS

This chapter is no exception to the rule set forth in every other chapter: be sure that you are working with the database as it was left at the end of the previous chapter. Otherwise you may find that things are not going to work like they are described here. As a review of the Plan section, Fig. 8-5 shows a picture representing the structure of our application's files as they will be by the end of this chapter.

Yet Another New File Format

The XFER File format is the first piece of this new module that must be built. It is relatively indistinguished in its structure, containing only six fields, all of which have been discussed in detail above. In the interest of experimenta-

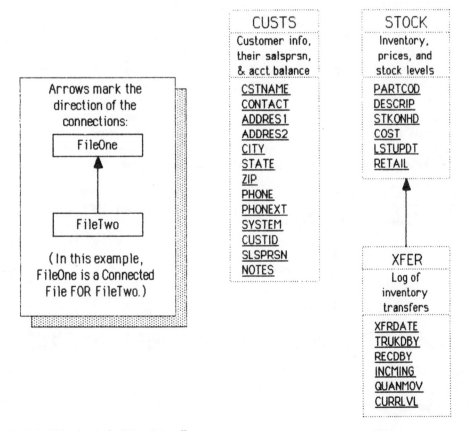

Fig. 8-5. This chapter's "big picture."

tion, we'll throw in a new twist anyway.

As we've done in the previous chapters, we'll be setting a few of these fields to be indexed. Two in particular are involved in an interesting dilemma. These two (TRUKDBY and RECDBY) are better off indexed, but because of their length, that could cause a problem. When Omnis 3 reserves space for a record in the Data file, it takes into account a few factors. The two most significant of those are the Field length and the *Index length*. The Index length is the "accuracy" with which Omnis 3 maintains an index.

With all field types, Omnis 3 saves space in the file on a byte-by-byte basis for both of these pieces of data. In a 25-character indexed field, for example, this means Omnis 3 is automatically taking up at least 50 bytes of disk space for every entry in that field, even if the entry is just a few characters long! This is not uncommon with database software, but it is not conducive to using many indexed fields on a computer where storage space is at a premium. But there is a hedge against this problem.

When determining which fields will be indexed in a File format, you can also vary the index length for that field. For instance, the TRUKDBY field will be set to 25 characters in length. When we set it to be indexed, the default index length will be 25 characters. We will manually override that size, and enter a more conservative figure. In this File format, we'll set the index lengths of both the TRUKDBY and RECDBY fields to be 6 instead of the default of 25. In the long run, that means that those two fields of each new record, will occupy at least 62 bytes of disk space, as opposed to the 100 bytes that they normally would have filled. The space saving is significant in a system where there is a large number of records to be entered.

But there is a trade-off involved in limiting the index length: the accuracy of the index. Considering the above situation, let's say you asked to use TRUKDBY as a sort field for a report. Omnis 3 would proceed to output records in index order. However, because the index length is only six characters, there would be a problem if two similar, but not equal, records were encountered (i.e.,

	Name	Type	Length	Dps	Indexed?
1	XFRDATE	Date			YES
2	TRUKDBY	National	25		YES
3	RECDBY	National	25		YES
4	INCMING	Boolean			NO
5	QUANMOV	Number		0	YES
6	CURRLVL	Number		0	NO
7					
8					
9					
10					

File format XFER

Fig. 8-6. The File format XFER.

142

"Gerald's Freight" and "Geraldine's Trucking"). Because only the first six characters are indexed, this situation would result in a "tie" for who would come first. This "tie" would have to be broken by the slower, disk-based method of sorting. In our application we can accept that chance, since it is obvious that a tie such as this would be very rare indeed. But be aware that limiting the index length to much less than six characters would probably result more frequent ties.

Now that we've put that behind us, we can build this File format:

☐ *Using Fig. 8-6 as your guide, create and build the XFER File format.*
☐ *Remember to set the index length of the TRUKDBY and RECDBY fields to 6:*

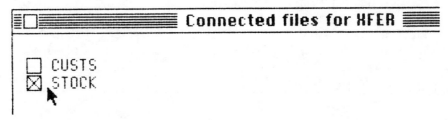

☐ *Don't close the window when you're done.*

As you remember from the above discussion, this file now must be connected to the STOCK file. Also, we'll check the organization of the Data file after these wholesale changes.

☐ *Choose **Set connections** from the Amend file format menu.*
☐ *Select the STOCK file as in Fig. 8-7.*
☐ *Use the **Reorganize data** command to check the Data file.*
☐ *Once you've satisfied your curiousity, go ahead and close all the open windows to save your new file.*

There are a few footnotes about File format creation. First, the actual order in which the fields appear in the list of fields is of no consequence. You can enter them in any order. Second, note that there is no reorganization necessary. As we discussed earlier, the process of connecting two files does not affect the connected file, only the primary one. Once the connection is made, Omnis 3 installs an invisible field into the primary file for the purpose of ultimately containing the record sequence number of the connected record. If data had been entered in the XFER file, then a connection had been made, that would ne-

Fig. 8-7. Connecting the STOCK file.

cessitate a reorganization of the Data file. But since there is no data in the file yet, it is still perfectly organized.

After all the talk of connected files earlier in the chapter, it is almost a letdown that it is this simple to connect two files! Let's continue into the Entry layout.

The Transfer Log Entry Layout

The form to be created here was discussed in great detail earlier, so the best approach to follow is to simply jump in and create the Entry layout now.

☐ *Using Figs. 8-8 and 8-9 as a guide, build the **XFRENTR** entry layout.*

No doubt you encountered a few problems in the construction. One of the most common is forgetting to set the field attributes properly. Only three fields in this layout are anything other than "Normal": PARTCOD is to be set as *Auto find* and *Upper case only*, and DESCRIP and STKONHD are *Local* and *Display only*.

Other than those attribute settings, the only peculiarities in this layout are the Defaults set for XFRDATE and INCMING. XFRDATE defaults to #D, which represents the current date. This is different from an earlier example, where we used #D as the Calculation for a field which needed no operator input. The difference here is that XFRDATE defaults to today's date, but it can be edited as well. The default for INCMING is 1 (one). Recall that it is a Boolean, or logical, field. By setting the default to 1, this in effect sets the default to YES. As with XFRDATE, this default value can be overridden by the user if it is not the appropriate response.

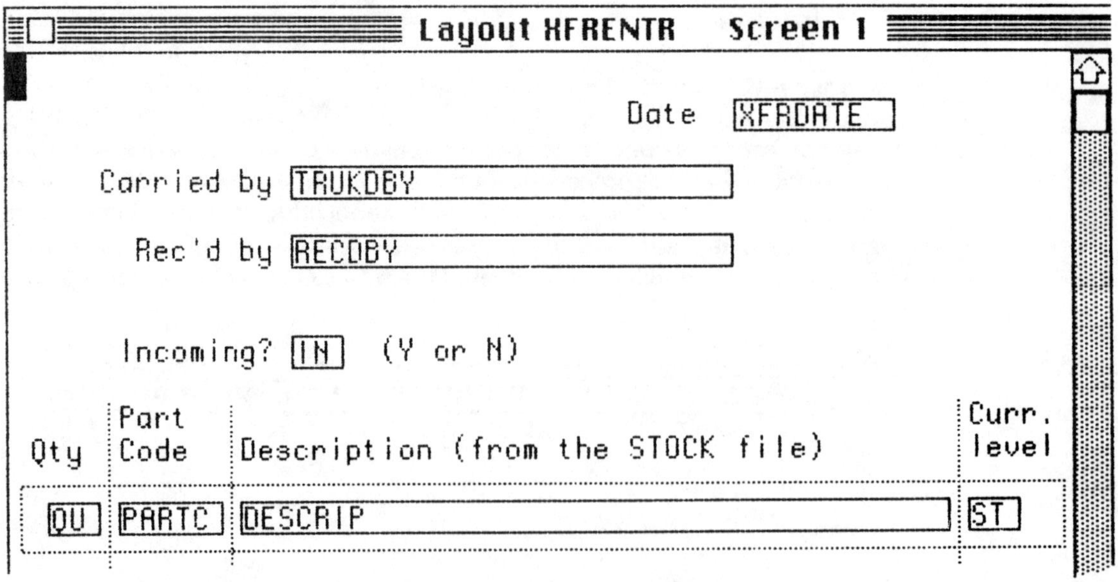

Fig. 8-8. The Entry layout XFRENTR.

```
ENTRY LAYOUT XFRENTR

           FILE     FIELD    VERTICAL  HORIZONTAL    ATTRIBUTES    LENGTH      JUST
--------------------------------------------------------------------------------

Screen 1
--------
1          XFER     XFRDATE     2        42                           9        Left
Def:chk    #0
2          XFER     TRUKDBY     4        17                          25        Left
3          XFER     RECDBY      6        17                          25        Left
4          XFER     INCMING     9        17                           3        Left
Def:chk    1
5          XFER     QUANMOV    14         3                           3        Left
6          STOCK    PARTCOD    14         7         FU                6        Left
7          STOCK    DESCRIP    14        14         LD               40        Left
8          STOCK    STKONHD    14        55         LD                3        Left


List of attribute codes:
          +   Calculated              I   Invisible
          M   Message field           D   Display only
          F   Automatic find          U   Upper case
          J   Unique indexed          V   Negative values allowed
          L   Local                   E   Zeros shown as empty
          P   Delete protected
```

Fig. 8-9. The Entry layout XFRENTR.

Recall that the order in which the fields appear on the Entry layout becomes critical when *Auto find* and *Local* fields are employed. Therefore, we need some mechanism for verifying that the fields are in the right "field number order" on the layout. Each field that is put onto the Entry layout is given a number, starting with 1 for the first field which is set up. *Auto find* fields must precede their *Local* brethren in number order. Sometimes they are input in random order, however, and the numbers don't line up properly. There must be a more convenient way of viewing these numbers than opening every field box one at a time. Of course, there is: in the *Amend layout* menu, there is an option to *Display numbers*. When this command is issued, Omnis removes the field names from all the small field boxes on the screen, and replaces them with the field numbers.

Here is a problem that could go undetected if this command were not used:

```
            Part
     Qty    Code    Description
     ┌───┐  ┌─────┐ ┌──────────────┐
     │6  │  │5    │ │7             │
     └───┘  └─────┘ └──────────────┘
```

As you can see, the fields were probably entered out of order. Luckily there is

145

a very fast and efficient means for righting this situation. Using the mouse, highlight the area of the layout containing the misbehaving fields, then click the Reorder button:

This command evaluates the fields in the selected area from left to right and top to bottom, and places their numbers in the correct order. The reason it does not automatically reorder all the fields on an layout is that it is sometimes preferable to have the fields input slightly out of order (you will see an example of this in the next chapter).

The Sequences

This chapter's sequences were discussed at length earlier. Fortunately, not much has changed since you first read about them. However, in this chapter, you will notice for the first time that we've built sequences that are necessary for the system to operate at all. Previously, our sequences have consisted mostly of warning boxes, data checks, and little helping hands along the way. Most of the commands were more efficient or elegant replacements for the commands in the *Enter data* menu.

This chapter's system will not work at all with out the help of its sequences; this is because quite a bit of the data manipulation will take place within them. For instance, if it weren't for the sequence, the connected file's data would never be updated properly, either when data is entered or deleted.

All of the new ideas have already been introduced in the Plan section, so let's give it a whirl right now!

☐ *Using Fig. 8-10 as a guide, build the sequences for the **XFRENTR** Entry layout.*
☐ *Remember to use Set Menu options to turn off display of the **Enter data** menu.*

You should get in the habit of completely commenting your sequences; it can be a real time-saver down the road. Figure 8-11 shows an example of simple comments inserted into a sequence. They will probably help later with enhancements, saving the programmer the trouble of stepping manually through the logic of the sequence to figure out exactly what it does.

Once the sequences are complete, try out the layout by entering a few transfers, using the Part codes from the Inventory database. Notice that as soon as you enter a Part code and Tab out of that field, Omnis 3 "looks up" the pertinent data and displays the required fields on your Entry layout. If you entered a number that isn't found in the file, you are given an error message, and you must reenter the field.

A new type of Delete sequence is used here, using a Yes/No Message box. This can easily take the place of the *Delete with confirmation* command, or any

SEQUENCES FOR XFRENTR

1 Inventory movements

2 Add a new transfer/A
Call sequence 21

3 Next/N
Next

4 Previous/P
Previous

5 Find/F
Find (prompted) [ ]

7 Delete this transfer/D
If QUANMOV<>0
    YES/NO message Bell [Do you really want to DELETE this transfer of ;XFRDATE;?]
    If Flag True
        Call sequence 22
    Else
        OK message [OK, this transfer was not deleted...]
    End If
Else
    OK message [There is no current record to delete!]
End If

21 Do something
Clear: Main file Connected files Other files
Prepare for Insert Enter data [ ]
If Flag False
    Quit sequence
End If
If INCMING=1
    Calculate STKONHD as STKONHD+QUANMOV
    Calculate CURRLVL as STKONHD
Else If STKONHD<QUANMOV
    OK message Bell [There aren't enough ;DESCRIP;'s for the Transfer (;STKONHD;).]
    Quit sequence
Else

Fig. 8-10. Listing of sequences and button definitions for the Entry layout XFRENTR.

```
        Calculate STKONHD as STKONHD-QUANMOV
        Calculate CURRLVL as STKONHD
    End If
    Update files

22 xfer deletion
    If XFRDATE=#D
        If INCMING=1
            * REMOVE the items from inventory
            Calculate STKONHD as STKONHD-QUANMOV
        Else
            * ADD the items back into inventory
            Calculate STKONHD as STKONHD+QUANMOV
        End If
        Delete
    End If
```

other command that requires the user to make a decision. The sequence continues once the user has clicked the Yes or No buttons in the box. The Flag indicates which button was clicked. If he or she clicked Yes, the Flag is set; No means the Flag is cleared. The other setting in this type of box is the decision as to which button is the "default," or the result which will be returned if the user presses Return. The default button will be highlighted, in the normal Macintosh way, by a thicker-than-normal black border around it.

Definitely the most complex of the Message boxes which you've used so far is the one found in the "Else if" clause in Sequence #21. It is displayed in if a part is requested in too great a quantity for current inventory levels. Notice that it displays two different fields, giving you an accurate error message, as well as the data needed to solve the problem. Figure 8-12 shows what would happen if you requested too many Macintoshes at a time that you only had 13

```
Commands
If XFRDATE=#D
  If INCMING=1
    * REMOVE the items from inventory
    Calculate STKONHD as STKONHD-QUANMOV
  Else
    * ADD the items back into inventory
    Calculate STKONHD as STKONHD+QUANMOV
  End If
  Delete
End If
```

Fig. 8-11. Using comments in your sequences.

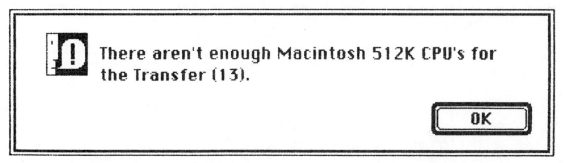

There aren't enough Macintosh 512K CPU's for the Transfer (13).

OK

Fig. 8-12. The message box warning of insufficient inventory.

in stock. Remember, any field value can be placed into a Message field or a Message box by enclosing its field name in semicolons anywhere in the text of the message.

Go ahead and enter a few Inventory transfers, both incoming and outgoing. Here is a suggestion for an enhancement:

☐ *Add a pertinent Message box for the case when the Transfer can't be deleted because the Date test fails in Sequence 22.*

The Transfer Log

Now that you have input a few transfers, we will proceed to build a simple report to print out the list of transfers. As was promised in the Plan section, this is a fairly simple report, considering the complex nature of the connected files involved in it.

Connected files in reports are completely transparent. You can assume that by the time a record gets to the point of being output in a report, it has already been "hooked up" with its connected record in the other file. Therefore, you can easily reference any field from either of the files as though they were both part of the same file! The only requirement is that Omnis 3 must know which file is the main and which is the connected file. This was discussed earlier; if it isn't perfectly clear, you can refer back to the Plan section for a review.

Let's get going and build this little report. "Little" here refers to the amount of effort invested, not the utility of the report. It is actually a very informative report, one which underscores the absolute simplicity of some of Omnis 3's most intimidating features. You'll once again be working from one of the Omnis 3 printouts, with a little graphic description as well. Let's do it:

☐ *The report is to be named* **MOVES.**
☐ *Using Figs. 8-13, 8-14 and 8-15 as guides, construct the layout (Fig. 8-15 is the view when the window is scrolled to the right. This report, as are most, is wider than the display screen.)*

The novelty item in this report is the use of a simple lookup table for the INCMING field. This is a very useful (if somewhat limited) feature of Omnis 3 (see Fig. 8-16). It allows you to interpret various field values as a different

```
REPORT FORMAT MOVES

     FILE      FIELD    LINE      POSITION      ATTRIBUTES      LENGTH        JUST
----------------------------------------------------------------------------------------
Detail
-------
Leave 0 line(s) and start new page if less than 4 lines available

     XFER      XFRDATE    1           1                            9          Left
     XFER      QUANMOV    1          11                            4          Left
     STOCK     PARTCOD    1          16                            6          Left
     STOCK     DESCRIP    1          23                           40          Left
     XFER      INCMING    1          72                            9          Right
Look up        Unknown/YES=Incoming/NO=Outgoing
               #S         2          11              +            35          Left
Formula        CON('Recd by: ',RECDBY)
               #S         2          46              +            35          Right
Formula        CON('Todays level: ',STKONHD)
               #S         3          11              +            35          Left
Formula        CON('Carried by: ',TRUKDBY)
               #S         3          46              +            35          Right
Formula        CON('Level at time of transfer: ',CURRLVL)

List of attribute codes:
     +    Calculated              B   Duplicate values blank
     C    Control character       I   Invisible
     F    Automatic find          E   Zeros shown as empty
     T    Totaled                 (   Shown like (123.4)
     X    No line if field empty  ,   Shown like 1,234.5
```

Fig. 8-13. Listing of the report MOVES.

value. Its main limitation is that you can only fit 70 characters in the text area, limiting the complexity of the lookup. But this is an example of a very handy conversion that makes this report more informative and easier to read. The first value must be the ''catch-all,'' or the value if all else fails. Successive values are in the form shown in Fig. 8-16. This type of field must be set as Normal for the lookup table to be available, or else this spot in the box is replaced with a Calculation or Message entry.

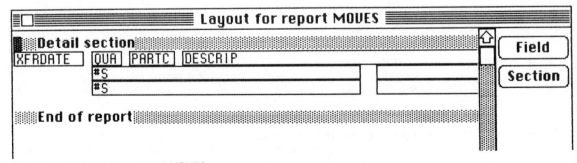

Fig. 8-14. Screen appearance of MOVES.

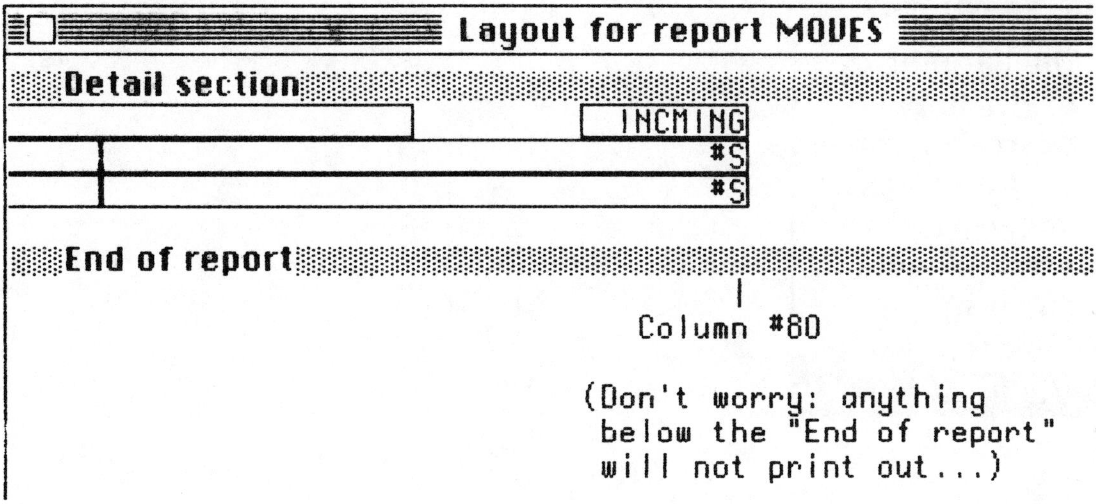

```
▤□▰▰▰▰▰▰▰▰▰▰▰▰ Layout for report MOUES ▰▰▰▰▰▰▰▰▰▰
░Detail section░░░░░░░░░░░░░░░░░░░░░░░░░░░░░░░░░░░░░░░░░░░
┌──────────────────────────┐  ┌─────────┐
│                          │  │ INCMING │
├──────────────┬───────────┘  ├─────────┤
│              │              │      #S │
├──────────────┴──────────────┤─────────┤
│                             │      #S │

░End of report░░░░░░░░░░░░░░░░░░░░░░░░░░░░░░░░░░░░░░░░░░░░░
│
│                               │
│                          Column #80
│
│                          (Don't worry: anything
│                           below the "End of report"
│                           will not print out...)
```

Fig. 8-15. View when the MOVES window is scrolled to the right.

This report also happens to be compatible with the *Print with Fonts* feature of Omnis 3. This feature doesn't usually work well with Macintosh fonts such as Geneva and New York, or most of the LaserWriter's fonts. This is because they are proportionally spaced, similar to the text of this book. Omnis 3 expects reports to be printed in fixed-space fonts, like the Imagewriter's draft mode, or Monaco and Courier on the LaserWriter. The reason that this report works better than most is that has no text typed directly on to the layout. This is what typically causes problems with Font reports because of spacing considerations. Try using the *Print with Fonts* setting in the Report Parameters, and gauge the result against some of the other reports in the earlier chapters.

Some suggestions for enhancements here are:

☐ *Add a command for this report to the Sequence menu.*
☐ *Find a way to make this a selective report, possibly limiting it to a date range. (Hint: you can enter a formula such as #D-3 to represent "the last three days" in an Omnis 3 Search.)*
☐ *Experiment with different Sort fields, and design a way for the user to be prompted for the Sort field at report time.*
☐ *Remove the capability for entry into the STKONHD field of the STKENTR Entry layout, because that figure shouldn't routinely adjustable.*

This has been a very busy chapter, but the last chapter will be even more action-packed. Take time to fully absorb the ideas presented here, and practice these new commands and methods extensively before continuing on to Chapter 9.

Look up table (for example Unknown/M=Male/F=Female/)

```
┌───────────────────────────────────────────────┐
│Unknown/YES=Incoming/NO=Outgoing                 │
```

Fig. 8-16. Using a simple look-up table.

Omnis 3

The DataBasics
Useful Reports
Search Formats
Custom Menus
Sequences
More Sequences
Expansion
Connections
The Array ⌘9

Adding the

Invoicing System

The Problem. This chapter will be the grand finale of our productive relationship with The Work Station, and we will produce our most ambitious module yet: the Invoicing System. The design goals for this system are:

1) No extensive operator intervention necessary.
2) Automatic debit of inventory levels upon execution of invoice.
3) Individual line items will be invalidated if they are out of stock.
4) The invoice totals will automatically adjust if situation 3 is true.
5) Invoice numbers assigned automatically.
6) Customers entered by their Customer ID number only.
7) Up to eight line items per invoice.
8) Invoice printing at the time of entry.
9) Capability to search for and view old invoices.

Good grief! They must know that our tenure at the store is nearly over, because they appear to have saved all the best assignments for the last. Let's see how we'll tackle this ominous set of requests.

THE PLAN

This chapter is unquestionably the most challenging yet. Because we have built up considerable momentum in the use of Omnis 3, we'll call upon tools acquired in every previous chapter to assist in the work on this one. One of the obvious results of this chapter's work will be a completing of the "circle" of Omnis 3's features. By the end of this part of the system, you will have worked extensively with every significant feature of the program, and will have built a rather impressive small-business retailing system.

Be forewarned, though; this still won't be a turn-key system! You will find a list at the end of the chapter that details some subtle "holes" in this seemingly elegant implementation. The list will be accompanied by suggestions and some examples of possible fixes for these deficiencies. There will also be guidelines and recommendations for future expansion, along with a few general hints and tips for future work with Omnis 3.

This chapter's material could very well fill an entire book on its own, and probably will someday. You will quickly see why Omnis 3 is often referred to as an "open-ended" program; there are very few real limits to the complexity of the systems you can build. As a matter of fact, one might say that the only limit is your own imagination. The more you learn about Omnis 3, the more possibilities will become apparent, even though it might be a little cloudy right now. We'll pull together most of the loose ends by the end of this chapter, and graduate you as an Omnis 3 authority!

Where to Start?

There seems to be a tremendous number of only loosely related requests in this chapter's problem. However, drawing on your knowledge of Omnis 3 architecture, we have to look at the information that is being requested. The central theme here is the invoicing system, so we'll have to design around that request. With every other major expansion of the system, we have started with new File formats, and this time is no exception.

In a situation very similar to the design of the Inventory transfer module in Chapter 8, we'll be working with Connected files again. If we look at the overall structure of the invoice, we see that the management has made a reasonable request; i.e., the customers are to be entered by customer code. In the last chapter, the request to enter parts by PARTCOD on the transfer forms resulted in the need for a connection between the STOCK file and the XFER file, and the use of an *Auto find* field. In that relationship, STOCK was a connected file for XFER. This direction of connection is significant, because the individual transfers in the XFER file can be connected to only one part in the STOCK file, while parts can certainly appear in many different transfers. Reversing the direction of the connection (making XFER a connected file for STOCK) would result in problems, because transfers would no longer be able to "find" their associated parts.

In the latest problem, our invoicing system, we will first need to create a new File format to hold the details of each invoice written. We'll name it IN-VOICE so we can remember it more easily. After all, this will be our fourth File format since the creation of CUSTS such a long time ago. INVOICE will contain the fields to track such details as *Invoice Number*, *Invoice Date*, *Method Of Payment*, *Tax*, *Invoice Total*, and *Cashier's Name*. If this all seems a bit familiar, this format is quite similar to the XFER file created in the last chapter. The *Tax* and *Invoice Total* fields are the by-now familiar Numeric type; *Invoice Date* obviously will be a Date field; *Cashier's Name* and *Method Of Payment* are text fields (National or Character: we'll decide later), and we'll set *Invoice Number* as a Sequence field.

If you remember the details of a Sequence field from the previous chapter, this type is perfect for invoice numbers. Sequence fields can't be edited, deleted, or reassigned, so this will guarantee the integrity of an invoice number once it is assigned. We won't have the nightmare of two customers ending up with an identical invoice number! This field will also automatically be indexed. Remember that Sequence fields are always indexed, because Omnis 3 maintains these fields regardless of whether or not you use them.

The connection picture for the INVOICE file is straightforward. Based on our experience with the XFER file, we can surmise that the following are true:

1) Each invoice from INVOICE can belong to *only one* Customer in the CUSTS file.
2) Each Customer in the CUSTS file can have *many* invoices from INVOICE connected to them.

What does this translate into? If you said, "CUSTS is a connected file for INVOICE," you are correct. Recalling the treatise on file connections, we know that, once we make the connection from INVOICE to CUSTS, Omnis 3 will add an invisible field to the INVOICE file. With each new record input to the INVOICE file, Omnis 3 will then store the Sequence number of the connected record from CUSTS in this invisible field, so the Invoices will forever know to which Customer they belong.

Uh-oh, here's trouble: What about the merchandise that the customer purchases? Certainly an invoice must have some sort of record of the items that the customer bought—and that is certainly true at The Work Station, where a typical computer system purchase totals upwards of $3000. We can't in good conscience give a customer a cash-register-type receipt for a purchase of that magnitude. We must figure out a way of itemizing the receipt if this invoice is to be acceptable to the customers. If we gather our thoughts for a moment, a possible solution becomes apparent.

In the last chapter, the Inventory transfers could very well have been used as psuedo-invoices because they referenced items in the inventory, and they actually handled debiting of inventory levels in an outgoing transfer. The inventory records in the STOCK file carry along with them the items' prices, and that is all that's really needed for the invoices. The method we employed to allow the XFER file to access these inventory records was the connection from the XFER file to the STOCK file. But we will have a connection from our INVOICE file going to the CUSTS file, and STOCK is already connected to XFER. How can we change this without affecting the function of what we've built already?

Luckily, Omnis 3 allows virtually unlimited networks of connected files within Libraries. Our example here would pose no problem. You can be assured that connecting the INVOICE file to the STOCK file would not affect the connections that are already in place. But think about this situation for a moment. The definition of a connected file, when applied to a connection between the INVOICE and STOCK files, would look something like this:

1) Each invoice from INVOICE can belong to *only one* part in the STOCK file.
2) Each part in the STOCK file can have *many* invoices from INVOICE connected to it.

Rule 2 poses no problem for our system as we visualized it in the beginning of this chapter, but look at Rule 1. We must be able to include up to eight items in an invoice, and each of those obviously would need to connect with a different record in the STOCK file. Figure 9-1 summarizes the current predicament.

We certainly didn't come this far with Omnis 3 to get shut out in the final inning, so we'll look more deeply into the capabilities of connected files and see if we can develop a solution.

What actually needs to happen in order to make this all work out is for us to build a fifth File format. Following this train of thought, we can use this file as a "Master" file for the invoicing system. Recalling Fig. 9-1's desperate picture, let's look at the feasibility of using this file as a "summit," with virtually all of our existing files being connected to it, each satisfying a different purpose by its connection. Figure 9-2 diagrams this hypothesis.

If we pause to step through this in our minds, it begins to become clearer. We can use this new File format to store the individual Invoice *line items*. The STOCK file will be a connected file for it, because each line item will certainly be for only one inventory item. It follows that the INVOICE file will also be a

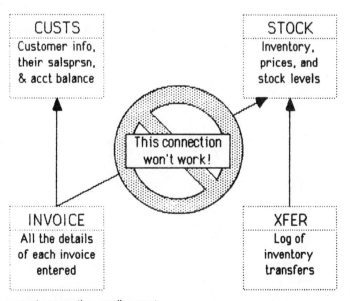

Fig. 9-1. The current connection predicament.

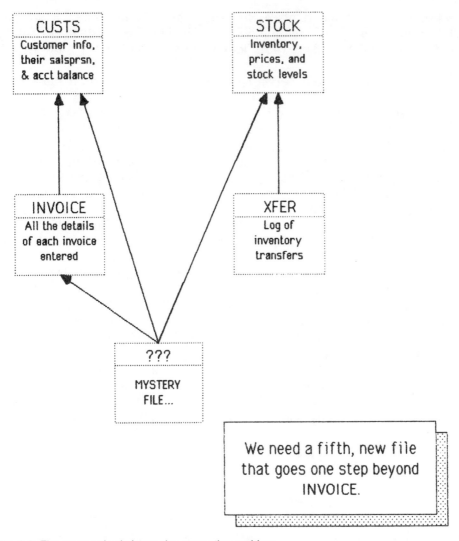

Fig. 9-2. The proposed solution to the connection problem.

connected file, since the line items are part of only one invoice. By extension, each line item belongs to a specific customer, meaning that the CUSTS file can also be connected to the line items file. In one swift stroke of your mouse, you can solve all of these potentially hideous data "traffic jams" by establishing a clear heirarchy using Connected files.

The actual construction of the LNITEMS file (as we'll call it) is strikingly simple. The reason for this is that we will be using it mostly as a connection point, although it will hold some data. The only field that's imperative to be stored here is the "quantity purchased" of that line's merchandise. The details of the merchandise itself are already stored in the STOCK file, which we will be connecting, so LNITEMS will have that invisible Sequence number field "pointing" at the appropriate part record. This relationship will be set through the use of an *Auto find* field when it comes time to design the Entry layout. Both the CUSTS and INVOICE files will be similarly represented in the LNITEMS file by invisible "pointer" fields. As you can clearly see, LNITEMS will have more *invisible* fields than visible ones! We will in fact be adding one more regular field to the file to hold the actual selling price for the item. This field will attend to the potential problem of a price change retroactively changing the totals of all the invoices written previously!

Now that we've found an elegant way out of our nasty predicament, an aside to the use of connected files and *Auto find* fields is needed here.

Omnis 3 is a member of a very exclusive club of high-powered database software. There are very few (if any at all) programs running on personal computers that manage data in such a manner as Omnis 3 does. Its *hierarchical* methods of working with files and records are commonly found in mainframe or minicomputer software. But conventional microcomputer programs, even highly powerful ones such as the immensely popular dBase III™, offer very few of these amenities. The invisible fields and that Omnis 3 so adeptly uses are replaced by regular fields in more common programs, and *Auto find* fields are only replaced by sophisticated command sequences.

For example, in order to build a system such as the one shown in Fig. 9-2, you would have to manipulate manually the Sequence numbers, as well as the record "pointers" (which are invisible in Omnis 3). The reason for this is that most other databases are "planar" in comparison to Omnis 3's very three-dimensional approach. To be fair, you *could* use dBASE III to do anything Omnis 3 can do, but there would be a phenomenal amount of programming required to build anything even close to the complexity of the model which we'll build in this chapter. But enough talk of the competition! Let's get back to the task at hand: the invoicing system.

The Invoice Entry Layout

The next step after constructing a File format is to design an appropriate Entry layout, and this case is no exception. This layout will bring together, on one screen, fields from almost every File format constructed so far. LNITEMS obviously will be represented, as will INVOICE, since both contain major components of a standard invoice. However, the STOCK file will be represented for each line item, along with the CUSTS file supplying customer information for the invoice.

Needless to say, we'll be using more than one *Auto find* field, but there are other issues as well. The complexity of this case warrants a detailed explanation.

The Next Step

Until now, life has been fairly simple for our Entry layouts. To be fair, we did add a level of complexity last chapter with the introduction of *Auto find* fields and Connected files—but that step pales in comparison to the jump we're about to make. As a preface to this discussion, consider the following train of thought.

We are building an invoice that will be storing, among other things, up to eight individual line items which will then belong to that particular invoice. We won't reserve space in the INVOICE file for these because we will end up with quite a bit of empty space in the file from empty line items being saved. Fine so far? But how can we construct the Entry layout for our invoice?

In the XFER example of the last chapter, we had no problem using the *Auto find* fields once they were explained sufficiently. But this example presents another problem: how can we put eight of everything on the Entry layout? After all, the *Auto find/Local* field process of locating records (in the STOCK file) will have to be repeated once for every line item, and there can be up to eight. When we issue the *Update files* command in the sequences to follow the data entry, how will Omnis 3 know enough to sort out the eight entries, get the LNITEMS file updated, and connect its records properly? The answer comes to us in the form of a special structure available in Entry layouts: the Omnis 3 *array*.

Array of Sunshine

For those familiar with conventional programming languages, arrays are considered standard equipment. But for the rest of us they can be rather intimidating. First, let's look at some of the details.

The dictionary defines an array as, "A systematic arrangement of numbers or symbols in tabular form." This definition can be readily applied to our example, because it is certainly in need of some arranging. The principle of arrays started with ancient mathematicians, who were constantly marveling over the order of things in nature. They envisioned systems, and these systems needed more than arbitrary order applied to them. A typical example of an early application for arrays in math was the advent of organized theater. When early entrepreneurs dared to start charging admission for theatrical events, they needed to account for the available seats in an auditorium. If you picture a typical seating arrangement of 26 rows of 30 seats, we have a good foundation for an example. Figure 9-3 shows a small model of this theater.

Each paying customer of the theater is given a ticket containing a seat assignment. A quick consideration of the distribution of seats yields an obvious scheme for referencing the seats: we can refer to the rows as A through Z, and the seats as 1 through 30 from stage left to stage right across each row. This system yields seat numbers starting at A-1 for the leftmost seat in the front row, and continuing throughout the seating. As obvious as this seems, let's look at it in depth. Each seat has a definite place, and there is a good order to things. Compared to a possible alternative, which might number the seats from 1 to 780, our first scheme makes finding your seat very easy indeed. Why is this?

What we have done is created a simple array, similar in scope to the Omnis 3 Array. We can see that if we are given seat F-19, there are two steps to find our seat:

1) First find our way to row F

An Imaginary Theater

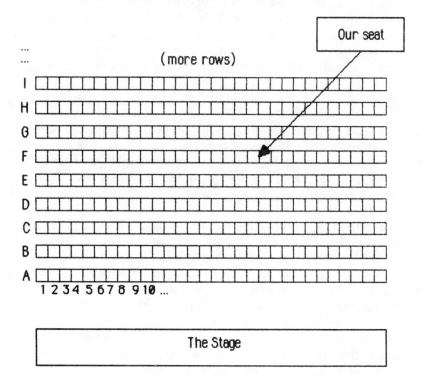

Fig. 9-3. A limited view of the theater.

2) Braving the popcorn tubs, simply climb over each person's knees until we arrive at seat number 19.

The structure imposed on this theater is the very essence of an array, because the key in building any array is to establish an index. We used the row as the index in this example, because it was the most convenient. It would be difficult to use the seat number as the index, as this would mean we would walk across the front row to 19, then climb back over five rows of theater seats, which is no mean feat! The index of an array is established by one of two factors: the natural order of things, or an arbitrary decision by the administrator of the system. Before this discussion degenerates into a lecture on systems theory, let's get back to the Omnis 3 array.

The index to our array should be apparent once a thorough inspection of the situation is made. Based on this inspection, the following conclusion arises: the line items will be arranged in an array where they are indexed on a line-by-line basis. Any alternative would be an unnatural organization, resulting in severe confusion at best. Once we've made this decision, we can press on and figure out how to build an array into our Entry layout.

Arrays are strange beasts, to say the least. They tend to bend the rules a bit, so they demand an open mind and a willingness to experiment. But they open a tremendous number of doors to you by the flexibility they facilitate. Therefore they are well worth the work involved in understanding them.

Arrays are similar to the theater example above because, to work simply, each indexed row should have the same number and type of elements. In your Entry layout, you will construct rows of fields to record the following data:

Quantity PartCode Description RetailPrice Extension

The first four fields are obvious, and the fifth field is the extended price, which is obtained by multiplying the quantity by the retail price. Omnis 3 will then be instructed by a sequence (which we'll talk about soon) to save data from each of these rows away as a separate record in the LNITEMS file. That is fairly straightforward, but how will Omnis 3 "know" which field is which? And what of the totals?

The key to arranging these fields is found in the array. Aside from the fields listed above, we'll begin each row of the array with a special invisible field. The temporary field #P is used for the index (see above) into the array. The index value (Omnis 3's term is *class*) is entered as the *Default:Check* for the field value, with the rows starting with a 1. For instance, in our eight-line invoice Array, the first line will be headed by a #P field with a Default:Check value of 1, the second line will also be #P with a Default:Check value of 2, and so on. Actually, the key to the use of these class fields is not the fields' positions on the layout, but their field numbers. All fields following #P(1) in field number order are considered to be of class 1, those following #P(2) are of class 2, and so on through the array. Two special values of #P further enhance the functionality of the array classes. Field #P(0) defines the class containing the totals of the array's components (similar to the method used in the Totals section of a Report) and #P(– 1) effectively "turns off" the class system, leaving all fields after it as standard (*unclassified*) fields.

A few of the "rules and regulations" involved in use of the array are that Omnis 3 allows the use of its string (#S) and numeric (#1-#10 only) temporary fields, enabling calculations to be done on a line-by-line or a cumulative basis; that #P can carry values up to 120, meaning that your arrays can have up to 121 rows, each containing copies of fields #1-#10, the S temporary string field, and copies of fields from any file involved in that Entry layout; and that you should use the #P(– 1) field to end the array in the right place, or the results can be unpredictable at best.

We will be employing many other new twists in this chapter's adventurous Entry layout, but they are all more easily understood when explained in the context of the exercises; that's why they are being saved for later. But we should speak now of the sequences involved in the invoicing layout.

So You Want to Be a Programmer?

This chapter offers an in-depth experience with a very complex sequence, the "program" which controls the disbursement of data into the two main files,

INVOICE and LNITEMS. Let's first look at INVOICE, the simpler of the two. The reason for looking at it first is that it will be the first file "updated" during the sequence.

To refresh your memory, we have decided to include six fields in the IN-VOICE file: *Invoice Number, Invoice Date, Method Of Payment, Tax, Invoice Total,* and *Cashier's Name.* An addition to the six regular fields, we will connect INVOICE to CUSTS, which will create a seventh, invisible field to handle the connection pointer. As the user makes a request to enter data using the Entry layout described above, the following will happen:

1. Our sequence will set the Main file for data entry to INVOICE. Omnis 3 is smart enough to adjust "back" a step and accommodate entries into LNITEMS in step 5, but it would not handle INVOICE's connections well if the Main file were set to LNITEMS (as you might think it should).
2. The invisible field is attended to by the use of an *Auto find* field, CUSTID from CUSTS. This connects this invoice to whichever customer's ID number is entered, so we can easily use a number of *Local* fields to display the details returned from the customer's record file.
3. In contrast to the rest of the customer's information, the salesperson's name can be edited because we'll make it a *Normal* field. This means that if the user changes the salesperson's name, that change will be written to the CUSTS file when the invoice is written.
4. Date, which defaults to today's date, and method of payment, which defaults to cash, are entered next.
5. The invoice line items are input last, one row (or class) at a time. Each row has only two fields of actual input, the quantity and the part code. The latter is the *Auto find* field which looks up the description and the retail price. The extended price is then calculated automatically.
6. The total is calculated "on the fly" as each of the line items changes. The tax and invoice total will be calculated only when the entire invoice is completed.
7. When the user clicks OK or presses Return to signal the completion of the Invoice, the sequence action begins. Figure 9-4 lists the complete sequence, which we'll now step through a section at a time.

The first action the sequence will take is to issue the *Redraw screen* command. This tells Omnis 3 to go through every field on the layout, recalculate it, then redisplay it. This takes care of the problem of not seeing the Tax and Invoice Total displayed on the screen. Once that has been done, we call the *Update files* command to write the Invoice details out to the INVOICE file. This helps to explain why the Main file was set to INVOICE. *Update files* will ignore the LNITEMS fields for now, because we have not referenced any fields from it.

But we also have to plan ahead here. We have a problem if the sequence commands after this point find an item which is in short supply. After all, we

2 Write an invoice/W

Set main file to INVOICE
Clear: Main file Connected files Other files # fields from 1 to 60 All copies of #1..#10 and #S
Prepare for Insert Enter data []
If Flag False
    Clear: Main file Connected files Other files # fields from 1 to 60 All copies of #1..#10 and #S
    Redraw screen
    Quit sequence
End If
Redraw screen
Update files
Calculate #13 as INVNBR (0 dps)
Calculate #16 as INVAMT (2 dps)
* For checking if there were any deletions!
Set main file to LNITEMS
Calculate #P as 1
Repeat
    Working message Repeat count [Processing line items and checking against inventory levels...]
    If LEN(PARTCOD)
        Calculate #11 as STKONHD-#2 (0 dps)
        If #11>=0
            Prepare for Insert with current values
            Calculate LNQTY as #2
            Calculate SELPRIC as RETAIL
            Calculate STKONHD as #11
            Update files
        Else
            OK message [Sorry, there are only ;STKONHD; ;DESCRIP;'s available. Item deleted...]
            Calculate #2 as 0 (0 dps)
        End If
    End If
    Calculate #P as #P+1
Until #P=9
Redraw screen
Calculate #14 as INVTAX (2 dps)
Calculate #15 as INVAMT (2 dps)
If #15<>#16
    * There must have been a deletion if these are not equal...
    Set main file to INVOICE
    Calculate INVNBR as #13
    Find on INVNBR with exact match []
    Redraw screen
    Prepare for Edit
    Calculate INVTAX as #14
    Calculate INVAMT as #15
    Update files
End If

Fig. 9-4. The complete sequence for data entry.

```
Calculate #S as CON(MID('A000',1,(5-LEN(INVNBR))),INVNBR)
YES/NO message Default to YES [Would you now like to print invoice #;#S;?]
If Flag True
    Set main file to LNITEMS
    Call sequence 23
End If
Clear: Main file Connected files Other files # fields from 1 to 60 All copies of #1..#10 and #S
Redraw screen
```

just updated the INVOICE file with the invoice prices! That is no problem, because we can always ask for that INVOICE record back later for necessary editing. So here we save away the Invoice number and the Total (at this point) with some calculations to temporary fields for later use.

Only now can we safely set the Main file to LNITEMS. The process of updating this file is far more complex than any other that we've seen because it is a flexible number of records, not just one. After all, the user can input anywhere from zero to eight line items on an invoice. Therefore, we must devise a more intricate *Update files* sequence for this situation.

As you remember, the key to an array is its indexes, or classes. The only way of "walking" through the rows is to use the *Repeat-Until* control structure. Programmers will notice the lack of the traditional For-To-Next structure in Omnis 3. This particular loop construct performs a particular operation a specified number of times, incrementing the loop index on each pass through, and then continues on with the rest of the program. However, you can easily build an alternative to this structure:

```
Calculate X as 1
Repeat
    (do something here)
    Calculate X as X + 1
Until X = 10
```

The only difference between the two is in readability, with the Omnis 3 example being slightly more convoluted yet functionally identical.

The first thing which must be done is to set the value of #P to 1, which is explained further below.

We'll make use of the last type of Message box in this loop, a Working Message. This is the type that Omnis 3 itself uses when printing. An option in the use of this box is the inclusion of a *Repeat count*. If placed within a Repeat-Until loop, the box will display a visual counter of the number of times the loop has been executed.

The tie-in between this structure and the use of the array is in the #P field. As the value of this field changes, Omnis 3 refers to different rows of the array. We will make use of this structure to increment the value #P and inspect the rows of the array one at a time. After all, if we try to use a field in the array, such as the price field (RETAIL), we have eight RETAILs on this Entry layout!

Omnis 3 determines *which* class we're speaking of by looking at the current value of #P.

This sequence uses LEN(), one of the Omnis functions, in an interesting way. As we have seen before, logical and relational expressions can be used in mathematical equations, because their truth values evaluate to either 0 or 1. But the LEN() function returns the number of characters in a text string, not a logical value. So how can it be used as a conditional test for an If-Then-Else expression if it doesn't evaluate to a truth value? The reason for the LEN(PART-COD) expression is to avoid processing lines with no entry on them. A close look at this situation reveals the answer.

If there are no characters in the value of that class's PARTCOD, there must be no entry in that class. However, any class that **does** have a PARTCOD will return a nonzero answer to the LEN(PARTCOD) function. The evaluation of conditional tests treats all nonzero results as True, so in this case this function's result is interpreted as a truth value.

If this test passes, we make a quick calculation to check the STKONHD figure to ascertain the current inventory level. This is done by subtracting field #2 (which is the Quantity temporary field) from it, and storing the result in field #11. Why #11? If you recall that the array can use fields #1-#10, we know that #11 is safely free from any class distinctions. This is important to remember when using temporary fields as "variables" within your sequences, or else you may find yourself accidentally writing over a value from your array. The calculated figure in #11 is then compared to zero. This determines whether or not this line's transaction will cause inventory to fall below zero, a situation which the system is supposed to prevent.

If the sequence determines that there are, in fact, not enough items, it "zaps" that line's transaction in the most direct way possible: it changes the Quantity figure to zero. This, in effect, zeros out the purchase of that line's inventory item. This becomes significant later when we recalculate the screen to determine whether there have been any deletions. A more sophisticated system might offer the opportunity to create an automatic backorder. Ours is not that mature, so we'll simply post a Message box and invalidate that line of the invoice.

As long as the inventory is going to be legal after the transaction, we'll go ahead and process this item. First, we have to put Omnis 3 into *Prepare mode* by issuing the *Prepare for Insert* command. After all, even though the users are not entering data at the keyboard, it is as if they were. Our sequence is "entering data" into the LNITEMS file on a record-by-record basis for us.

The actual processing involves a few calculations, the first of which sets the LNQTY field to be the value of the temporary field #2. (Because of the way in which Omnis 3 handles the array, it is best to use Temporary fields for any normal input fields. The program is a little careless about "initializing," or clearing, fields before they are used. If we put more than one LNQTY on the layout, Omnis 3 will have problems keeping track of the Main file. We set it to INVOICE, but this field would foul up that setting, since it is from one "level" above it.

There also are calculations done to arrive at the SELPRIC field, obtained from RETAIL, and the STKONHD field. STKONHD is part of a connected file

(STOCK) but, just as before, we can assume that we have access to this field because it has been located and read into memory by the *Auto find* operation.

Once all the values are set, the record can be written to the disk using the *Update files* command. This is the equivalent of the user entering a record and then pressing Return. First, Omnis 3 looks at the current records in memory from the STOCK, INVOICE, and CUSTS files. Since each is a connected file LNITEMS, the Sequence numbers of the records are recorded along with the LNITEMS record which is written to the disk. It is important to note that issuing the *Update files* command takes Omnis 3 out of Prepare mode. Therefore, this sequence has to continually reset this mode before writing another record.

The last step in this particular loop is to increment the value of #P and then check to make sure that it is still less than 9. An array is in no way limited to only eight elements; this example was kept to eight classes only to keep the layout as simple as possible. However, this last step is one of the only things about this example that would have to change. For example, if you had 16 rows of line items on your layout, you would only have to change this last step to read "Until #P = 17" to accommodate the increased size.

After all the processing, we need to do some fancy footwork to determine if the invoice needs to be adjusted for deleted items. We can determine this by comparing the two total figures: before and after the line-by-line processing. If they aren't equal, this signals us that we need to recall the INVOICE record. To recall that record, we first set the Main file back to INVOICE, then set the Invoice number to the correct value and do a Find operation to locate it. Once found, we put Omnis 3 in *Prepare for Edit* mode, then recalculate the values of the Tax and Invoice Total figures from the saved values. When we finally issue the *Update files* command, the INVOICE record has been adjusted and all references to the deleted item are gone.

As we continue to explore the invoice processing sequence, we reach the last portion, which offers the user the chance to print the invoice. In real life this step would be unnecessary, since the invoice probably would have to be printed at the time of entry. This step is included in order to show off an interesting method of converting Omnis 3 Sequence number fields into realistic-looking Invoice numbers. The Sequence number fields are simple Numeric fields, with values such as 13 or 150. Normal numbering systems for documents like invoices would have these numbers look like "0013" or "A00150." This is impossible on an Omnis 3 Entry layout because Sequence numbers are not assigned until after the record is written to the disk. That doesn't keep us from using some string manipulations to get this number to show up in a more standard-looking format. The #S temporary string variable is filled with this string, because we can't do calculations in a Message box.

The calculation makes use of the MID( ) function, which returns a part of a string. There are three *arguments* or *parameters* to this function. The first is simply the string itself, which can be a quoted string or, as in this case, a temporary field. The second argument is the character position (numbered from the left) at which Omnis 3 is to start counting, and the third is the number of characters to copy into the returned value. We're using a few of the string functions together to preface the actual invoice number with some "padding" to make it look better. We'll use this function again in the printing of the invoices. Here's a step-by-step breakdown of what this function does:

1) Converts the invoice number temporarily to a string (i.e., 150 converts to "50"), and then counts the number of characters in it.
2) Subtracts that number from 5.
3) Using the preface "A000," it starts at the beginning and counts off enough characters to make the resultant string exactly five characters long.

Based on the response of the user to the Yes/No message, we'll either print the invoice or skip past that sequence call and just clean up the screen.

This is the most complex sequence presented in all the examples in this book. As a matter of fact, it might be the most involved that you'll ever write. But whether or not you fancy yourself a budding programmer, the most important rule to remember to make your programs more understandable is: "Comment your programs clearly." The example in Fig. 9-4 uses very few, because the comments are here in the text. You should include some of the text above as comments in your version of this sequence.

Note that this sequence is just about as large as it can be. If you choose to add "too many" comments, you may wish to break up some of the individual routines into subroutines by making them into different sequences. They can then be accessed via CALL( ).

Before we go on to talk about the reports that will handle the chore of printing the invoices, there is one other feature we'll build in to the Entry layout. As simple as it may sound, adding a Find command to an Entry layout that uses an array is anything but trivial. The reason for that is you actually have to use *two* different Find operations: one to Find the INVOICE record, and another complex sequence to search out the LNITEMS. The Find sequence is listed in Fig. 9-5.

The first command, *Goto screen 2*, is a new one. Screen 2 will be prepared as another entry screen with only one field, field #13. The reason for using this field is that Omnis 3 has message boxes for Yes/No questions, but not for fill-in-the-blanks types. To keep things simple, we'll limit ourselves to finding a particular invoice by number. So the only field will be a temporary Numeric field for the invoice number to be input. We'll simulate data entry by simply calling *Prepare for Insert* and *Enter data*, then exiting the layout without calling *Update files*.

If the user clicks OK, we'll do a quick calculation to set the INVNBR field to whatever was input in field #13. Whether or not the user clicks OK, we'll go back to Screen 1, because that's where the invoice will be displayed. The reason for calling *Redraw screen* is that Omnis 3 gets lazy during the execution of a sequence. Even if you call *Goto screen 1*, it won't actually take you there until there's something to be drawn on the screen!

Once we're back at the screen, we'll perform our string manipulation to turn the invoice number back into the more recognizable "A0013" form.

4 Find an invoice

Goto screen 2
Clear: Main file Connected files Other files # fields from 1 to 60 All copies of #1..#10 and #S
Prepare for Insert Enter data []
If Flag False
    Goto screen 1
    Quit sequence
Else
    Goto screen 1
    Redraw screen
    Calculate INVNBR as #13
End If
Calculate #S as CON(MID('A000',1,(5−LEN(INVNBR))),INVNBR)
Set main file to INVOICE
Find on INVNBR with exact match []
Options: Restore current record at end of sequence
Redraw screen
Set main file to LNITEMS
Calculate #P as 1
Find on INVNBR with exact match []
If Flag True
    Repeat
        Working message Repeat count [Searching files for Line Items from Invoice #;#S;...]
        Calculate #2 as LNQTY (0 dps)
        Calculate #P as #P+1
        Next with exact match
    Until #P=9
Else
    OK message [Sorry, invoice #;#S; doesn't have any entries in it...]
End If
Calculate #P as 1

Fig. 9-5. The sequence for finding an invoice.

The first half of the real work is to find the INVOICE record. This is done with the sequence *Find* command, which is similar to prompted Find, except it doesn't ask the user for a value. The parameters are supplied along with the command. In this case, we are instructing it to find whatever we have just placed in the INVNBR field above. If a match is found, we call *Redraw screen* to display the record on the invoice layout.

Next comes the tricky part. We have to search out the line items one at a time. This routine is actually the reverse of the routine that sent them off in the first place, although some of the logic changed a bit because there were more calculations to do on the outbound trip. After the Main file is set to LNITEMS, we can start. We do another Find with exact match to start with; if a match isn't found the next steps are all skipped and a message is posted. As we did before, we'll use #P to classify our array as we fill it in. We need to fill one line at a time, so we'll do a loop (incrementing #P on each pass) looking for INVNBR again. This can be done because INVOICE is a connected file for LNITEMS. There is a tremendous amount of processing done internally by Omnis 3 during this sequence, because every time it looks at a LNITEMS record, it must trace down its connected record in INVOICE and inspect its INVNBR field. (Try doing this in another database program!)

The *Next with exact match* instruction is the key to this routine. Once the initial Find is done, this command repeats the operation, and will return a cleared Flag if no more matches were found. Otherwise, the next record is found and read into the array, since #P has been set to the right line number. Finally we set #P back to 1 to tell Omnis 3 that all the classes in the array (starting at 1) will be displayed when the screen is redrawn.

These two sequences can be optimized and are not intended to be the gospel on the use of the array. But they do work well and demonstrate simply how to access the array from within your sequences.

Your Receipt

An obvious concern in an invoicing system is getting the information down on paper. This section details the strategy for building the two reports for this chapter, the invoice itself and a "digest" of invoices. We'll cover the invoice itself first, as that is the primary purpose here. Just as the Find operation was quite complex, printing an Invoice is no simple matter, either. First, let's talk about the Report format itself, then we'll list the sequence that will print it.

The heading section of the invoice will look very much like the top part of any retail invoice. It will have the store's name, the customer's name, the date, invoice number, method of payment, and salesperson. It is here that the justification for the file connection between CUSTS and LNITEMS becomes apparent. This connection allows the Main file to be set to LNITEMS for this report and guarantees that the correct customer's information is directly available to the report. The other alternative would involve a far more complicated report, as well as a more involved sequence. In the long run, the extra few bytes per record for the connection are worth it because of the added ease of use.

The Detail section is fairly basic, listing just the data from the invoice. It is only one row deep, so the invoice line items will print out directly below one another. If you wished them to be double-spaced, you could add a blank line to the Detail section.

This report uses a Subtotals section but no Totals section. Omnis 3 has a direct relationship between the Sort fields and Subtotals. The Sort fields are numbered from 1-9, and correspond to up to nine levels of Subtotals. This gives you the ability to set up hierarchical reporting, separating out groups of related information for appropriate subtotals. We'll use this method, along with an invisible sort, to group together or line items. Subtotals sections behave just like Total sections in that the fields in them correspond to fields within the Detail section that are marked as Totaled. We'll calculate the total, although we'll simply use the stored value of the tax and invoice total for those fields.

Omnis 3's definition of Report sections becomes critical here. The Headings section borrows its data from the first available record in the Detail section. This is important because this report is not going to be printed in the manner which you are used to. We're going to use a Repeat-Until loop to print it. Figure 9-6 lists the sequence.

This sequence borrows much of its logic from the Find command we built for the Entry layout. The major difference here is in the two new Printing commands, *Print record* and *Print totals*; the former holds a special significance, in that it prints the Heading section automatically. It tells Omnis 3, "Print one copy of the Detail section for the current record, then wait a moment." In other words, rather than printing the entire report as we've done in the past, this command breaks down the report into smaller pieces.

The *Print totals* command tells Omnis 3 to wrap up the report and print whatever totals sections are defined. In this case we have used the Subtotals section, but it was defined to break across separate invoice numbers, so it is printed here. If we had defined a different subtotalling arrangement, Omnis might have taken the initiative to print some subtotals along the way if appropriate.

The invoice digest report is similar in concept to the invoice itself, but lacks some fancy touches such as its own sequence. It uses Subtotals to arrange its records in the right order. However, it also has more informative fields on the report format. Since this report is for the benefit of salespeople and management, we will include profit-oriented information such as overall invoice margin, line-by-line profit figures, and a calculated salesperson's commission. These fields are all standard fare, but are in the Subtotals section because they will be calculated on an invoice-by-invoice basis, not for the entire report. The Totals section isn't used in this report, but it could be used to total all of the invoices printed in this report. You could further enhance this report by adding a level

```
23 Print current invoice
----------------------

Options: Restore current record at end of sequence
Select Report INVPRT
Find on INVNBR with exact match []
If Flag True
     Repeat
          Working message Repeat count [Printing invoice #;#S;...]
          Print record
          Next with exact match
     Until Flag False
     Print totals
     Quit sequence
End If
```

Fig. 9-6. The sequence for printing an invoice.

of subtotaling for Saleperson, or possibly even a Search format for a date range, such as a particular month.

Now that we've seen the basics of using the array, let's put it to use and build the final phase of The Work Station's system.

THE STEPS

Because of the detailed nature of this chapter's Plan section, the Steps are rather minimal. Most of the work has been detailed extensively above, so you'll be doing most of the work from included listings and diagrams.

The process of implementing the Invoicing module of the system begins, as have all previous modules, with the File formats. The two files which are to be added here are INVOICE and LNITEMS. The key to the success of this system depends on the proper connection scheme being implemented, so take care to be methodical and accurate.

Feel free to experiment in this section, but be careful to make frequent backup copies. You may find yourself redoing a lot of work if you accidentally destroy some component of the system, such as a set of sequences. Any experienced programmer will have war stories of hours or days of lost work that will surely elicit the following response from you: "Oh, that's terrible, but it'll never happen to me."

It is inevitable. It *will* happen to you. So be careful.

The File Format

Enough of the frightening rhetoric; let's get to work.

☐ *Using Fig. 9-7 as your guide, build both the* **INVOICE** *and* **LNITEMS** *File formats.*

☐ *The* **connections** *for LNITEMS are to be set as in Fig. 9-8.*

☐ *The only* **connected** *file for INVOICE is CUSTS.*

The *Reorganize data* command will not be necessary, but it never hurts to use it to satisfy any doubts you might have as to the integrity of the Data file. The rule of thumb for using the command is to gauge whether the changes made to the Library file have had any effect on the data already stored in the Data file. A connection or a new field added to an existing File format, such as STOCK, would necessitate a reorganization. An alternate command that is sometimes required is *Partial reindexation*. This is required if the only change to the File format is the addition, deletion, or modification of the index on a field.

Now that the foundation for our invoicing system is built, we can build the Invoice Entry layout on top of it.

The Entry Layout

This layout is very complex, and will no doubt take a significant amount of time to complete. There are a number of shortcuts which, if employed, will make this task less painful:

```
--------------------------------------------------------------------------
FILE FORMAT LNITEMS

        NAME        TYPE      LENGTH   DEC PLACES   INDEXED?   INDEX LEN   DATA LEN
--------------------------------------------------------------------------
1       LNQTY       Number              0            YES        6           6
2       SELPRIC     Number              2            NO                     6


Connected files:
   INVOICE    STOCK   CUSTS

--------------------------------------------------------------------------
FILE FORMAT INVOICE

        NAME        TYPE      LENGTH   DEC PLACES   INDEXED?   INDEX LEN   DATA LEN
--------------------------------------------------------------------------
1       INVNBR      Sequence                         YES        4
2       INVDATE     Date                             YES        2           2
3       MOP         Char        1                    NO                     1
4       INVAMT      Number               2           YES        6           6
5       INVTAX      Number               2           NO                     6
6       CASHIER     National   20                    NO                     20

Connected files:
   CUSTS
```

Fig. 9-7. The File formats INVOICE and LNITEMS.

1) **Undo.** If you use a Macintosh, you already know how it works. Use it often.
2) **Cut, Copy,** and **Paste** in the Edit menu. Omnis 3 can use the Clipboard in constructing Entry layouts and Reports. This is particularly useful in building your array, since the fields are all repeated and are identical in each class (with the exception of the #P fields).
3) **Print layout details** command. The only way of getting a "bird's-eye view" of your layout.
4) **Display numbers.** Gives you a more useful perspective than viewing the field names.

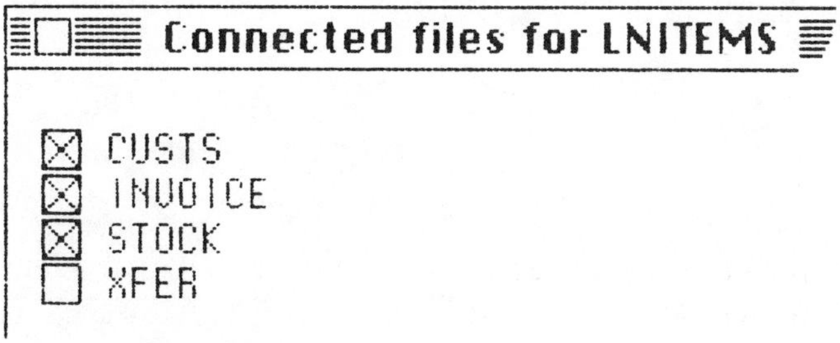

Fig. 9-8. The connections for LNITEMS.

5) **Reorder** button. The field number order is critical to the success of this layout.

As a quick preview of the components of our Entry layout Array, see Fig. 9-9. Armed with this set of tools, you are ready to work on the Invoice layout.

☐ Using Figs. 9-10 and 9-11 as a guide, build Screen 1 of the INVENTR Invoice layout.
☐ On Screen 2 of INVENTR, you need only place the temporary field #13

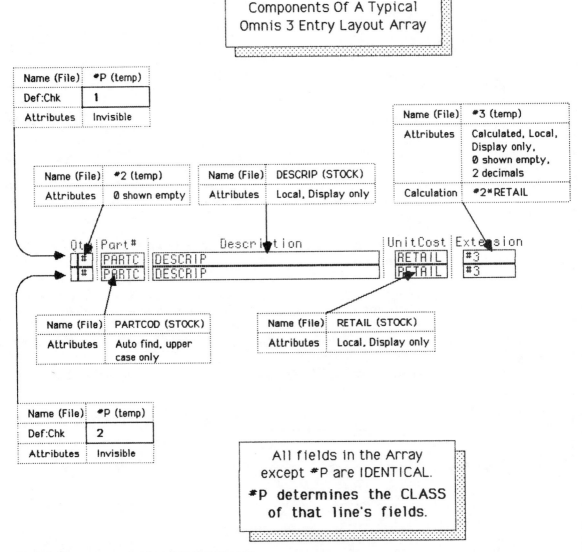

Fig. 9-9. The components of an Entry layout array.

```
ENTRY LAYOUT INVENTR

            FILE     FIELD    VERTICAL   HORIZONTAL   ATTRIBUTES   LENGTH   JUST
Screen 1
--------
1          INVOICE  INVNBR      1           52         DE           9      Left
2          CUSTS    CUSTID      1           37         F            4      Left
3          CUSTS    CSTNAME     1            1         LD          30      Left
4          CUSTS    ADDRES1     2            1         LD          35      Left
5          CUSTS    ADDRES2     3            1         LD          20      Left
6                   #S          4            1         +LD         45      Left
Formula    CON(CITY,'   ',STATE,'    ',ZIP)
7          CUSTS    PHONE       5            1         LD          12      Left
8          CUSTS    PHONEXT     5           14         LD           5      Left
9          CUSTS    SLSPRSN     5           36                     10      Left
10         INVOICE  INVDATE     2           52                      9      Left
Def:chk    #D
11         INVOICE  MOP         3           52         U            2      Left
Def:chk    'C':(MOP='C')!(MOP='X')!(MOP='G')


        Here follow the eight sets of Array entries.
        Each is identical, except for the first field (#P):
        It's DEF:CHK is 2 for the 2nd field, 3 for the 3rd, etc...


12                  #P          9            1         I            1      Left
Def:chk    1
13                  #2          9            2         E0           2      Left
14         STOCK    PARTCOD     9            5         FU           6      Left
15         STOCK    DESCRIP     9           12         LD          30      Left
16         STOCK    RETAIL      9           44         LD           7      Left
17                  #3          9           53         +LDE2        7      Left
Formula    #2*RETAIL


        (The above six fields in this Array would repeat 7 more times)


60                  #P         18            1         I            3      Left
Def:chk    0
61                  #3         18           52         + E2         9      Left
62         INVOICE  INVTAX     19           52         +LDE         9      Left
Formula    #3*.065
63         INVOICE  INVAMT     20           52         +LDE         9      Left
Formula    #3+INVTAX
```

Fig. 9-10. The Entry layout INVENTR.

Screen 2
----

1   #13   10   26   0   5   Left
Def:chk 0:(#13>0)&(#13<9999)

List of attribute codes:
        +   Calculated   I   Invisible
        M   Message field   D   Display only
        F   Automatic find   U   Upper case
        J   Unique indexed   V   Negative values allowed
        L   Local   E   Zeros shown as empty
        P   Delete protected

on as a Normal field with 0 decimals, as in Fig. 9-12. This is the screen
for entry of the Find parameter.

If all went smoothly you should take a break, because your eyes are probably
falling out of your head by now! It is probably also a good time to make one

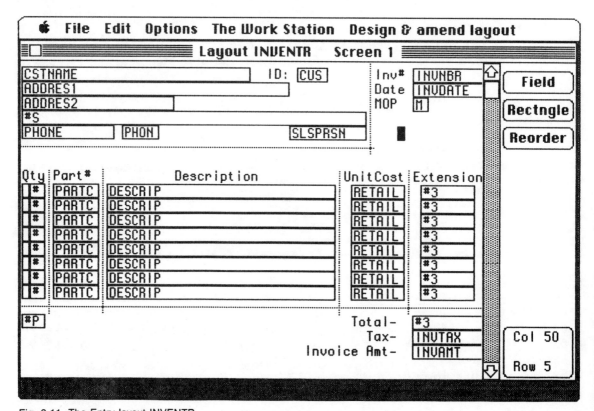

Fig. 9-11. The Entry layout INVENTR.

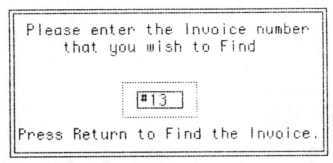

Fig. 9-12. Screen 2 of the Entry layout INVENTR.

of your now (I hope) frequent backups. You stand a good chance of thoroughly trashing both the Data file *and* the Library file once we start playing around with the complex sequences at the next step.

Before we launch into the sequences, another tenet of good programming becomes apparent:

Draw diagrams or pictures whenever possible.

In the construction of this particular example, a simple diagram like the picture in Fig. 9-13 is very useful. This particular one is a network diagram of the connection system in this database. When working with a more complex system such as this invoicing application, it becomes almost impossible to remember all the details of connections, fields, files, and overall hierarchy. A basic picture can help to clarify the many interrelationships and the overall flow of the systems.

The Sequences

As tempting as it may seem to jump right in and enter a couple of invoices, recall that this layout is functionally useless without its accompanying sequences. The sequences for this module are quite complex, so it is important to be methodical in constructing them. Most important, try not to "take dictation," which means simply entering the sequence line-by-line without a clear understanding of each step. If all else fails, that is certainly an alternative, but you should make every effort to comprehend the logic behind the steps. Refer back to the explanation in the Plan section if any of the steps are particularly unclear, and make a backup of the Data file. Let's get it built!

☐ *Figure 9-14 lists Sequence #2, which does the Invoice processing.*
☐ *Figure 9-15 lists Sequence #4, our Find command, along with other information such as button assignments.*
☐ *Remember to use the **Set menu options** command.*

You probably had one major problem with the sequences as listed here. Omnis 3 won't allow you to set the *Main file* to LNITEMS. Why did this

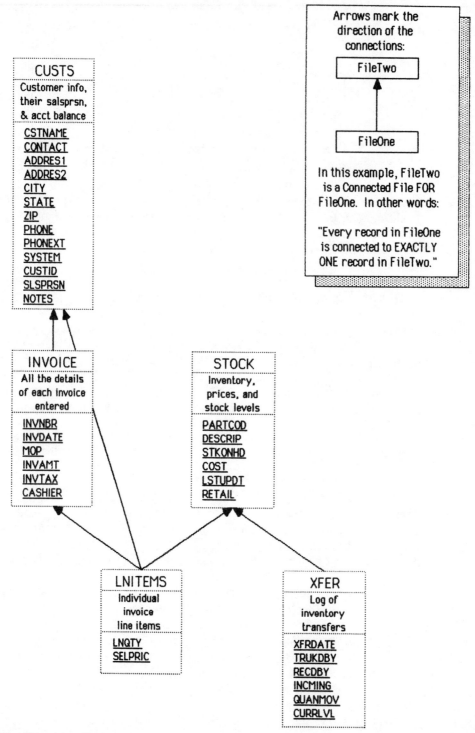

Fig. 9-13. The "big picture."

2 Write an invoice/W

Set main file to INVOICE
Clear: Main file Connected files Other files # fields from 1 to 60 All copies of #1..#10 and #S
Prepare for Insert Enter data []
If Flag False
    Clear: Main file Connected files Other files # fields from 1 to 60 All copies of #1..#10 and #S
    Redraw screen
    Quit sequence
End If
Redraw screen
Update files
Calculate #13 as INVNBR (0 dps)
Calculate #16 as INVAMT (2 dps)
* For checking if there were any deletions!
Set main file to LNITEMS
Calculate #P as 1
Repeat
    Working message Repeat count [Processing line items and checking against inventory levels...]
    If LEN(PARTCOD)
        Calculate #11 as STKONHD-#2 (0 dps)
        If #11>=0
            Prepare for Insert with current values
            Calculate LNQTY as #2
            Calculate SELPRIC as RETAIL
            Calculate STKONHD as #11
            Update files
        Else
            OK message [Sorry, there are only ;STKONHD; ;DESCRIP;'s available. Item deleted...]
            Calculate #2 as 0 (0 dps)
        End If
    End If
    Calculate #P as #P+1
Until #P=9
Redraw screen
Calculate #14 as INVTAX (2 dps)
Calculate #15 as INVAMT (2 dps)
If #15<>#16
    * There must have been a deletion if these are not equal...
    Set main file to INVOICE
    Calculate INVNBR as #13
    Find on INVNBR with exact match []
    Redraw screen
    Prepare for Edit
    Calculate INVTAX as #14
    Calculate INVAMT as #15
    Update files

Fig. 9-14. Sequence 2, which does the invoice processing.

```
End If
Calculate #S as CON(MID('A000',1,(5-LEN(INVNBR))),INVNBR)
YES/NO message Default to YES [Would you now like to print invoice #;#S;?]
If Flag True
     Set main file to LNITEMS
     Call sequence 23
End If
Clear: Main file Connected files Other files # fields from 1 to 60 All copies of #1..#10 and #S
Redraw screen
```

happen? For the simple reason that there are no fields from that file used in the INVENTR layout. Therefore, the way to work around that is to open up the INVENTR Entry layout and just place a field from LNITEMS (LNQTY or SEL-

```
4 Find an invoice
----------------
Goto screen 2
Clear: Main file Connected files Other files # fields from 1 to 60 All copies of #1..#10 and #S
Prepare for Insert Enter data []
If Flag False
     Goto screen 1
     Quit sequence
Else
     Goto screen 1
     Redraw screen
     Calculate INVNBR as #13
End If
Calculate #S as CON(MID('A000',1,(5-LEN(INVNBR))),INVNBR)
Set main file to INVOICE
Find on INVNBR with exact match []
Options: Restore current record at end of sequence
Redraw screen
Set main file to LNITEMS
Calculate #P as 1
Find on INVNBR with exact match []
If Flag True
     Repeat
          Working message Repeat count [Searching files for Line Items from Invoice #;#S;...]
          Calculate #2 as LNQTY (0 dps)
          Calculate #P as #P+1
          Next with exact match
     Until #P=9
Else
     OK message [Sorry, invoice #;#S; doesn't have any entries in it...]
End If
Calculate #P as 1
```

Fig. 9-15. Sequence 4, our Find command.

178

6 Print invoice list

Select Screen
Select Report INVLIST
Print report

23 Print current invoice

Options: Restore current record at end of sequence
Select Report INVPRT
Find on INVNBR with exact match [ ]
If Flag True
    Repeat
        Working message Repeat count [Printing invoice # ;#S;...]
        Print record
        Next with exact match
    Until Flag False
    Print totals
    Quit sequence
End If

Screen 1 (The Work Station Invoice) Primary

Button 1 (Write 1) Sequence 2
Button 3 (Find 1) Sequence 4

Screen 2 (Invoice Find...) Primary

Button 1 (Go ahead!) Sequence 0

PRIC) anywhere on it. Then return to the sequences and enter the correct command. However, remember to go back to the layout and remove the field added above. Once the command is entered properly, Omnis 3 will not complain again.

You might have noticed what looked like a typographical error, the assignment on Screen 2 of Sequence 0 to Button 1. This is no mistake; we need a way to hide all the default buttons from the screen, and there is no simple way of doing this. Remember, Omnis 3 will display the standard complement of eight buttons if you don't define any buttons of your own. But we are using Screen 2 as a temporary window, and there are no commands associated with it other that the standard OK and Cancel buttons. Therefore, we set Button 1 to be Sequence 0, which tells Omnis 3, ''I do have a button, so don't display the default set; but my button is blank, so don't display it, either.'' This is a bit of trickery, but playing dirty with Omnis 3 is OK if you are aware of the consequences of your actions.

We also are setting the sequences for the invoice printing and the invoice digest, even though we haven't built those Report formats yet; if you are going to try to write an invoice now, you will have a problem when the sequence reaches the point where it expects to find the Reports on the disk. Hold off for just a while longer before trying to do any work with the system.

The Reports

The highlight of this entire process is the printing of an invoice using all the components of The Work Station's system. We'll build two reports here: INVPRT and INVLIST. The first is the report, described in the Plan section above, which collaborates with Sequence #23 to output the printed invoice. The second will output a page-by-page, invoice-by-invoice synopsis of all of the transactions processed up to that point.

The INVPRT report is first, so let's build that one now.

☐ Figures 9-16 and 9-17 show the Report format, the second showing the screen after scrolling it to the right.
☐ Figure 9-18 lists the details of the fields to be included.
☐ Figure 9-19 shows the **Sort fields** to be set.

Text such as the store's name and address obviously, are completely optional, so you can add your own name or even leave it blank. The most important part is getting the fields in the correct order, and getting their attributes set correctly. Before you go any farther, make sure that the INVPRT Report's *Parameters* are set correctly.

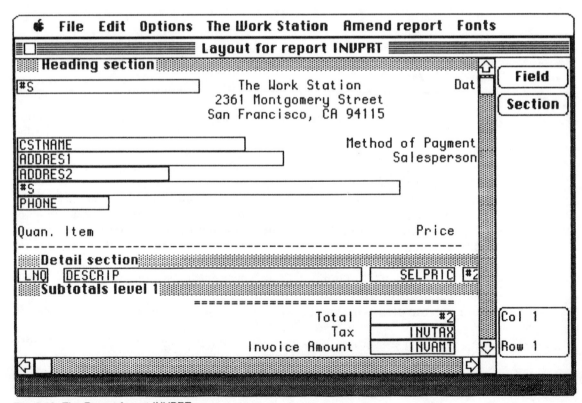

Fig. 9-16. The Report format INVPRT.

```
╔═══════════════════════════════════════════╗
║ ▤☐▤▤▤▤▤▤▤▤▤▤▤▤▤  Layout for re            ║
╟───────────────────────────────────────────╢
  on              Date  │INVDATE      │
  treet
  94115

  Method of Payment: │MOP          │
        Salesperson:  │SLSPRSN       │

  ┌──────────────┐
  └──────────────┘



            Price
  ─────────────────
 ▤▤Detail section▤▤▤▤▤▤▤▤▤▤▤▤▤▤▤▤▤▤
  ┌─┐┌────────┐┌──┐
  └─┘│ SELPRIC│ #2│
 ▤▤Subtotals level 1▤▤▤▤▤▤▤▤▤▤▤▤▤
  ===============
  │       ┌──────────┐
  │       │       #2 │
  x       │ INVTAX   │
  t       │ INVAMT   │
          └──────────┘
```

Fig. 9-17. The Report format INVPRT scrolled to the right a bit.

- ☐ If you choose **Print with fonts**, make sure you select a font such as Monaco or Courier, as opposed to Geneva or Times.
- ☐ Check the **Always send to printer?** box, since you want the printed invoices always sent to the printer.

The anxiety is probably unbearable, so the time is ripe to try out the Invoice printing sequence. Let's give it a whirl!

- ☐ Choose Enter data with INVENTR.
- ☐ Go ahead and enter an invoice, using Customer ID's (CUSTID) from CUSTS, and inventory item Part codes (PARTCOD) from STOCK.

After all is said and done, and you responded that you did, in fact, want to print the invoice, it should have come out like the one in Fig. 9-20. This particular example used fonts (Monaco 12), because that is the size which works best for the spacing in the INVPRT layout. The layout certainly can be adjusted for a smaller font, but there is hardly enough information here to make that necessary.

The final step is the construction of the INVLIST report. This one doesn't use sequences because it has fields and sections which do all the work for it. The Subtotals section handles breaking the pages and stopping for totals

```
REPORT FORMAT INVPRT

     FILE      FIELD     LINE      POSITION      ATTRIBUTES      LENGTH      JUST
Heading
-------

               #S        1         1             +               24         Left
Formula        CON('Invoice number: ',MID('A000',1,(5-LEN(INVNBR))),INVNBR)
    INVOICE    INVDATE   1         63                            11         Left
    CUSTS      CSTNAME   5         1                             30         Left
    INVOICE    MOP       5         63                            10         Left
Look up        Unknown/C=Cash/X=Check/G=Charge
    CUSTS      ADDRES1   6         1                             35         Left
    CUSTS      SLSPRSN   6         63                            15         Left
    CUSTS      ADDRES2   7         1             X               20         Left
               #S        8         1             +               50         Left
Formula        CON(CITY,', ',STATE,'  ',ZIP)
    CUSTS      PHONE     9         1                             12         Left


Detail
------

Leave no blank lines

    LNITEMS    LNQTY     1         1                             4          Right
    STOCK      DESCRIP   1         7                             39         Left
    LNITEMS    SELPRIC   1         47            T,              11         Right
               #2        1         59            +TI2            4          Left
Formula        SELPRIC*LNQTY

Subtotals #1 to #9
------------------

Leave 1 blank line(s)

               #2        2         47            ,2              11         Right
    INVOICE    INVTAX    3         47            ,               11         Right
    INVOICE    INVAMT    4         47            ,               11         Right

List of attribute codes:
        +     Calculated              B     Duplicate values blank
        C     Control character       I     Invisible
        F     Automatic find          E     Zeros shown as empty
        T     Totaled                 (     Shown like (123.4)
        X     No line if field empty  ,     Shown like 1,234.5
```

Fig. 9-18. The details of the fields for INVPRT.

automatically. This report uses a lot of calculations (and more could certainly be added) but let's see INVLIST in its standard variety first.

☐ Figures 9-21 and 9-22 show the Report format.
☐ Figure 9-23 lists the details of the fields.
☐ The **Sort fields** are to be set the same way as with INVPRT.

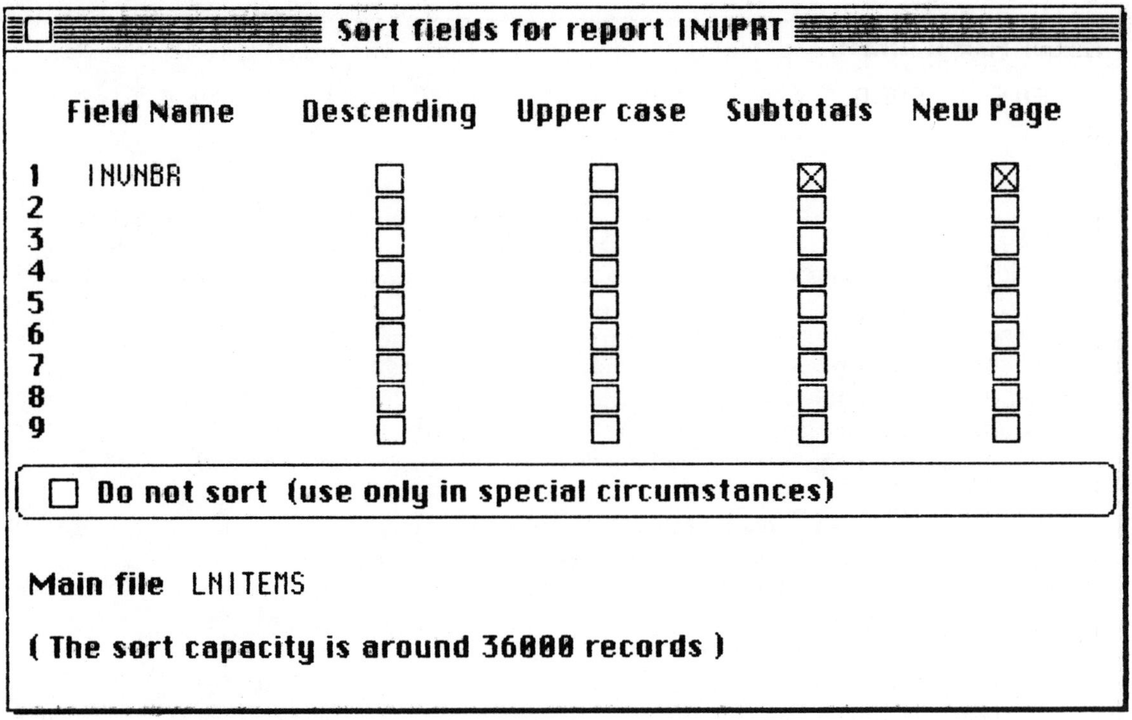

Fig. 9-19. The Sort fields for INVPRT.

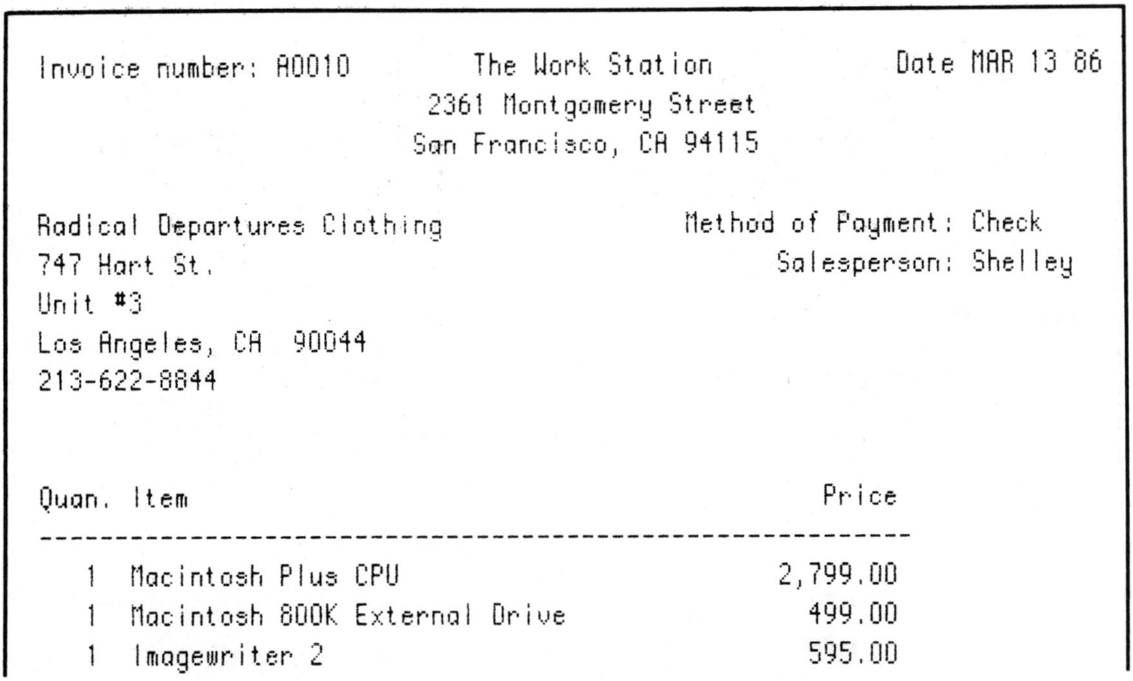

```
Invoice number: A0010        The Work Station        Date MAR 13 86
                          2361 Montgomery Street
                          San Francisco, CA 94115


Radical Departures Clothing          Method of Payment: Check
747 Hart St.                              Salesperson: Shelley
Unit #3
Los Angeles, CA  90044
213-622-8844



Quan. Item                                   Price
----------------------------------------------------------------
   1   Macintosh Plus CPU                  2,799.00
   1   Macintosh 800K External Drive         499.00
   1   Imagewriter 2                         595.00
```

Fig. 9-20. A printed invoice!

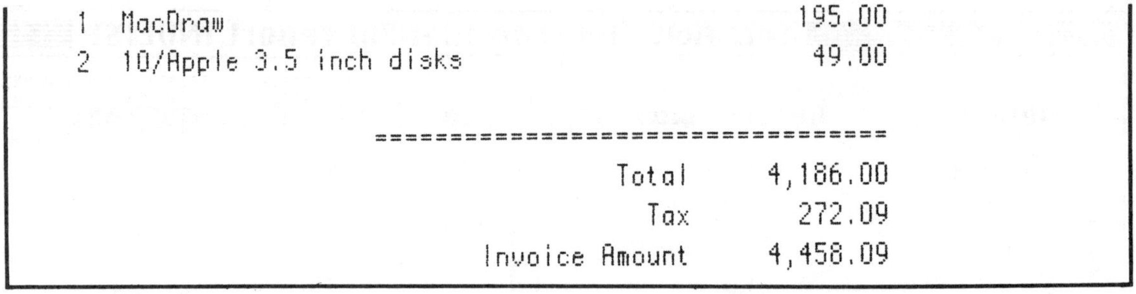

```
      1  MacDraw                                    195.00
      2  10/Apple 3.5 inch disks                     49.00


            ===================================
                                 Total    4,186.00
                                   Tax      272.09
                         Invoice Amount   4,458.09
```

This report works from the Invoicing menu of the INVENTR Entry layout, so you'll have to bring up that layout for data entry in order to access this report. If all goes well, the result should be as shown in Fig. 9-24. This example, of course, is printed to the screen. If the report is directed to the printer, be aware that it will take a full page for each invoice because of the settings in the Sort fields.

Did you try out the Find command? That one is very showy, utilizing the message box in Fig. 9-25 as it searches for Line items from the requested invoice.

There are a number of things which could have gone wrong in this process. The system was tested thoroughly prior to publication, and it worked fine. However, numerous factors, including typos in the text here and entry errors on your part, can contribute to the failure of one or more components of the invoicing sequences. Persistence and awareness are a developer's best aptitudes, and it is recommended that you make the most of these traits in debugging your system.

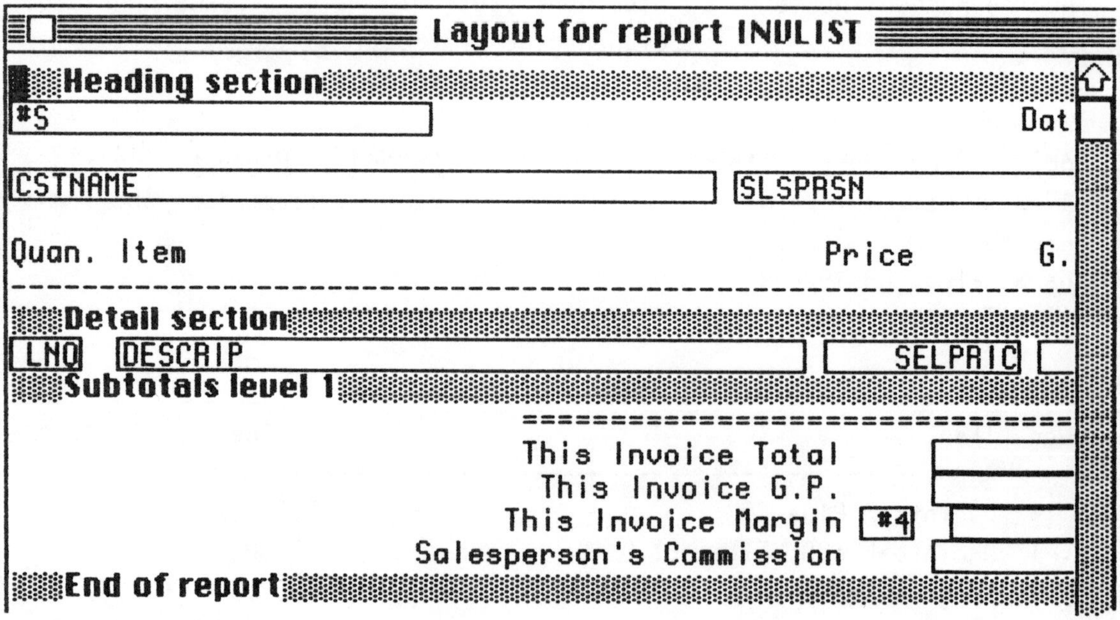

Fig. 9-21. The Report format INVLIST.

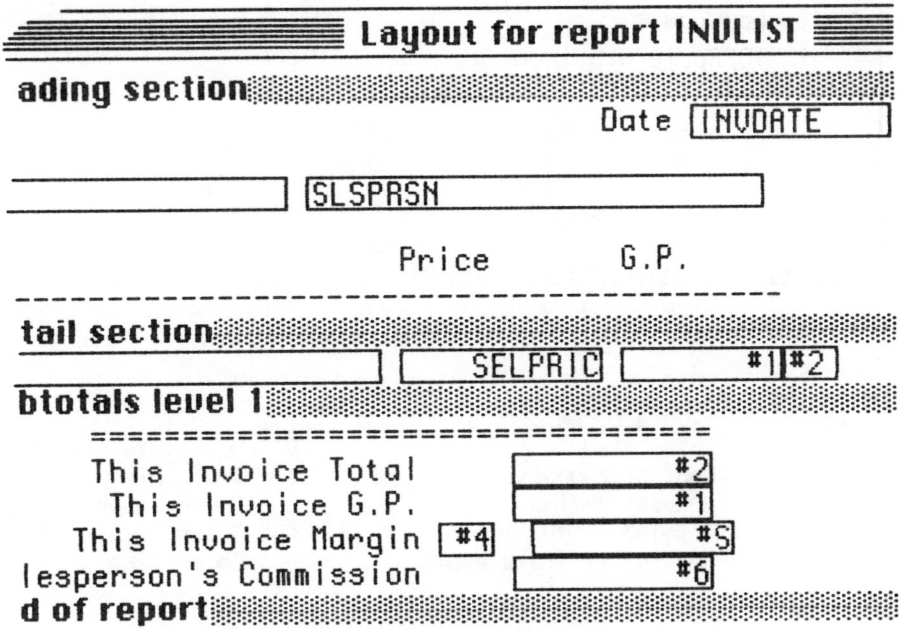

Layout for report INVLIST

ading section

Date INVDATE

SLSPRSN

Price   G.P.

----

tail section

SELPRIC   #1 #2

btotals level 1

=====================================

This Invoice Total   #2

This Invoice G.P.   #1

This Invoice Margin #4   #S

lesperson's Commission   #6

d of report

Fig. 9-22. The Report format INVLIST scrolled to the right a bit.

REPORT FORMAT INVLIST

FILE	FIELD	LINE	POSITION	ATTRIBUTES	LENGTH	JUST
Heading						
	#S	1	1	+	24	Left
Formula	CON('Invoice number: ',MID('A000',1,(5-LEN(INVNBR))),INVNBR)					
INVOICE	INVDATE	1	63		11	Left
CUSTS	CSTNAME	3	1		40	Left
CUSTS	SLSPRSN	3	42		25	Left
Detail						
Leave no blank lines						
LNITEMS	LNQTY	1	1		4	Right
STOCK	DESCRIP	1	7		39	Left
LNITEMS	SELPRIC	1	47	T,	11	Right
	#1	1	59	+T,2	9	Right
Formula	(SELPRIC-COST)*LNQTY					
	#2	1	68	+TI	3	Left
Formula	SELPRIC*LNQTY					

Fig. 9-23. The details of the fields for INVLIST.

```
Subtotals #1 to #9
------------------
Leave 1 blank line(s)

          #2        2         53              ,              11      Right
          #1        3         53              ,2             11      Right
          #4        4         49              +I              3      Right
Formula   (#1/#2)*100
          #S        4         54              +              11      Right
Formula   CON(#4,'%')
          #6        5         53              +2             11      Right
Formula   #1*.11


List of attribute codes:
     +    Calculated           B    Duplicate values blank
     C    Control character    I    Invisible
     F    Automatic find       E    Zeros shown as empty
     T    Totaled              (    Shown like (123.4)
     X    No line if field empty   ,   Shown like 1,234.5
```

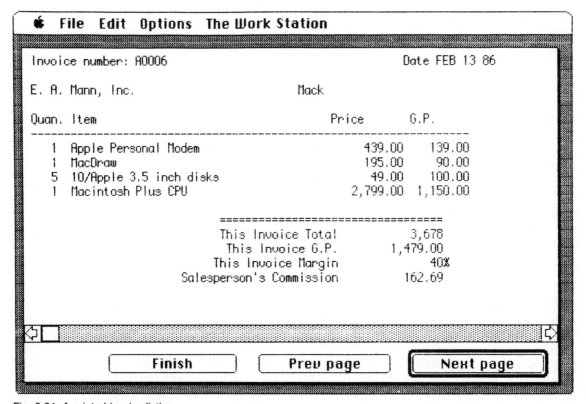

Fig. 9-24. A printed invoice listing.

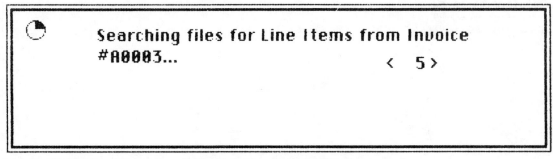

Searching files for Line Items from Invoice
#A0003...   ‹   5 ›

Fig. 9-25. The Working message box displayed during our special "Find" command.

What Comes Next?

Now that The Work Station's system has (I hope) come together successfully, the obvious question is: "What else can I do with it?" The answer is "Plenty!" There are numerous paths for expansion of this system, and a few of them are listed below. As I stated from the very beginning, this system was not designed to be commercial-grade. However, it could certainly evolve into a useful product with enough attention and hard work.

Expand the Invoice array to allow more items on the invoice. You can make the array appear on a second entry screen, but in this example, you will have to move the Find command's entry screen to #3 or beyond. You can then make screen #2 a secondary screen for #1. The process for putting the array on a second screen is covered in the example "Time & Cost" database included with your Omnis 3 package.

Build some simple accounts receivable capability into the system. This can be started in a few steps. First add a BALANCE field into the CUSTS file, then add another choice to the MOP field on the invoice: Charges. Then, have your sequence examine the contents of the MOP field when the invoice is written, and if it indicates a Charge transaction, debit the Customer's balance with a simple calculation.

Implement the invoice CASHIER field. The CASHIER field was purposely not used, but it could certainly add to the utility of the invoice if it were implemented. Reports could then be produced on a cashier-by-cashier basis.

Add a Search format to the INVLIST report to selectively output invoices, maybe by salesperson and date, or just by date. This would be simple to do, and would significantly enhance the utility of the INVLIST report format created in Chapter 9.

Enhance the invoice processing sequence so it will not throw out items that are overallocated. To accomplish this, it could execute a loop of instructions to determine how many are available, and ship just that many. If there still weren't enough, then it could throw away that item as it does now.

Add the capability for invoices to be refunded (incoming) as well as normal sales. This could easily be implemented in a manner similar to the method used in the inventory transfers. The inclusion of a Boolean field would do the trick. The sequence would then have to be smart enough to examine the Boolean field when the invoice was processed. It could do something like this:

```
If BooleanField = 0
    * a NO entered above means that the invoice is a refund!
    Calculate LNQTY as LNQTY * ( – 1)
End If
```

The rest of the sequence could then proceed as normal, but note that the prices will be negative, and the STKONHD field will be *incremented* because of the negative value of LNQTY. Normally STKONHD is decremented because LNQTY is subtracted from it.

A new file could be added specifically for the salespeople, which could be updated for actual commission figures as the invoices are written. You could also base it on a sliding commission scale, instead of the fixed 11 percent of gross profit figure we used here. It would have to be a connected file for CUSTS, as well as LNITEMS and INVOICE.

Allow editing of the prices charged to customers (discounting). This is a neat capability for the system that can be implemented with a bit of trickery. It would be useful to see quick lookup of not only the stock on hand, but also the cost of an item. But you wouldn't want wandering eyes to happen upon the cost figure. Therefore, we can use some string manipulation to "disguise" the cost as part of a nonsense string of characters at the bottom of the screen, such as in Fig. A-1.

This evolutionary change can be implemented by setting another screen of the INVENTR layout up as this entry screen. Then enter the fields shown in Fig. A-2. All the fields except PARTCOD must be entered as Local or this will not work. Can you remember why? The two temporary string fields are simply concatenations of the numbers returned by RETAIL and STKONHD respectively. The last field is not so simple. It, too, is a Local field, but its calculation is more complex. Actually, it is just a simple CON() function with lots of foreign characters (use the Option key on your Macintosh's keyboard), and a COST field stuck in the middle, as in Fig. A-3. Normally, this COST part will just stick a "0" in the middle of the string, but once a part is located, that field will be recalculated to display the "hidden" cost. The simple sequences needed are shown in Fig. A-4.

Add the discounting capability mentioned above. This could be done in

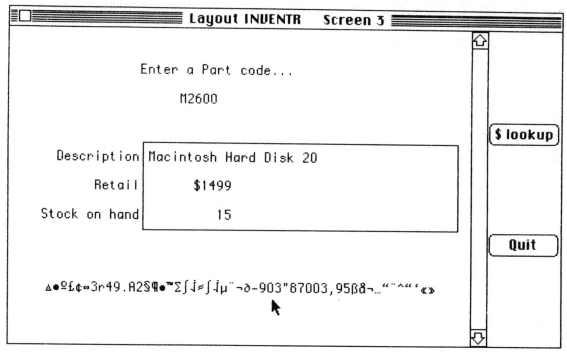

Enter a Part code...

M2600

$ lookup

Description	Macintosh Hard Disk 20
Retail	$1499
Stock on hand	15

Quit

∆•º£¢₩3r49.A2§¶•™Σ∫∫≠∫∫µ¨¬∂–903"87003,95ß∂¬…""^"''«»

Fig. A-1. Simple camouflage for cost figures.

at least two ways. The first, and easiest, would be to add a field to the CUSTS file for Discount Percentage (DISCPCT?). This field could then be used to multiply each line item's price by to reach the final prices.

Enter a Part code...

PARTC

Description	DESCRIP
Retail	#S
Stock on hand	#S

#S

Fig. A-2. Fields for an inventory-editing scheme that allows discounting.

The second way, item-by-item discounting, is far more complicated. It might seem at first to be trivial. After all, we allowed the SLSPRSN field to be edited, so why not the RETAIL field? Remember though, any changes made to SLSPRSN were written *permanently* to the CUSTS file. We certainly don't want our retail prices changing because one person was given a discount! In order to make it work, you would have to add at least one new field to the array. This field could be inserted somewhere before the RETAIL field. It would have to be an invisible, temporary Numeric field. Its calculation would simply be the current value of RETAIL. Then, after the user completes data entry, the SELPRIC could be set equal to RETAIL, then RETAIL could be reset to its actual value.

There is a problem here, however. Can you see it? It is very subtle, and took hours of testing to uncover during the development of the book. Everything works fine as developed unless the user tabs *backward* through the array to make a change. Local fields are calculated whenever the field to which they belong changes, or is tabbed through. The problem is that the second time the user tabs through the temporary field, it *recalculates*, causing its value to assume the *changed* value of RETAIL. Can you think of a way around this predicament using the current version of Omnis 3? After hours of toiling with it, I found that there is no apparent way of fixing this, except to wait for the new release of the program.

These suggestions are certainly not the only way to go about expanding this system. You may come up with an unconventional solution to one or more of the above applications. If you do, recall the immortal words of some man wiser

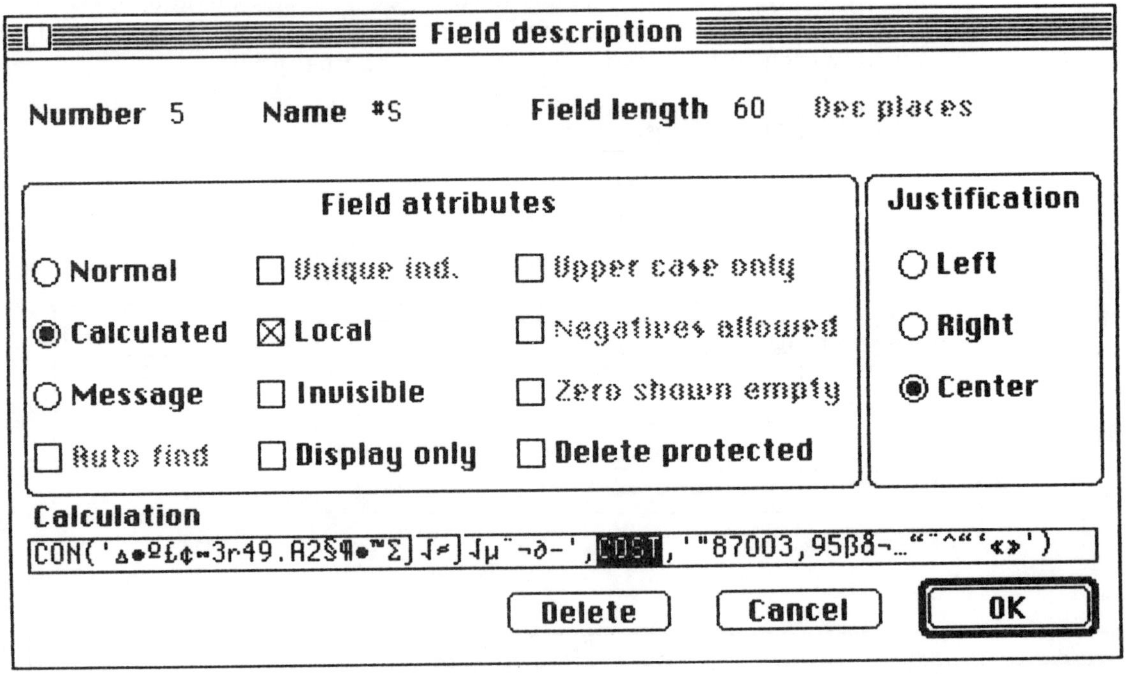

Fig. A-3. Location of the hidden Cost field.

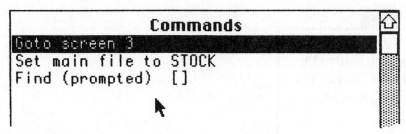

Fig. A-4. Sequences needed to implement the discounting feature.

than both of us:

> *If it works, don't fix it.*

Good luck with Omnis 3, and happy developing!

The DataBasics
Useful Reports
Search Formats
Custom Menus
Sequences
More Sequences
Expansion
Connections
The Array
Appendix ⌘B

Omnis 3 Reference Section

This section's purpose is to supply a quick reference for the sequence commands and the special functions. This is simply a supplement to the text of this book and the Omnis 3 User's manual.

SEQUENCES REFERENCE

What follows is a basic overview of Omnis 3's sequence commands. Commands are listed in the order that they appear in the opening screen of the Sequences editing window. Each is accompanied by a simple explanation. Examples can be found for most commands in the text.

Find/next/etc

Next	The equivalent of the *Next* command in the *Enter data* menu. Uses the current Sort field(s) and/or Search format.
Previous	The equivalent of the *Previous* command in the *Enter data* menu. Uses the current Sort field(s) and/or Search format.
Search	The equivalent of the *Search* command in the *Enter data* menu. Uses the current Sort field(s) and/or Search format.

Find (prompted)	The equivalent of the Find command in the *Enter data* menu. Uses the current Sort field(s) and/or Search format. If text is entered in the Message area, the first Message field in the entry layout will display that prompt. Field data may be included in the message using ;NAME; notation.
Find	Used to perform a Find operation on a predetermined field and value. You must specify an Indexed field and desired text or value, or a calculation which contains the indexed field name.
Exact match	If set, implies that a Next or Previous command must satisfy an exact match on the current indexed Find. Otherwise, requires a Find to be an exact match.

Edit/insert

Prepare for . . .	Places Omnis 3 in *Prepare mode*. This must be done before any manipulation of data, and a subsequent *Update files* command. You can prepare for Edit, Insert, or Insert with current values.
. . . Edit	Edit current record
. . . Insert	Clear the fields and get ready to add a new record.
. . . Insert with current values	Same as Insert, but the current record is not cleared first.
Enter data	Prompts the user for input in the standard manner, making the OK and Cancel buttons available. Will display a message in the first message field on the Entry layout if there is one present. Field data may be included in the message using ;NAME; notation.
Update files	Causes all changed data in memory to be securely written to the Data file. Must be called to ''save'' your data in a sequence before

proceeding to another record.

Delete   Erases the current Main file record. No confirmation is requested unless the option below is selected.

Ask for
confirmation   If selected, prompts the user for confirmation using the supplied message string. Field data may be included in the message using ;NAME; notation.

Print

Print record   The selected report is used to print one copy of the Detail section for the current Main file record. Report headings, if they are required, are printed using this field's data.

Print totals   The selected report is used to generate Totals, then the report is terminated.

Print report   The selected report is printed in it's entirety, unless a Search format is in effect.

Clear data

Main file
Connected files   Removes all field data from memory for these files
Other files

Range of
 # fields   Restricts the initialization of temporary numeric fields to the selected range.

All copies of
#1..#10 and #S   Effectively clears all of the temporary fields in the array. The array itself is not cleared completely unless all files contained therein are cleared also.

Redraw screen   Causes Omnis 3 to recalculate all fields using the latest values available. Fields are not automatically redrawn when their values are changed by a sequence.

Selected fields only	If set, this option restricts the drawing to the selected range of fields on the layout. These are the numbers assigned on the layout itself.
Goto screen	Causes Omnis 3 to make the selected screen the current Entry layout. The initialization sequence for that screen is executed when it becomes current.
Set main file	Causes the selected file to be made the Main file. The list of available files is gathered by inspecting the current Entry layout. If there are no fields from a given file anywhere in the layout, that file *cannot* be set as the Main file.
Select	
Report	Sets the current report to the name entered below. This does not cause it to be printed. That must be done with the *Print report* command.
Report (prompted)	Presents the user with the list of available reports in that Library. It then sets the current report to the name selected by the user. This does not cause it to be printed.
Search	Sets the current Search format to the one named below. Can only activate searches; they cannot be deactivated easily. See Chapter 5 for an example of how to deactivate a search.
Search (prompted)	Presents the user with the list of available Search formats in that Library. It then sets the current Search format to the one selected.
Output(prompted) Printer Screen	Determines the destination for reports. Overrides any settings in the report parameters.

Set options

Totals at the end of sequence

Assures that the currently printing report will be ended normally, with its totals correctly printed.

Restore current record at end of sequence

Assures that the record in memory at the start of a sequence will be restored in memory when the currently executing sequence ends.

Set field range

Restricts entry to the selected number range during subsequent Insert or Edit operations. These are the numbers assigned on the layout itself.

Message

OK Message

Displays the text entered in the message field in a Macintosh standard Alert box. Field data may be included in the message using ;NAME; notation. Contains a default OK button, and the user can press Return as an alternative. Option: *Sound the bell.*

Yes/No Message

Same as OK message, but has two buttons. Flag is SET if the user clicks OK. Normally, the Default button is No. Option: *Default to Yes.*

Working

Displays an Alert which stays posted until there is activity on the screen, or its enclosing control structure terminates. Options: *Show repeat count* and *Show cancel button.*

Comment

Inserts a comment line into a sequence. Can be used for any text, as it is completely ignored by Omnis 3.

Calculate

Perform a calculation within a sequence.

Field name

Any field is legal here, as long as it is contained within the layout, or is a temporary field (#1..#60 or #S).

Calculation	Any mathematical, relational, or logical operators, or special Functions can be included, as long as the overall length is 70 characters or less. Number of decimals is only prompted for when the field is a temporary numeric field. Flag is SET if the result $<\ >0$.

Test

Test for record in memory	The flag is SET if there is a Main file record available in memory. Otherwise, the flag is CLEARED.
Test data against Search format	The flag is SET if the current record passes the current Search format. Otherwise, the flag is CLEARED.
Test if Cancel box is selected	When a working message box is being displayed, executes a *Quit all sequences* if command-(.) is pressed or the Cancel button is clicked.

If/repeat/etc

If/Else If Else/End if Repeat/Until	Omnis 3's control structures. See chapters 5-9 for examples and descriptions of their uses.
Flag true Flag false Calculation	Conditional tests which are done for the If, Else If, and Until keywords. Calculation follows the same rules as the Calculate command.

Call/quit

Call sequence	Passes control to the enumerated sequence, then regains control when the called sequence finishes executing.
Quit sequence	Immediately terminates the execution of the current sequence. Options: *Set* or *Clear* the Flag.

Quit all sequences	Immediately terminates the execution of the current sequence and all calling sequences.
Quit layout	Terminates all sequences, then removes the current Entry layout and any corresponding menus from the screen.

FUNCTION REFERENCE

This is an overview of Omnis 3's special functions. They are listed in no particular order. Each function is listed along with the type of value which it returns, and some examples of its implementation. More examples can be found for many functions in the text.

ABS(Number)

Numeric   Returns the Absolute value of the given number.

$$ABS(-1) = 1$$
$$ABS('-2') = 2$$
$$ABS(1) = 1$$
$$ABS('Jim') = 0$$

CHK(CheckString,String1,String2)

Boolean   Evaluates the following equation:
(CheckString $>$ = String1) & (CheckString $<$ = String2)
on a character-by-character basis.

$$CHK('94105','00000','99999') = TRUE$$
$$CHK('A0209','A0000',A0200') = FALSE$$
$$CHK('A0209','00000','9999') = FALSE$$

CMP(IntRate,Periods)

Numeric   Returns a compound interest multiplier for use in deriving payment figures by the following formula:

$$(1 + (IntRate/100))_{Periods}$$

$$CMP(15,12) = 5.35$$
$$CMP(12,25) = 17.00$$
$$CMP(12,6) = 1.97$$

CON(String1,String2,StringN, . . .)

    String

Returns the string resulting from the concatenation (combination) of the strings which are its parameters.

    CON('Cynthia',' ','Smith') = 'Cynthia Smith'
    CON(ABS(-3*5),'th') = '15th'
      CON(#D,' is my birthday!') = MAR 15 86 is my birthday!

DAT(String)

    Date

Converts the string into a date value. Strings of incompatible format are ignored, and an undefined date is returned.

    DAT(CON('MAR ',3*5,' ',86-1)) = MAR 15 85
    DAT('April 15 1986') = APR 15 86
    DAT('The quick brown fox') = 0

DTD(Date)

    String
    Numeric

Returns the day portion of a date as the appropriate type, either a string or a number, depending on how it is to be used. The default is a string value.

    DTD(DAT('15 Mar 85')) = '15th'
    DTD(DAT('15 Mar 85') + 6) = '21st'
    DTD(DAT('15 Mar 85')) + 6 = 21

(notice how it is used as a number in the last example)

DTM(Date)

    String
    Numeric

Returns the month portion of a date as the appropriate type, either a string or a number, depending on how it is to be used. The default is a string value.

    DTM(DAT('15 Mar 85')) = 'March'
    DTM(DAT('15 Mar 85') + 6) = 'September'
    DTM(DAT('15 Mar 85')) + 6 = 9

(notice how it is used as a number in the last example)

DTY(Date)

String
Numeric

Returns the year portion of a date as the appropriate type, either a string or a number, depending on how it is to be used. The default is a string value.

DTY(DAT('15 Mar 85')) = '85'
DTY(DAT('15 Mar 85') + 6) = '91'
DTY(DAT('15 Mar 85')) + 6 = 91

(notice how it is used as a number in the last example)

INT(Number)

Numeric

Truncates (removes the fractional part) of Number, and returns the remainder. This function *does not* round off Number.

INT(3.483) = 3
INT(20/3) = 6
INT('.999') = 0

LEN(String)

Numeric

Returns the length in characters of String. All numbers are converted to strings before processing.

LEN('Greetings, Earthling!') = 21
LEN(200/5) = 2
LEN('Timbuktu') / 2 = 4

MID(String,StartNumber,NumberOfChars)

String

Returns the substring of String which begins at StartNumber characters from the beginning, and is NumberOfChars in length.

MID('abcdefghijklm',3,1) = 'c'
MID('13 September 1959',4,9) =
    'September'
MID('AnyString',1,LEN('AnyString')) =
    'AnyString'

NOT(AnyExpression)

Boolean

Reverses the truth value of AnyExpression. Nonzero values are evaluated as True, and zero values are considered False.

NOT(1) = 0
NOT(0) = 1
NOT('-200.35') = 0
NOT('Steve') = 1
NOT(INT(.3)) = 1

POS(SubString,String)

Numeric

Returns the position of SubString within String. Evaluates to 0 if SubString is not found in its entirety within String. Function is case-sensitive.

POS('An','Andrea') = 1
POS(3*2,'1986') = 4
POS('case','UPPER CASE') = 0

PWR(Number,Exponent)

Numeric

Returns Number raised to the power of Exponent.

PWR(3,2) = 9
PWR(2.5,3) = 15.625

SQR(Number)

Numeric

Returns the square root of Number.

SQR(2) = 1.4142
INT(SQR('1986')) = 44

UPP(String)

String

Returns String in uppercase characters.

UPP('case') = 'CASE'
UPP('13 Sep 1959') = '13 SEP 1959'
CON('UPPER',UPP(MID('lower case',6,4)))
    = 'UPPER CASE'

Index

MASTERING OMNIS EXAMPLES DISK OFFER

An appropriate companion for a book of this nature is an Examples Disk, and *MASTER-ING OMNIS 3* is no exception. Included are files that will assist you in your work on The Work Station's Omnis 3 system.

△ Library files containing versions of the system at various places during its development, allowing you to check your own work against the actual example files that were used in the writing of the book.
△ Data files with all the data described in the book entered for you. This will save you the time and trouble of entering enough data to get significant reports from the system.
△ A Library file which implements some of the enhancements in Appendix A.
△ A few special surprises, including Public Domain and Shareware programs to help you in your work with Omnis 3.

To order the **MASTERING OMNIS 3** Example Disk, send a check or
money order for **$24.95**, along with this coupon to:

PROGRESSIVE MICRO SYSTEMS
2443 FILLMORE STREET
SUITE 293
SAN FRANCISCO, CA 94115

(make the check payable to: Progressive Micro Systems)

△ △ △ △ △

Please take a moment to answer these questions:

1) Version # of your Omnis 3 _____ 3. _____   4) If not, why?_____
2) For how long have you   _____
   been using Omnis 3?   _____   5) How would you describe
3) Did this book meet   your use of Omnis 3? _____
   your expectations?   _____   _____

Name _____

Address _____

City/ST/Zip _____

TAB No. 2674

Other Bestsellers From TAB

☐ **THE ILLUSTRATED DICTIONARY OF MICROCOMPUTERS—2ND EDITION—Hordeski**

Little more than a decade after the introduction of the first microprocessors, microcomputers have made a major impact on every area of today's business, industry, and personal lifestyles. The result: a whole new language of terms and concepts reflecting this rapidly developing technology . . . and a vital need for current, accurate explanations of what these terms and concepts mean. Michael Hordeski has provided just that in this completely revised and greatly expanded new second edition of *The Illustrated Dictionary of Microcomputers*! 368 pp., 357 illus., Large Desk-Top Format 7″ × 10″.

Paper $14.95   **Hard $24.95**
Book No. 2688

☐ **MACINTOSH™ ASSEMBLY LANGUAGE PROGRAMMING**

Delve below the surface-level capabilities of your Macintosh and discover the incredible power that assembly language can unlock. You'll learn all about the fundamentals of machine code . . . gain an understanding of editors and assemblers . . . and tap into the 68000's addressing modes and instruction set. It's a book no Mac owner can afford to miss! 208 pp., 31 illus., 7″ × 10″.

Paper $16.95   **Hard $24.95**
Book No. 2611

☐ **DATA COMMUNICATIONS AND LOCAL AREA NETWORKING HANDBOOK**

With data communications and LANs being the area of greatest growth in computers, this sourcebook will help you understand what this emerging field is all about. Singled out for its depth and comprehensiveness, this clearly-written handbook will provide you with everything from data communications standards and protocols to the various ways to link together LANs. 240 pp., 209 illus., 7″ × 10″.

Hard $25.00   **Book No. 2603**

☐ **JAZZ!™—Bolocan**

Let software expert David Bolocan guide you masterfully through all of Jazz's capabilities—word processing, spreadsheet analysis, database management, communications, and business graphics capabilities. Written in easy-to-understand, plain-English, this hands-on tutorial takes you from an introduction to using Jazz on the Macintosh and fundamental commands to exploring its tremendous applications and integrating them. 304 pp., 249 illus., 7″ × 10″.

Paper $17.95   **Hard $24.95**
Book No. 1978

☐ **MACINTOSH™ PROGRAMMING USING MS-BASIC™ 2.0—Vile, Jr.**

This unprecedented manual shows how you can make the most of the special interactive features of MS-BASIC 2.0. With an emphasis on learning-by-doing, expert programmer Richard Vile guides you through techniques for using the menus, windows, buttons, edit fields, dialog boxes, mouse, quickdraw graphics, and other conveniences. Includes more than 20 ready-to-run programs. 288 pp., 117 illus., 7″ × 10″.

Paper $16.95   **Hard $24.95**
Book No. 2621

☐ **THE COMPUTER SECURITY HANDBOOK—Baker**

Electronic breaking and entering into computers systems used by business, industry and personal computerists has reached epidemic proportions. That's why this up-to-date sourcebook is so important. It provides a realistic examination of today's computer security problems, shows you how to analyze your home and business security needs, and gives you guidance in planning your own computer security system. 288 pp., 61 illus., 7″ × 10″.

Hard $25.00   **Book No. 2608**

☐ **MACINTOSH™ EXPANSION GUIDE**

What kind of accessories and add-ons are available for the Mac? Which ones are the best buys for the applications you have in mind? How can products from other manufacturers be interfaced with the Macintosh? You'll find the answers to these and just about any other question you have on Macintosh peripherals here, in this exceptionally thorough, time-saving guide. Far more than just a product listing or a rehash of manufacturers' sales brochures, these are the best of the peripherals currently on the market for the Mac . . . each one chosen for value and performance after exhaustive testing and examination. In addition, the authors provide you with evaluative reviews of the products and tables that list the vital statistics and features for quick comparative analysis. 224 pp., 31 illus., 7″ × 10″.

Paper $16.95   **Hard $22.95**
Book No. 2601

☐ **ONLINE RESEARCH AND RETRIEVAL WITH MICROCOMPUTERS—Goldmann**

This time-saving guide shows you how to turn a micro into an invaluable research "tool" for digging up information from databases across the country. Using Nahum Goldmann's "Subject Export Searching Technique," businessmen, engineers, physicians, lawyers, professors and students can quickly and easily retrieve information in the comfort of their work station. 192 pp., 119 illus., 7″ × 10″.

Hard $25.00   **Book No. 1947**

Other Bestsellers From TAB